More Praise for *Into the Forest*

One of the *Wall Street Journal*'s 10 Books to Read in September 2021
One of *Hey Alma*'s 8 Jewish Books You Should Read This September 2021

"Page-turning . . . an even more improbable fairy tale about rescue, reunion, and romantic love."
—*The Forward*

"An extraordinary story."
—*Booklist*

"A gripping story of one family's courage and resourcefulness under life-threatening conditions."
—*Kirkus Reviews* (starred review)

"Inspirational . . . Readers will be on the edge of their seats."
—*Publishers Weekly*

"An excellent choice for serious book clubs that have previously chosen challenging titles like Tatiana de Rosnay's *Sarah's Key* and Irène Némirovsky's *Suite Française*."
—*BookTrib*

"Frankel demonstrates the resilience of the human spirit, even when all appears to be lost."
—Peter Bergen, author of *The Rise and Fall of Osama bin Laden*

"One of the most moving, thrilling, inspiring books anyone will read all year, fiction or nonfiction!"
—David Rothkopf, author of *Traitor*

"Gave me goose bumps, actual goose bumps . . . Thrilling and heartwarming, without masking horror and tragedy."

—David Plotz, former CEO of *Atlas Obscura* and author of *Good Book*

"Set in one of the world's last remaining primeval forests, this story of horror and heroism has the trappings of a grim fairy tale: Once upon a terrible time, after so much loss and devastation, one unlikely couple found their happily ever after."

—Ilana Kurshan, author of *If All the Seas Were Ink*, winner of the Sami Rohr Prize for Jewish Literature

"Hard to put down . . . A tragic, yet uplifting tale of human fortitude and love that needs to be told and widely read."

—Allan Levine, author of *Fugitives of the Forest*

"What makes *Into the Forest* truly memorable is Frankel's uncanny empathy for her characters. . . . She never allows us to look away, nor do we want to, no matter how terrible the events of this powerful narrative."

—Glenn Frankel, Pulitzer Prize–winning journalist and author

ALSO BY REBECCA FRANKEL

War Dogs

Into the Forest

A HOLOCAUST STORY OF SURVIVAL, TRIUMPH, AND LOVE

REBECCA FRANKEL

ST. MARTIN'S GRIFFIN
NEW YORK

Published in the United States by St. Martin's Griffin, an imprint of St. Martin's Publishing Group

www.stmartins.com

All photos in this work are courtesy of the Lazowski and Langerman families.

Designed by Meryl Sussman Levavi

The Library of Congress has cataloged the hardcover edition as follows:

Names: Frankel, Rebecca, author.
Title: Into the forest : a Holocaust story of survival, triumph, and love / Rebecca Frankel.
Description: First edition. | New York : St. Martin's Press, 2021. | Includes bibliographical references and index.
Identifiers: LCCN 2021016349 | ISBN 9781250267641 (hardcover) ISBN 9781250267658 (ebook)
Subjects: LCSH: Rabinowitz family. | Jews—Belarus—Dzíátlava (Hrodzenskaíá voblastś)—Biography. | Rabinowitz, Miriam Dworetsky, 1908–1981. | Rabinowitz, Morris, 1906–1982. | Lazowski, Philip. | Holocaust, Jewish (1939–1945)—Poland. | World War, 1939–1945—Jews—Bialowieza Forest (Poland and Belarus) | Holocaust survivors—Connecticut—Hartford—Biography.
Classification: LCC DS134.7 .F73 2021 | DDC 940.53/18092224788—dc23
LC record available at https://lccn.loc.gov/2021016349

ISBN 978-1-250-87490-0 (trade paperback)

Our books may be purchased in bulk for promotional, educational, or business use. Please contact your local bookseller or the Macmillan Corporate and Premium Sales Department at 1-800-221-7945, extension 5442, or by email at MacmillanSpecialMarkets@macmillan.com.

First St. Martin's Griffin Edition: 2023

3 5 7 9 10 8 6 4 2

For Gail

For Miriam and Luba
For Ruth and Toby
For sisters

Contents

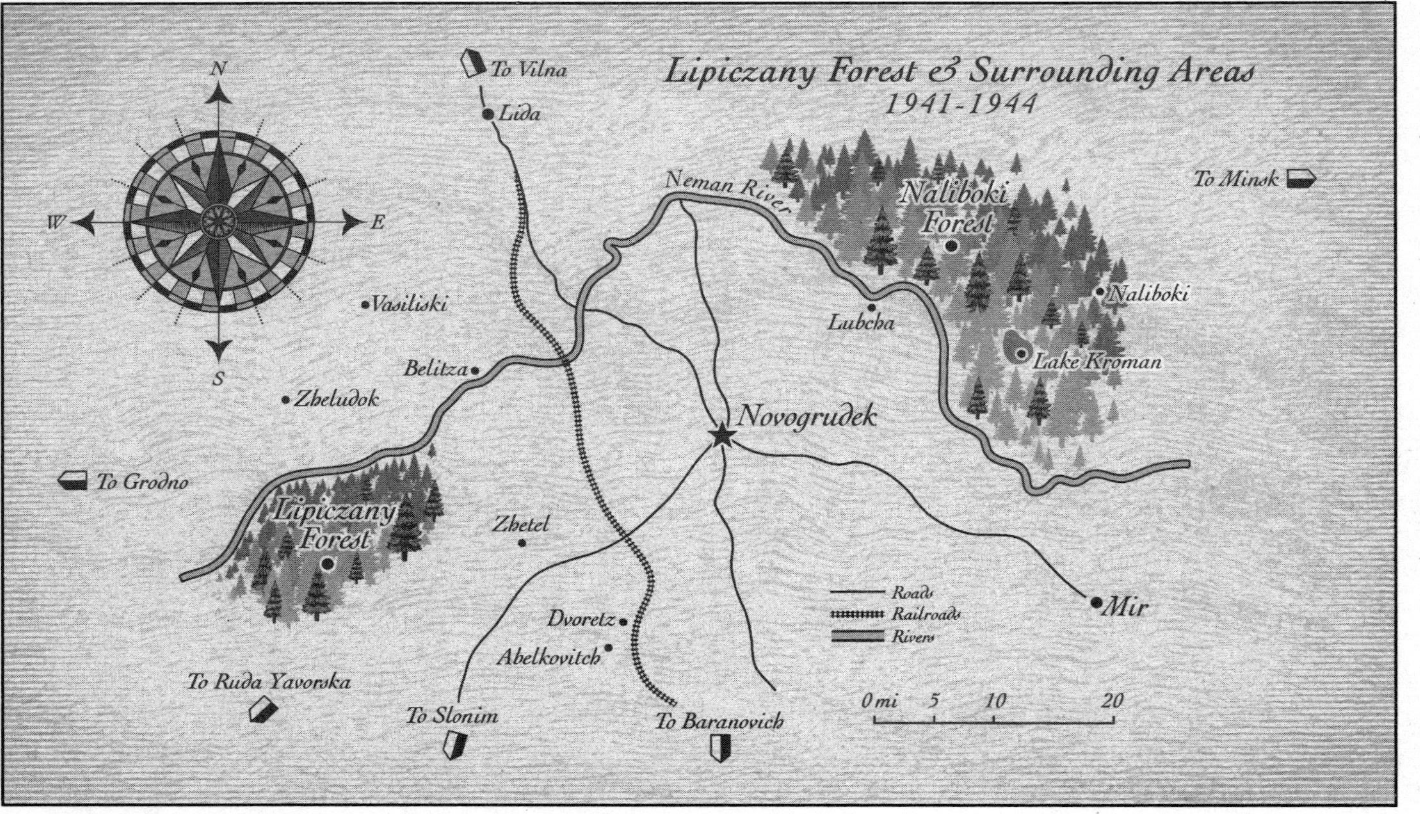
Lipiczany Forest & Surrounding Areas
1941-1944
N
S
W
E
To Vilna
Lida
Vasiliski
Belitza
Zheludok
To Grodno
Lipiczany Forest
Zhetel
Dvoretz
Abelkovitch
To Ruda Yavorska
To Slonim
To Baranovich
Neman River
Novogrudek
Lubcha
Naliboki Forest
Naliboki
Lake Kroman
To Minsk
Mir
Roads
Railroads
Rivers
0 mi
5
10
20

Prologue

A Wedding in Brooklyn

In the New York City clerk's archive there are 1,049 lined ledger pages dutifully cataloging Brooklyn's newlyweds in 1953. Somewhere among the marriage certificate numbers and the columns of dates recorded in looping black scrawl are the names of a couple who said "I do" on a May afternoon in a small catering hall in one of the borough's Jewish enclaves.

Their wedding was the flashpoint of multiple time lines—an event that determined the course of more than a dozen lives and upon which at least one fated love story hangs. Which is why it's all the more curious that, at least in this specific sense, the bride and groom are inconsequential. Their role in this story is merely a footnote; even their names have long been forgotten. Far more remarkable is who attended their wedding and the extraordinary thing that occurred between them.

Among the newlyweds' reception guests that day was a young Yeshiva University student named Philip Lazowski. Morning after morning, this dark-haired young man with his compact build and bookish intensity hopped on the subway from Brooklyn and rode it all the way up to Manhattan's West 185th Street to attend classes, only to make the return trip back to the Flatbush Avenue station so he could take night courses at Brooklyn College. Though he had been in New York for nearly five years, the twenty-three-year-old immigrant with a halting accent hadn't adjusted to his new life in the United States.

Reluctant to attend this spring wedding of his fellow Yeshiva student, Philip drifted uncomfortably through the crowd of American twentysomethings sashaying around him in their sports jackets and crinoline skirts. When music filled the hall and partygoers rose to join the newlyweds on the dance floor, Philip, ill at ease in his borrowed suit, stayed seated at his table. So did a young woman with raven-swept hair and bright brown eyes occupying the chair next to his. They started talking and discovered they had much in common. Her name was Gloria and she was also taking night courses at Brooklyn College. She was from a small town in Poland, as was Philip. And like him, Gloria had escaped Nazi slaughter by fleeing to the Białowieża Forest to live alongside the partisan fighters in the woods.

When Gloria heard that Philip was from a village called Bilitza, her lovely face lit up. "I know a woman who once saved a boy from Bilitza," she told him. The woman was the mother of her friend, a girl she'd met in a refugee camp in Italy, who was now living in Connecticut. In fact, she had just been to see them. "Only the woman doesn't know if the boy survived," Gloria said.

"How did she save him?" Philip wanted to know.

Gloria told him the story of how her friend's mother had risked her own life and the safety of her two young daughters to keep the boy from death during the first ghetto massacre in Zhetel.

As he listened, Philip's heart began to pound—he already knew this story. "That was me," he told her. "I am that boy."

A few minutes later, Philip was racing down a flight of stairs to the pay phone in the catering hall basement. Excitement buzzed through him as he dialed the operator while the wedding party whirled on above.

The operator's voice sounded in his ear. After he deposited the correct change for the long-distance call, she asked who he was trying to reach. "Rabinowitz," he replied. But there were six Rabinowitz residences listed in Hartford. What, she asked, did he want her to do?

Philip felt around inside his pocket—there weren't enough coins to pay for a second call. He took a deep breath. "Try the first one," he told her.

The line rang.

A woman answered.

It was her—Miriam Rabinowitz, the woman who had saved him. He'd found her at last.

❧

Weddings are life-affirming rituals with a hopeful view of the future implicit in their ceremonies. But they are also bridges between individuals, families, and formative years. So it is fitting that this serendipitous encounter should have transpired at a wedding.

Even then, in 1953, nearly a decade after World War II officially came to a close, there were still some people for whom a Jewish union like this one would be viewed as something of a marvel. The world had just emerged from one of the darkest periods in modern history, collectively having to rebuild on the loss of some sixty million lives. Of the six million European Jews killed in the Holocaust, three million were from Poland. By 1950, only 45,000 of the more than three million Jews counted in Poland in 1933 remained. An even smaller percentage of those who fled to the Belorussian woods survived.

As if fortune needed to signal just how powerful its hand had been in reuniting Philip Lazowski with Miriam Rabinowitz, on

May 23, 1953, just one week after that wedding, Gloria Koslowski, the captivating brunette from the Brooklyn reception, was killed by a drunk driver while crossing Pitkin Avenue. Her death in any shape would have been tragic: that an intelligent, vibrant young woman should be robbed of her hard-won existence on a rain-slick street in Brooklyn more than four thousand miles away from where she had outrun the Nazis was a senseless death, devoid of any natural symmetry or justice.

But Gloria's life would still give way to new life. She would become both the connective thread between two families and the seed from which a third would grow—all because she reunited the boy from Bilitza with the woman who saved him.

There are many stories of love and survival from the Holocaust, stories of extraordinary perseverance and bravery that defy all fathomable depths of human endurance. Many of them have twists of fate, and there are even a few with miraculously happy endings.

They are the great love stories of a terrible time—and this is one of them.

PART I

Before

CHAPTER 1

A Wedding in Vilna

IN THE END, IT WAS A BEAUTIFUL WEDDING.

Even if, according to the bride and groom's parents, the occasion was long overdue and perhaps, for their sophisticated hosts, the event was a touch slapdash. Fortunately, there was far more to celebrate than there were reasons to complain. Not the least of which was the venue, a grand apartment in a posh Vilna neighborhood, a city that was no doubt flush with cosmopolitan allure for a young provincial couple exploring its delights in 1933.

It was actually the young lovers' second attempt at a marriage ceremony. The first try for a romantic but no-frills elopement came to a panicked halt when the bride abruptly changed her mind. Game as she had been to buck tradition, and with it a Jewish ceremony—prepared even to be married by Vilna *goyim*—her whole being had rejected the scene around them at the Vilna courthouse. *No,* she thought, *I cannot get married like this.* Waiting in front of them in the long, colorful line of besotted couples was a man wearing a hat with the brim tilted in a smug slant across his forehead. "Like a gangster!" the scandalized bride would later scoff. The groom, perhaps registering the look on his future wife's face, took his cue and raised no protest. The wedding was put off.

But rather than leave Vilna unwed, the couple was rescued by the groom's well-to-do relatives. The ceremony and reception took place at Number 8 Daichishe Road, at the home of Saul and Batsheva Rabinowitz. Saul was the owner of not one but two lucrative textile businesses and this, their luxurious city home, was staffed by no fewer than two maids and a nanny for their two young boys.

The wedding, an intimate affair, numbered guests in the twenties. In addition to family, the couple's circle of friends, already in Vilna for the city's annual fair, comprised the majority of celebrators. The ceremony was simple—the young Jewish couple made their vows and then, as it was a Saturday, enjoyed a small Kiddush before the splendid supper was served. The elaborate feast of fish and meat was procured by the bride's father and prepared by the groom's mother.

A young woman liberated for her time, the twenty-four-year-old bride eschewed at least one principal wedding tradition: the white dress. Instead, she wore a long black evening gown; her rippling curls, dark and thick, framed her small oval face in a fashionable bob. Standing six feet tall—nearly a foot higher than his betrothed and large enough to fill a doorframe—was the groom. At twenty-five, his dark hair, which he was fond of slicking back and to the side, was already beginning a gentle retreat into two narrow peaks. Above a generous nose his brown eyes shone warmly; he was mad for the spitfire at his side.

It was September 30, 1933, and Miriam Dworetsky and Morris Rabinowitz were married at last.

*

The day Miriam Dworetsky finally chose an eligible suitor from a good Jewish family must have come as no small relief to her father, Gutel Dworetsky, who had himself been a widower for more than two decades. His wife, Rochel, died during labor with their fourth child. Delivery complications claimed the lives of both mother and baby, leaving Gutel, who was still a relatively young man in 1913, with three small children—Miriam, five; a son, Beryl, three; and finally Luba, who was just one.

Intent on devoting himself fully to his bereaved young family, Gutel vowed never to marry again. For a man of his time, this was something of an outwardly peculiar decision. Gutel was financially comfortable; he owned homes in both Novogrudek and Zhetel, neighboring towns that, at the time, were still under Russian rule. Taking a new wife appeared both personally and parentally practical. But Gutel was of the mind that his children would be scarred by the sudden presence of an unfamiliar woman and was seemingly content avoiding the business of a new marriage. Still, he wasn't prepared to raise a family alone, so Gutel's niece Itka came to the Dworetsky family home in Novogrudek to help with the children.

Itka, the daughter of Gutel's sister, was too young to be a spinster, but presumably old enough that her family determined her own marital prospects were lacking. This was likely because Itka, as the family delicately put it, was simpleminded. In whatever ways she was limited, Itka was equal to the task of caretaker to her young cousins and slipped into the role of their surrogate mother. What Itka thought of the arrangement was never really clear but enough could be gleaned through the happiness of the children she helped to raise, who, despite growing up in the murky shadow of Rochel's death, never felt they were without a mother.

Gutel was a religious if not strictly devout man. The Dworetsky family observed the Jewish holidays and their corresponding rituals and traditions. Every year without fail, he would take the children to synagogue for the Yizkor memorial services in remembrance of their departed mother. As they got a little older, Miriam and Luba became aware of how the congregants' glances lingered over them; they noticed how elderly women's eyes welled with tears watching their widower father and his motherless children. But their pity baffled the girls. "What are they crying for?" they whispered to each other. They understood they had no mother, but their father was doting, Itka was always with them. What, they wondered, could they be missing?

Of the children, only Miriam remembered Rochel. But as time passed, her mother's form and figure faded even further until all that remained with tactical clarity were scattered scenes from the funeral, the feeling of hands and arms lifting her up so she could see above the mourners. But even those memories were devoid of the palpable sting of loss; the connection to Rochel became ever more remote. Whether Miriam was ultimately the product of a too-lenient single father or if she had inherited her self-guiding streak from her mother was something no one, least of all Miriam, could ever really be sure of. But the elder Dworetsky daughter, who made a regular habit of defying convention, would soon provide her father with plenty to worry about.

As a young woman, Miriam didn't possess stereotypical, head-turning feminine attributes. Her pointed features and diminutive size, paired with the contemporary styles—the cropped finger wave hairdos and the shapeless dresses with their hanging forms—deprived Miriam of the womanly shape that time and future tailoring trends would reveal. Miriam's dark gray eyes and fair complexion matched against her deep brown hair gave her face a muted polish. When Miriam posed for photos her face would set in an almost grim expression that belied the high-spirited nature within. She may not have been a classic beauty, but Miriam's lively personality, her beguiling laugh, gave her an irresistible zing.

By the time she was a teenager, Miriam had become a popular and outgoing girl. Called Manya by most everyone who knew her, she was active in local Zionist youth organizations, where she enjoyed fast friendships and her own opinions. Miriam was easy to laugh. Her friends liked to say she was the perfect audience for a joke—*any* joke. "Just show Manya two fingers, and she laughs," they teased. Light of heart but hardly frivolous, Miriam also excelled at academics and went to work in a local drugstore after graduating from high school. Always a careful study, she quickly learned how to handle prescriptions from the shop owner, Mr. Lazarofski.

One day, Miriam overheard the local inspector telling Mr. Lazarofski that one of the small patent medicine shops in the neighboring town of Zhetel had closed, meaning that the space would be available to a new proprietor. The idea for her future hatched right then and there.

Patent medicine shops weren't pharmacies exactly, but rather places where people could get things like soaps, vitamins, salves, and other over-the-counter remedies. Strictly speaking, patent medicine shops weren't allowed to carry medications—it was illegal for prescriptions to be filled by anyone other than a certified pharmacist—but the practice was an accepted enough convention. Many shop owners had a little hiding room, and as long as they were smart enough to keep the medications out of sight, the inspectors limited their reprimands. Still, Zhetel only allowed a few of these stores at any given time, so permission to occupy and operate such a business had to be approved by the local council. Miriam wasted no time getting to Zhetel to present her petition, and soon the proper paperwork was arranged and the little shop was hers.

Gutel either relented to his daughter's plans, or more likely had never been asked permission. There's no reason to think that by then Miriam Dworetsky was anything other than her own woman.

It was sometime in 1927 that twenty-year-old Miriam packed up her things and left the family home in Novogrudek, striking out on her own for Zhetel on little more than a few borrowed zlotys from her father and the steam of her own gumption.

Her determination was tested before she even opened her shop doors. The drugstore business was something of a family-wide trade, and when an uncle in Lida offered Miriam inventory from his store's supply to help her get going, she accepted without hesitation. It didn't take long for her to discover that he'd sold her expired medications, leaving her with useless goods and a hefty dent in her seed money.

Her early career was further hampered by an already crowded market. Given the community's small size, the few nearby shops were all in competition to secure the lion's share of local business as well as the nearby farms and neighboring small towns. One of the other stores' proprietors was another relation, an older cousin of Miriam's who wasted no time in launching his campaign to outsell her, bringing his brazen tactics right to her doorstep. Waiting in the street, he would trail after her customers, angling to see what they'd purchased. If it was medicine, he would lean in, a sly conspirator, and ask, "How much did you pay? I'll give it to you for cheaper."

Miriam refused to be rattled. The people in Zhetel quickly came to rely on "the Dworetska woman," as they called her, trusting how confidently she handled her medicines and wares. She was so successful, in fact, that the other patent medicine shop owner in Zhetel, Hinke Merskeh, was forced to shutter her own business for good. And when the older woman approached Miriam and offered to sell her the remainder of her stock for a song, Miriam was jaded just enough to refuse her.

❧

Assuming that Gutel was proud of how quickly his daughter established herself as a successful business owner, he couldn't overlook that she was still an unattached young woman, living by herself. So, after some investigation in Novogrudek, he went to Zhetel with a proposal for his wayward daughter, a plan to acquire the one thing that could shift her life into respectable place: a husband.

"Manya, listen," he broached, hedging toward his point. "I've heard about a very good *shadchan*." He had done his homework, he said, and this matchmaker's reputation was of the highest caliber.

Miriam laughed her easy laugh. "Papa, I'm not going to marry through a *shadchan*." And that was possibly the very last time Gutel shared his opinions on how his daughter should run her life. Miriam may have been more ambition-driven than many of her female contemporaries, but she had also cultivated a healthy recreational life. She was universally well liked among her social circle, mostly comprised of members of Hashomer Hatzair, a Socialist Zionist youth movement. She regularly hosted their informal meet-ups, as well as the after-parties, in the back room of her Zhetel shop, where she also lived. It was the ideal location—free from the eyes and judgment of parents, where they could let loose their independence in all its many forms.

When it came to men, Miriam never fell short of options. Of all the eager bachelors with their eyes on Miriam, perhaps none would regret the bungling of his pursuit more than Leibel Neski. Active in the same Zionist organization, Leibel was a few years older than the other members, and perhaps it was his age that buoyed his confidence enough to give Miriam his undivided attention during these gatherings, where he made his intentions toward her clear. But though she had no trouble enjoying company, sadly for Leibel, Miriam never took his advances seriously.

He would certainly rue the evening he decided to bring along a friend to a meeting at Miriam's. The younger tagalong—who was endowed with the elusive trifecta of being irrefutably tall, dark, *and* handsome—worked with Leibel at the Zhetel lumber mill. His name was Morris Rabinowitz.

Even in his early twenties, Morris wasn't just a tall man but a sizable one, with large hands and fingers as thick as sausage links. In a tailored suit, tie, and hat, he was easy to spot in a crowd and not just because he stood shoulders above it. Whether a flat cap or fedora, the hats Morris wore never rested quite as low on his head as they seemed to do on other men. Instead, the brims sat slightly aloft, as if they couldn't quite manage the job of covering his manly brow; but there wasn't one he didn't pull off with unmistakable swagger.

If Morris attracted instant attention with his dimensions, he also had no trouble holding an audience. Morris was something of a genial carouser; he loved a good card game and crowd, and he especially enjoyed taking in local sports. Eventually, he would develop an appetite for cultural indulgences like Italian opera, indicating that beneath all his small-town bravado lay more sensitive inclinations. Despite having never finished high school, Morris was sharp-witted and shrewd, and he had a knack for cultivating trusts and friendships with people of all sorts by operating on confidence and easy charm. His was the kind of ambition that, paired with the right opportunity, was poised to pop like a champagne cork.

The moment Leibel walked Morris in Miriam's direction marked the end of possibility for the rest of her suitors. She'd found the man for her, and she felt it in her bones before Morris had even said hello. As Miriam herself would later describe their introduction, it was simply "love at first sight."

❧

Morris wasn't a member of the Hashomer Hatzair and had very little interest in officially joining the group. But when Miriam invited him to come back for another meeting he obliged. And then another, and another. And so began two years of unhurried courtship.

Their slow start was due in part to the fact that shortly after they met, Morris left to serve a brief stint in the Polish army. But his time away didn't keep their feelings from building, and when Morris came back, the two quickly reignited their romance. Soon he was visiting Miriam at her shop every evening. The couple carried on like this happily for many months. Matrimony was set not aside but ahead for some undetermined point in the future.

It was an attitude that soon exhausted their families' more traditional expectations.

"What are you waiting for?" Morris's parents, the well-established Zhetel couple Berl and Beyla Rabinowitz, wanted to know. Still, Morris and Miriam would not be rushed.

In 1933, a fire ravaged Zhetel, leaving half the town in charred ruins. Like many small, forest-adjacent villages, Zhetel was essentially an intricate labyrinth of timber. And like so many others in the Novogrudek province, it was regularly plagued with fires, big and small, that gnawed their way through the tightly packed streets, jumping from one wooden home to the next before the modestly equipped fire brigades could intervene. Sadly, this particular blaze destroyed Berl and Beyla's house.

The Rabinowitzes moved quickly to rebuild their home. The process of putting it back together, piece by piece, seemed to trigger a deeper stirring in the older couple—perhaps having learned a harsh lesson in life's fragility. Berl and Beyla began their appeals for marriage to their son with fresh zeal. The room for acceptable delay had run out. "Why are you carrying on like this?" they demanded. "Enough is enough."

In the face of this renewed pressure, Morris and Miriam finally marched their way to the altar and had their Vilna wedding. If their extended (presumed) engagement had been unconventional, their relationship also appeared to be something closer to an equal match of true individuals—a union of two strong, capable people who entered into a marriage purely for love.

It was a foundation that would have set the newlyweds up for a happy family life at any time, but for the trying circumstances ahead, it would prove something more like miraculous. Just as the life Miriam and Morris were building together was taking shape, so too were the darkening clouds gathering over a not-so-far-away country.

Newly appointed German chancellor Adolf Hitler and his Nazi Party were on the precipice of unfurling their violent campaign against the Jewish people of Germany and unleashing Hitler's plot to take over Europe: lebensraum—expansion by conquering. An early Nazi slogan for the idea that only true Aryans were entitled to the idyllic pastoral life of the countryside, *Blut und Boden* (blood and soil) became a popular political banner and justification for the policy of lebensraum.

Earlier that year, on April 1, 1933, Hitler had launched a Jewish boycott. For a single day, SS storm troopers marked the windowpanes of Jewish-owned German businesses with the Star of David and the word *Jude*, intimidating anyone who attempted to enter those shops. The fear and demoralization of this day were hard felt, and not just by the Jews in Germany. The tailstreams of the Nazi Party's growing influence—born out of a discontent that had roiled the German populace since the end of the last great war—were twisting their way into Poland. Its fearmongering propaganda against the Jews was gaining a foothold among the Polish people and meddling in their politics.

The trouble this would eventually bring to the Rabinowitz family's doorstep—to all the Jewish doorsteps in Poland—was still years away. For now, it was a ripe old time to be young, Jewish, and in love, and living in the town of Zhetel.

CHAPTER 2

The Town Named After a Bird

ZHETEL WAS AN OLD, STORIED PLACE. ITS LONG, TURNOVER HIStory could be traced by its many different names dating back to the twelfth century, when it was called Dyatel, the Russian word for woodpecker. It wasn't technically even considered a small town until Lithuania's Grand Duke Alexander declared it so in 1498, calling it Zietela. When the first Jews arrived on the scene some eighty years later, the village had a total of five streets, 118 houses, and a single market. It was then ping-ponged around in the Grand Duchy of Lithuania, with a brief stint under Swedish rule, until the late 1700s, when it became part of the Russian Empire. During the Great War, Germany ruled Zhetel until March 1918, when for not quite a year it became part of the Belorussian People's Republic. In 1919, occupying Polish troops captured the town, but it wasn't until the Peace of Riga treaty that Zhetel was officially brought into the Second Polish Republic in 1921 and given its Polish name: Zdzięcioł. By then the town was populated with telephone lines and a telegraph, a power station, a post office, a hospital with an ambulance, two churches and four synagogues, and even a veterinary clinic. To its Jewish residents, whose ancestors had flourished there for some three hundred and fifty years, this town would forever be known by its Yiddish name, Zhetel.

Tucked away against the Białowieża Forest, the two-river town was far from everything big but close to every place big enough to keep in touch with the wider world. It was roughly the same distance of twenty-five miles to the towns of Lida, Slonim, Baronovich, and slightly closer to Novogrudek, the regional capital. Travelers coming in and out of Zhetel utilized the town's network of buses—small motorized wagons that made regular trips to neighboring villages and the nearest train station seven miles away—though just as often the townspeople ventured the journey on foot.

Laid wide in cobblestone, the vast market square was the town's bustling center. It was surrounded by buildings; a few stood solid in sturdy brick but mostly they were clapboard structures with steep gabled roofs, jumbled together along the raised sidewalks. There were banks and schools, restaurants and shoe shops. The streets were crowded with single-horse-drawn buggies and carts, strolling pedestrians, and men riding bicycles.

There was a pleasing, reliable rhythm to Zhetel life. Two mornings a week, well before dawn, the market square would fill with vendors, and farmers and peasants would make the journey from their homes by the forest to shop as well as sell and trade their fresh produce and meats. On Fridays, the town hushed before sunset when stores and restaurants with observant Jewish proprietors closed early for Shabbat. On Sunday mornings, the streets would echo with the clanging calls of bells ringing from the long end of the square, where a great white church rose like a mountain above the town. Completed in 1646, it was a gargantuan structure, dwarfing Zhetel's otherwise stumpy skyline, and a testament to a time when Christians dominated the area. The largest synagogue easily spanned the length of a city block, with its double chimneys and rows of tall, arching windows, though it didn't come close to matching the church's cloud-reaching height.

Every once in a while, the big world came to Zhetel. It was a known hub of talent and craftsmanship, and the reputations of its skilled artisans—its shoemakers, carpenters, tailors, and masons—exceeded the bounds of the little town. One year, the priests and cardinals from Vilna came to see Lazerowich the shoemaker, and ordered his finely stitched shoes. Even Vilna's world-renowned Yiddish theater troupe—which burst onto the international stage in the 1920s with its inaugural performance of S. Ansky's *The Dybbuk*, whose actors would bring their acclaimed productions to New York, London, and Paris—had graced the local theater.

Zhetel boasted plenty of its own excitement. There were bazaars and balls, concerts and movies at the local *kino.* It even had its own competitive soccer team. The heartbeat of Zhetel was its young people, a vivacious and eclectic group engaged in politics and dreams of life in Palestine. Most evenings, bands of teenage boys and girls belonging to Jewish youth groups traipsed through town, singing songs in Hebrew and Yiddish, their voices rising over the streets.

"It was a very happy little Jewish town," said one man reflecting on his childhood in Zhetel.

Perhaps if you were to strip Zhetel down into its Jewish parts—its synagogues and schools, its kosher butchers, and its shopkeepers—it would have appeared quite similar to its neighboring vistas. Another former Zhetel resident described his native home as such: "All the towns near Zhetel looked the same. The market was in the center. The windmill was operated either with or without water. Every town had its own matchmaker, joker, fool, and Shabbat gentile. Week after week, year after year, life in Zhetel followed the same pattern."

This may very well have been true. But even if Zhetel resembled the hundreds of shtetl villages and towns in Poland, this small little hamlet was unique, full of character and qualities that made it a highly unusual place. And those differences would provide its residents with unpredictable advantages in the years ahead.

Of all its charming irregularities and agreeable quirks, the distinguishing dynamic of Zhetel was its inclusive nature among Jews and non-Jews alike. After the Great War, the town's population ebbed and flowed; but as 1930 kicked off a new decade its residents—primarily Jews, Poles, and Belorussians (White Russians), and a small representation from the region's Tatar Muslim community—numbered about five thousand, nearly 80 percent of whom were Jewish. Yiddish was the primary language, but Polish, Belorussian, and Hebrew were on regular rotation, and most people in town spoke all four, with a smattering of German for those who were of age during the war.

Where many nearby Jewish communities represented a fraction of the towns and cities in which they lived, they also tended to be far more homogeneous and insulated as a result. They were either Orthodox or secular, Zionist or not. But Zhetel's Jewish life teemed with great variety. Its boundaries were elastic enough to hold a multitude of beliefs—religious and political. There were Orthodox, observant, secular, and "Lefties, Righties, Zionists, Communists, Bundists, Jewish Socialists," said one former resident taking stock of all its social layers. In Zhetel, there was room for everyone.

It was true there was a divide between gentile and Jewish neighbors, but there was far less outwardly displayed anti-Semitism or resentment of "the other." There were friendships forged across the kind of social and cultural lines that in larger cities had no real reason to exist.

As another Jewish resident at that time would fondly remember: "An unusual city, unusual people. Very good people, nice people. We stick together," she recalled, "and this is what it was."

It was this distinction that would soon make a great deal of difference.

❧

After they were married, Morris and Miriam moved out of Miriam's tiny shop-apartment and into a larger house on Zhetel's main square, just across the way from the big church and down the street from Morris's parents. It was a comfortable house with an equally comfortable yard surrounded by a wooden fence with a swinging wooden gate.

Tacked inside one of the street-facing windows was an advertisement for vitamins featuring the famous Dionne quintuplets. Their pink cherubic faces and jet-black curls winked out from behind the glass. The five Canadian sisters were an international sensation, and their sweet likenesses branded all manner of products from dental creams to corn syrup, and were a signal of the purchasable goods inside. The front door opened into the main floor of the house, which was occupied by Miriam's patent medicine shop; the walls were lined with towering hutches, their tall cabinets and long counters were made out of a polished blond wood. A short flight of stairs to the second floor led to the family's living quarters, which included a modest kitchen with a large hearth, a dining room and a living room with a tall white fireplace, and the family bedrooms. The house didn't have indoor plumbing; a water carrier would come regularly to deliver pails of fresh water for cooking, the wash, and the baths that were taken in tubs. The outhouse was in back beyond the shed that Morris used to store his bicycle and piles of firewood.

It was during their second summer as husband and wife that Morris and Miriam welcomed the first new member of their family, a baby girl, born on July 16, 1935, at the Novogrudek hospital. Following the Jewish tradition of naming a newborn child after a departed loved one, they decided to call her Rochel in honor of Miriam's mother.

When Miriam became pregnant again a little more than a year later, Morris prayed for a boy. But on June 9, 1937, Miriam gave birth to another baby girl, Tania. Having descended from a long line of male-begetting-male heirs, Morris was beside himself that he and Miriam had failed to produce a son. Misogynistic countryisms were long infused into Zhetel's culture and his shame was practically a public affair. When friends and family offered their sympathies on Morris's bad luck—"Oh, Maeshke, you had another girl. Why couldn't you have had a boy?"—it ground like salt in a wound. "I have to hang my own head that I should bring another girl into the world so soon after the first," he'd say, a lament he repeated for years.

Still, if Morris's disappointment in the gender of his offspring ran deep, it never surfaced in how he treated his daughters. From the time they were toddlers he was an enthusiastic and engaged father. In the warmer months, Morris brought Rochel and Tania along to the local soccer matches, hoisting them one at a time onto his strong shoulders so they could see over the crowds. In the winter, he bundled up the girls in their bulky coats and took them ice skating on the frozen Pomerayke River, or piled them onto a little sled so he could pull them across the ice.

For Miriam's part, motherhood was a welcome joy that didn't hamper her attendance in the shop. After Rochel was born she hired a Muslim girl named Manya to fill in as housekeeper and nanny. Short with dark hair, the younger Manya's culinary gifts outdid those of the lady of the house, and while Miriam was happy to relinquish her kitchen duties, there could only be one Manya in the family, so the Rabinowitzes fondly addressed their helper as Marysa. When Tania was born, further reinforcements were required. Cousin Itka came once again to keep after children and a home that weren't hers. And just as she had loved and cared for Miriam, she loved and cared for Miriam's daughters.

Rocheleh and Taibeleh, as they were called at home, were growing into darling, beautiful girls, each of them with apple-cheeked grins and shining brown eyes. Miriam often dressed them in matching outfits. The girls posed for a photo in the family's backyard when Rochel was four and Tania two. The sisters wore the same red buckle shoes and wool coats, each fashioned with a wide, curving collar and giant circle buttons. They held hands and their smiles stretched as big as pieces of pie.

But little more than the girls' clothes were similar; Rochel's features, dark and round like her father's, were decidedly of Rabinowitz descent. Tania's complexion was lighter, and while she resembled her older sister, her face was more angular like their mother's. Where Rochel was the precocious rule-follower and always eager to please, Tania was mischievous. By the time she was three years old, her epic misbehaviors had earned her the nickname "little devil." The crowning episode occurred when she found her way into the kitchen to an unattended pot of soup, which she pulled from the stove. Its simmering contents scalded the side of her face, and though it left no real visible scars, the injuries permanently damaged the hearing in her left ear. The Rabinowitz sisters shared a bedroom and confidences, and a genuine affection between them. Rochel would often help to hide Tania's bad behavior because she couldn't bear to see her punished.

Like most happy children, they were being raised in an environment that allowed each sister to feel she was the center of her own small life—both girls were adored by the family that surrounded them. Rochel, old enough to play outdoors unaccompanied, used to thrill herself by racing back and forth along the street to her grandparents' house until she was out of breath.

Large and warm, Berl and Beyla Rabinowitz's home was an enticing destination.

After the fire of 1933, they resurrected their house on a grander scale, making it one of the stateliest in town: two towering white columns flanked the front door, setting off the facade's painted white brick. They had cordoned off part of their spacious domicile into an informal inn where they offered rented rooms and indoor dining. Beyla, who had cultivated a reputation as a consummate cook, prepared lunch and supper for the guests. With its prime center-of-town location, their home also served as something of a local salon; their living room was always a churn of activity, brimming with lodgers and guests who provided a constant hum of grown-up voices bantering over politics and local gossip. Behind the din of chatter, oil sizzled in hot pans while the oven pumped out wafts of sweet blintzes, freshly baked potato kugels, and tzimmes, the air heavy with the sultry aromas coming from Bubbe Beyla's famous kitchen.

The mother of five—two daughters and three sons (which included a set of twins)—Beyla Rabinowitz was amply constructed with robust head-to-toe curves. She was a woman of plenty in all respects—her face was a wide canvas with full eyebrows and penetrating brown eyes. Her shining black hair curled with a bounce just below her ears.

A fitting match for Beyla, Berl Rabinowitz was a big man with a personality equal to the size of his reputation. Though he descended from a long line of rabbis dating back to the fifteenth century in Padua, Italy, Berl had broken with the male-Rabinowitz tradition to pursue the life of a businessman in the lumber trade. Just as the passion for a religious vocation seemed to have passed him by, so did any distinctly Semitic features. Instead, Berl resembled a Slavic cowboy. The span of his classic gunslinger mustache was so voluminous that when Rochel sat on his lap, she could twirl its whiskery ends all the way around her fingers. His handsomeness, like his steel-colored eyes and bluntly shorn head, had a rugged severity, and he carried the air of an outdoorsman even in a suit.

The extended Rabinowitz family was large, and Rochel and Tania were often in the pile-on company of doting aunts, uncles, and cousins who lived nearby. In closest proximity, there was Aunt Cherna, Morris's sister, who helped Beyla run the inn's dining room and overnight accommodations. Like her mother, Cherna was full-figured, but she had inherited her father's honey-fair complexion. Her nose and sparkling blue eyes were small and neat, and her petal-pout lips closed into a near-perfect heart. It could hardly be a coincidence that the Yiddish term *zaftig* was coined just as Cherna was coming of age.

Of all the relatives in their close family circle, the Rabinowitz girls adored their Aunt Luba most. Miriam's younger sister was a frequent guest in Morris and Miriam's home, making regular trips from Novogrudek, where she worked as a French teacher, to see her little nieces. Tall, with a willowy posture, Luba had eyes the color of a settled sea, and they were just as serene as her temperament. Her affectionate nature spilled over on the girls—she was always wrapping them in her arms or pulling them onto her lap. Luba's ear for language made her a natural and patient listener. When Rochel came home one day from kindergarten and confided that she was envious of another girl's blouse—a white shirt with colorful embroidered flowers—it was Luba who found a pattern and fashioned one just like it for her niece.

From the inside of their home to the outer reaches of their community, Morris and Miriam had, in just a few short years, built a very rich life for themselves. Their house was happy and so were their children. True to their independent natures, their marriage had room enough for both husband and wife to each establish prosperous professional lives.

Morris, like Berl, had carved out a name for himself as a dealer in the local lumber business, working with Leib Kaplinsky. As he learned how to navigate the forests in order to sort through its ancient trees determining which would become the best timber for floors, walls, and roofs and turn a profit for the mill, Morris became intimately familiar with its wooded groves. His job took him to the town's edges and deeper into the Polish Christian farming community, where Morris traded not just in lumber, but in the currency of relationships. He came to know the local farmers well; the forester had become a trusted friend.

Miriam's business continued to thrive. She had been married for more than six years now, but the sign hanging over the shop entrance still bore the Russian styling of her maiden name: *Dworetska*. The sign was a small point of contention in her marriage. While Morris didn't like it, that's how her customers would always know her. And Miriam was proud, even if secretly, that her independence had outlived—and even outshined—her married self.

The day would come when Miriam would be known by her husband's name. But it would take a force more powerful than convention to push that maiden self-reliance to the side.

"I was Dworetska until the war," Miriam would say. "Then I became a Rabinovich."

❧

In the years after the Great War, the Jews of Poland enjoyed a period of relative calm and inclusion under the near decade-long leadership of Marshal Józef Piłsudski. A former revolutionary, Piłsudski had been a juggernaut of political force in Poland for decades. He refused the presidency after successfully executing a coup d'etat in 1926, instead assuming the role of minister of military affairs from which he ruled over a popular quasi-dictatorship. When Piłsudski died of liver cancer in May 1935, Poland's defenses against Hitler's aggression were unquestionably weakened, and the country's Jewish population, which at that time exceeded some three million people, lost his protecting influence.

As Hitler's power reached its pinnacle during the latter half of the 1930s, so too did his appeal with Germany's receptive neighbor to the east. Many officials in Poland's highest echelons of government openly championed Hitler's anti-Semitic rantings and believed he had the right idea about treating the country's Jewish citizens as unwelcome foreigners. They promoted legislation for economic boycotts and forced emigration.

During this time, the Polish Catholic Church was a source of mixed messaging when it came to the country's anti-Semitism and the Jewish community. In his broadly circulated 1936 pastoral letter titled "On the Principles of Catholic Morality," Cardinal August Hlond addressed "the Jewish Problem." He warned, "It is a fact that Jews are waging war against the Catholic Church, that they are steeped in free thinking, and constitute the vanguard of atheism, the Bolshevik movement, and revolutionary activity." While he emphasized that "it is forbidden to assault, beat up, maim or slander Jews," he also urged the Catholic community to "skip over" Jewish businesses. "So long as Jews remain Jews," Hlond wrote, "a Jewish problem exists and will continue to exist." Among Polish priests, what support there was for Hitler and the Nazi Party ranged from quiet backing to full and open admiration. One popular and highly influential Warsaw priest went so far as to call Hitler "the whip of God."

Radical nationalist groups escalated their protests to mob violence, and a wave of pogroms soon followed that resulted in hundreds of Jewish deaths. While the Polish government never sanctioned or supported these attacks—indeed members of the Socialist Party and representatives on the political left condemned, even protested, the brutalities against Jews—it proved feckless in curtailing the unrest. The perpetrators of the abuse, even those found guilty of murdering Jews, received light sentences. And rather than inhibit the riots, these verdicts were seen as passive permission to continue them.

It may have been much later than the rest of Poland, but in 1938, Hitler's influence eventually made its way to Zhetel.

One morning, the town woke to find that the market square had been defaced—the surrounding buildings were graffitied with anti-Semitic language. "Go to Palestine," one read in Polish. Plastered on the walls of the great Catholic church, signs called for the "death of all Jews."

Appalled, the Catholic priest immediately had the signs torn down. A progressive man, it was his stewardship of the non-Jewish population that was in large part responsible for the town's singular harmony. In his Sunday sermon, the priest condemned the vandalism and the hate behind it, renouncing those responsible. "The Church will not allow this to happen," he told the assembled worshippers, and warned his congregation not to be swayed by such bigotry. Then in a public show of remorse, he apologized to the Jewish community.

For a time after the priest's rebuke, the appearance of Nazi propaganda and related menacing incidents in Zhetel lost much of their visible momentum. Their volume dropped to a lower frequency, retreating into the quiet space of shadows. Sneers of "dirty Jew" were spewed during drunken rantings, Jewish boys were heckled in the street. Supporters of the right-wing National Democratic Party, known as Endeks, traveled from larger cities to encourage the surrounding farming communities to purchase their goods only from other Christians rather than fill Jewish pockets with money, and a campaign for a Jewish boycott grew more conspicuous.

In the spring of 1939, the graduating class of Zhetel's public Polish high school celebrated the milestone event with a group field trip to Warsaw and the seaside port of Gdynia. One of the few Jewish students graduating that year was especially thrilled to be traveling with her classmates on such a big adventure. When they arrived in Gdynia, she saw that posted all along the port were signs with grotesque depictions of Jews and hateful anti-Semitic slogans. The shock and fear she felt seeing those signs by the waterfront—the understanding that she might very well be in the midst of a crowd of people who felt this way about Jews—all but extinguished any excitement she had felt about visiting the big city. All she wanted in that moment was to go home to Zhetel. "In a way, Zhetel was a cocoon, especially for children," another Jewish student realized later. It offered "a sense of safety from the hatred that was all around us."

Around the same time, there were attacks against Jews in Lublin. When word that Poles were harming and even killing Jews spread to Zhetel, its Jewish population became fearful that pogroms would eventually come to their town as well.

In the last days of summer, that anxiety would only swell. On August 23, 1939, news that envoys from Germany and Russia—Reich foreign minister Joachim von Ribbentrop and Soviet foreign minister Vyacheslav Molotov—had signed a non-aggression pact ricocheted around the world. Hitler's path to Poland had lost its last barriers. Radio airwaves and newspapers were immediately abuzz with speculation that a German attack on Poland was imminent.

❧

When Hitler pulled off his stunning victory in the German election of 1934, he became both *Führer* and *Reichskanzler*, consolidating an extraordinary amount of political power into a single governing office. In the wake of the news, foreign correspondent

Frederick T. Birchall surmised in his front-page story for the *New York Times* that the win gave Hitler "dictatorial powers unequaled in any other country, and probably unequaled in history since the days of Genghis Khan."

At the time, Birchall was considering hypothetical power, amassed but so far untapped, but the reporter took a long look down the stretch of Hitler's potential reach. "No other ruler has so widespread powers nor so obedient and compliant subordinates," he warned. "The question that interests the outside world now is what Chancellor Hitler will do with such unprecedented authority."

The world was about to find out.

PART II

The War

CHAPTER 3

The Russians Invade

BEFORE THE SUN ROSE ON THE MORNING OF SEPTEMBER 1, 1939—not even ten days after the Molotov-Ribbentrop treaty was inked in Moscow—the German air raids on Poland began. The Luftwaffe's first strikes were not military targets but highly populated towns, among them: Wieluń, Białystok and Grodno, Łódź, and Kraków. At nine o'clock, the capital city, Warsaw, was hit.

Attacking from the north, west, and south, Hitler launched the force of Germany's military—1.8 million troops, 2,500 tanks, and naval ships—at Poland from air, land, and sea. Caught unaware, Polish forces were slow to mobilize and could only muster a mere fraction of the military manpower in response. Most of their tanks and planes were destroyed within days.

For months the Jews of Zhetel had hovered anxiously around the few radios in town, waiting to have their worst fears confirmed. That morning they tuned in to the BBC broadcast as announcer Lionel Marson broke the news that Germany—without any declaration of war—had invaded Poland. Two days later, on

September 3, Britain and France declared war on Germany, but neither country sent military aid to their foundering Polish ally.

In a rush to fortify the front, Zhetel's able-bodied men of age were called to join the Polish soldiers fending off the country's invaders. Morris Rabinowitz, just two months shy of his thirty-fourth birthday, was among them. On the day the buses came to ferry the drafted men to war, Miriam and the children walked with him to the town square to see him off. They said their goodbyes and lingered to watch Morris board the bus. Rochel kept her eyes on her father's tall figure as she waved goodbye, holding her hand as high as she could reach to catch his attention one last time.

As the German forces swiftly pushed their way into Polish cities and towns in the west, a great number of frightened Jews fled to the small rural communities in the eastern part of the country. Many Zhetel families opened their homes to these refugees. They brought news from the west, and reports of Poland's armed forces had not improved. There was talk among Zhetelers that if the Germans overran the Polish army, forcing their troops to retreat, the Jews would follow them rather than stay and be subjected to German rule.

But this would not be necessary.

On September 17, the secret protocol of the Russia and German nonaggression treaty was put into action: Joseph Stalin's Red Army invaded Poland from the east, under the auspices of protecting and liberating Belorussians and Ukrainians. Poland continued to fight, now engaging multiple attackers on all sides. Its efforts collapsed within weeks. On September 27, Poland surrendered to Hitler's armies. Germany and Russia quickly harvested their victory and, as outlined in their accord, split the country in two, cutting a jagged division along the river Bug. The territory to the west now belonged to Germany, the area to the east—including the Novogrudek region—to the Soviet

Union. As the Nazis marched across their newly claimed land, they stopped just fifty miles short of Zhetel.

❧

The Russians rolled into town on a parade of might and metal. The great grinding caterpillar tracks of the Soviet army's massive tanks pressed so heavily onto Zhetel's streets they imprinted a trail behind them, unsettling the ancient cobblestones that forever afterward would remain uneven.

The crowd of Jewish residents waiting to welcome the Russian soldiers did so with joy. They tossed flowers before their marching feet and floated kisses into the air; some even ran off the sidewalk to press their lips against the tanks. Children chased the procession, running up to point at the soldiers' hats emblazoned with a hammer and sickle inside the big red star, calling out to them in broken Belorussian. The soldiers smiled and handed down their caps.

On October 6, the very last fighting men of the Polish army, still holding out their defenses near the town of Kock, put down their weapons and surrendered to the Germans. The units of temporary troops were disbanded, and Morris returned to an occupied hometown and uncertain days ahead.

❧

After their initial exuberant relief at the Russians' late September arrival, the Jews of Zhetel were forced to contend with their new reality. Their Soviet occupiers were clearly the lesser of two evils, but the changes to their lives under Communist rule—which benefited some but crippled others—were drastic and immediate.

The big cities' campaign of anti-Semitism, and the menacing violence against Jews that had crescendoed in Poland just before the outbreak of war, came to a standstill. Under their Soviet occupiers, Jews weren't discriminated against or relegated to the margins just for being Jews—some were even given high-ranking government jobs, or made factory foremen.

The Soviet educational system—which came with a helping of Soviet indoctrination and fealty to Stalin—was not only more academically rigorous than both Zhetel's Polish public-school curriculum and its private Hebrew schools, it was also free. Nor was there any cost for the healthcare dispensed at the newly established hospital. This appealed to many Jews in Zhetel, and for many others—especially the younger generation—there were ideological reasons to be enthusiastic about Communism. "The theory behind it sounded very good, above all they claimed every person is equal, with equal opportunities and equal rights," one former student said. "For a Jew in particular, this sounded like a utopia."

All religious institutions were shuttered and repurposed: the synagogues and churches were turned into government storehouses and offices. Religious worship and celebrations—Shabbat and all Jewish holidays—were effectively canceled. The garden belonging to the Catholic priest was transformed into a public park. The great main square was put to new use as an outdoor cultural center and a gathering place for the town's young people. In the warmer months, concerts and dances filled the evening air with music.

But the Soviet occupation would not be benevolent to the Jews or the Polish community. The NKVD, the Soviet secret police, rounded up members of the Polish elite from doctors to political leaders. Many were arrested and jailed, others were beaten and tortured. It soon became clear that having certain ideas was dangerous, and even a whisper of Zionist or Socialist views was enough to earn the accused a one-way ticket to Siberia. "Nothing was private anymore," one Jewish Novogrudek resident remembered. "Our 'liberators' were caricatures of freedom." Almost immediately after their arrival in Zhetel, agents of the NKVD rounded up three Jewish families—the Kablinskis, the Padlechewskis, and the Zalsteins—charged them as counterrevolutionaries, and deported them to Siberia. As time went on, the NKVD doubled down on its investigations into Zhetel's township, encouraging a culture of informants that stoked suspicions and pitted neighbor against neighbor. In school, children were told to keep their ears open at home, and to come forward if their parents spoke against Stalin.

Slightly less dangerous but perhaps equally problematic in a Communist-ruled society was being a capitalist—especially a wealthy one. Rich families, Polish and Jewish alike, fled in the wake of the Russian invasion, while others were deported to Siberia in the early days of the occupation.

By Zhetel's standards, the Rabinowitz family was hardly rich, but they were certainly well-off, and therefore undeniable beneficiaries of capitalism. Morris and his father, Berl, owned two of the largest homes on the town square; Miriam and her mother-in-law, Beyla, were the proprietors of the patent medicine shop, and the inn and tavern. One after another, Jewish business owners were brought into the police headquarters across from the kosher butcher shop and interrogated by NKVD officers, but somehow the Rabinowitzes skated through these sweeps unscathed. The family's livelihood, however, did not.

When the Russians nationalized all businesses in October, they commandeered Berl and Beyla's brick house and the Dworetska shop, forcing Miriam to turn over her entire inventory with it. Just weeks earlier, the newly arrived Russian soldiers, unaccustomed to open commerce and stores with such full shelves, set upon Zhetel in a buying frenzy. With their pockets full of zlotys and rubles, they cleaned the local merchants out of most everything they had in stock. Acting quickly, Miriam collected first-aid supplies and medicines, including her store of drugs, and stowed them in the false-bottom drawer in one of her giant hutches. When the family vacated the house, they were able to take their furniture—and the stashed goods—with them.

Without a home of their own, Morris made hasty arrangements to rent rooms from a lawyer who owned a sizable house at the edge of town. They had barely settled there, when the Soviets forced the lawyer and his family to give up their house as well. This time Morris and Miriam moved outside of town to a farm owned by a Christian family, the Belskys.

The Belskys were kind people who took a lasting interest in the well-being of their new Jewish tenants and their doe-eyed daughters, and let them a large room off the kitchen of the main house. It was close quarters for their foursome, but Morris and Miriam used the wide oak cabinets from Miriam's shop to break up the space, attempting to create the illusion of rooms and possibly a shred more privacy.

When the Soviets halted the town's once robust commerce—distributing all food, clothing, and wares through government storehouses—basic necessities were soon in short supply. Morris purchased a dairy cow and installed her in the Belskys' barn so there would always be fresh milk for Rochel and Tania. The milking fell to Miriam, who, raised a Novogrudek city girl, had never in her life been so close to a cow. But under Mrs. Belsky's patient tutelage Miriam learned the demanding task of filling the buckets as best she could until the older woman relieved her to strip the last of the milk from the cow's udders. The physical toll was unexpected. At night Miriam would massage her aching hands; some evenings her fingers were so stiff she could barely manage to close a fist.

One morning when Mrs. Belsky came over to inspect Miriam's progress, she drew back, pleased to find the job was already done. "Oh, you finished this time," she said, smiling. "Now, you know how to do it from beginning to end." Quietly, Miriam's pride swelled. She was still a woman defying expectations, even in a barn.

For a time, the Rabinowitzes' life at the Belskys' was calm and content. But money soon became an issue—there simply wasn't enough of it. The Soviet authorities registered both Morris and Miriam as merchants, making it extremely difficult for either of them to find new work. There were few jobs to be had, and most of the positions had gone to Jews who spoke fluent Russian early on in the occupation. The leftover alternatives—manual labor and risking trade on the black market—were less than ideal and opportunities for either in Zhetel were scarce. When Morris finally found a job, it was thirty miles away in Slonim. Things were so dire he had no choice but to take it, and he was apart from Miriam and the girls for long periods at a stretch.

It was a precarious time for Zhetel. The Soviet authorities were always on the hunt for counterrevolutionaries. After being hauled into the NKVD offices for interrogation, people sometimes disappeared without a word.

Like many other mothers and wives in Zhetel, Miriam had busied herself preparing *sukeris,* a bland hearty bread typically eaten on long journeys. She hung sacks of it from the ceiling to keep it ready in anticipation of the short notice they would receive if the NKVD decided to send them to Siberia. The fear that she and the children could be deported while Morris was miles away in Slonim frayed Miriam's nerves. When it became clear that their circumstances were not going to change, husband and wife packed up their daughters, piled their belongings into a wagon, and left Zhetel, trading Morris's hometown for Miriam's.

❧

The region's capital city, Novogrudek, was settled in a valley dip between large, rolling hills. Just beyond its outer edge, high on the steep green-grassed incline known as Mount Zamkovaya, stood the medieval ruins of a magnificent castle built in the twelfth century. All that remained of the once-formidable citadel were two crumbling towers with their vaulted archways and a far-reaching wall. Their bricks and stones had a washed-away look, worn by centuries of wars and weather.

More than twice as large as Zhetel with a population of thirteen thousand (not quite half of which was Jewish), Novogrudek was world renowned for its matzah and as the hometown of one of Poland's most famous literary heroes, early nineteenth-century poet Adam Mickiewicz.

The sprawling Mickiewicz estate—which boasted, among other luxurious features, endless green lawns, a barn, and a gazebo—was located in Novogrudek's center and the heart of the city's Jewish neighborhood. On Racelo Street, which ran adjacent to the famous property's high stone wall, among the wooden houses topped with tiled roofs, was the home of Gutel Dworetsky. It was the house where he'd lived with his wife, Rochel, and their young children, and where he'd carried on as a widower for the better part of his adult life. And after the crash of 1929, when his lucrative lumber business grew thin, the walls of this house had provided. Gutel rented the basement space to some local dairy farmers. Damp and cool, the brick room had provided the perfect temperature for aging cheese. For years, giant wheels hung from the low ceiling, a constellation of suspended circles. The Mickiewicz wall cast a shadow, perpetually keeping the light from entering Gutel's bedroom, but every fall the chestnut trees that grew on the other side dropped their nuts onto the street, to the delight of the neighborhood children.

Returning to Gutel's house with her family intact surely gave Miriam some welcome relief after months of worrying about separation and Siberia. Since moving away to Zhetel, she'd made many trips back to Novogrudek to visit her father and siblings.

After she and Morris were married, she'd returned to patronize Novogrudek's higher-end merchants to furnish their home; it's where she had her finest dresses made. It was in the Novogrudek hospital that she'd given birth to Rochel. (There hadn't been time when Tania came so she was born at home in Zhetel.) It was her childhood home, where she and Luba and their brother, Beryl, grew up under the helping hand of Cousin Itka.

The Rabinowitzes moved in with a Dworetsky cousin, a lawyer who owned a large house not far from Gutel's, where they did their best to keep a low profile. Though it was a risk, Morris and Miriam decided ahead of time not to register their departure from Zhetel or their arrival in Novogrudek with the Soviet authorities in the hopes that a fresh start and a little anonymity would improve Morris's employment prospects. This meant keeping Tania and Rochel, who was coming up on her sixth birthday, at home.

Rochel watched other children in the Jewish neighborhood going off to school and couldn't understand why she wasn't able to join them. She'd loved her kindergarten in Zhetel and desperately wanted to repeat the experience. When Rochel appealed to her aunt for an explanation, Luba told her, "When your family left Zhetel, your parents did not tell the government. If you were to go to school here in Novogrudek, they would have to register you." And that, she told Rochel, "would not be good." It was an answer that did little to placate Rochel, but she detected a warning in Luba's voice and decided it was better not to ask any more questions.

There were other things in Novogrudek to pique the children's interest: both girls were over the moon to be living so close to Luba, but better still, they had discovered their aunt was in love. Sweet, sensitive Luba had fallen for a young painter, who set his brushes to canvas depicting the local landscapes. It was perhaps no surprise that Luba should become enchanted with an artist or that his temperament should complement her own. But theirs wasn't the only brewing romance. Beryl Dworetsky was engaged to a young woman named Chana. Soon the whole family was caught up in the expectant thrill of a wedding.

Budgets being what they were in the time of Soviet occupation, there was little money to grant the occasion its usual fanfare. In the end, it didn't matter; it was a wedding all the same and very exciting. Rochel stood close to her mother, wide-eyed, as she watched the women help Chana get ready. Miriam brought a roll of gauze from her collection of patent-medicine shop wares and, with Luba's help, they fashioned the wispy material into a veil for the bride. A rabbi came to the house of a family friend where they held the ceremony and a small reception.

Even under Communist rule, the business of being a Jewish family persisted (albeit more quietly) under the Dworetsky roof. The family found ways to keep their traditions. When Passover came that spring of 1941, they held the Seder supper in Gutel's house. Perhaps the meal was scanter than years' past, but still there was matzah and that meant the children's favorite part of the evening—the finding of the *afikomen*—was on as usual. In Seder tradition, the middle matzah is broken in two, and one piece, the *afikomen*, is hidden away for the children of the house to find. Later in the service, they are meant to barter their bounty for treats or *gelt* (pocket money), because as tradition dictates, without the full *afikomen*, the meal and the Seder cannot be completed.

That night Rochel was the one to find the *afikomen*. Her spine tingled as she tucked it away for safekeeping. But after dinner when she went to retrieve the *afikomen*, the piece of matzah was gone. Rochel was in a panic—she couldn't return to her grandfather's table without the matzah, but how could she admit that she had lost such a sacred part of the meal? In a flash, she snuck out of the house and ran across the way to the neighbors. She knocked on the door, and asked for a piece of matzah, which the neighbor retrieved for her without question, and back Rochel scurried with the necessary half in hand.

How her heart must have pounded when she surrendered that matzah piece to her grandfather. Rochel, who never so much as bent the rules, was now an impostor. Later that night, when she pulled back the covers to climb into bed, there was the original *afikomen* in between the blankets. It hadn't been lost, just overlooked. It would be far worse to confess the sin of losing the matzah now, so Rochel swallowed down her guilt and confided in no one, not even Luba.

It was a heavy secret for such a pure heart to hold.

The year pressed on. Morris and Miriam made do. Work was found and money, if only paltry sums, was made. Much had changed in the months since the invasion; they were now a family living through war. Whatever the guiding principles and ambitions of their marriage had been before, only one thing really mattered now: the family must stay together.

This period in Novogrudek had the air of impermanence. Life under the Russians had its drawbacks, but they, like most of the Jewish people across eastern Poland, were faring far better than those living under Nazi rule—of that they were certain. Just how much better off, Morris and Miriam could scarcely imagine.

CHAPTER 4

The Germans Invade

SUNDAY MORNING, JUNE 22, 1941, PASSED IN A STRANGE quiet. It was the kind of quiet that builds around something invisible—a premonition, a clamping anxiety. It was as if the whole city of Novogrudek was holding its breath. Just before noon, people came out into the streets to gather in front of windowsills and lean into doorways, waiting while their neighbors fiddled with radios. The air snapped and buzzed as the broadcast began. The tinny sound of a marching band came through, trumpeting the upbeat tune of a town parade. Then, in measured cadence, Foreign Commissar Vyacheslav Molotov addressed the citizens of the Soviet Union: "Today at 4 o'clock A.M., without any claims having been presented to the Soviet Union, without a declaration of war, German troops attacked our country."

Earlier in the still-dark hours before dawn, Count Friedrich-Werner von der Schulenburg, Germany's ambassador in Moscow, had come to Molotov's Kremlin office to deliver the communique from Reich foreign minister Joachim von Ribbentrop. Not only had Russia "broken its treaties with Germany," Ribbentrop's missive accused, it was readying "to attack Germany from the rear."

Ribbentrop concluded, "The Führer has therefore ordered the German Armed Forces to oppose this threat with all the means at their disposal." The 1939 nonaggression pact, in which both Schulenburg and Molotov had, together, put so much faith, was dead: their countries were at war.

When Schulenburg finished reading, Molotov turned to face his now former ambassador-in-arms. "Why did you sign the non aggression pact if you were prepared to break it so easily?"

Schulenburg was at a loss. Widely trusted among his diplomatic circles, he had a reputation for being erudite and charming. At sixty-five, the career diplomat who'd held his post in Moscow since 1934 had been an adamant and vocal supporter of keeping the peace with his host country. Despite (or likely because of) his recent and repeated urgent telegrams to Berlin expressing concerns over growing reports of Germany's borderline provocations—rumors that, he was careful to note, were an "obvious absurdity"—Schulenburg's own leaders had kept him in the dark. Hitler had lied when he personally assured Schulenburg during a late-April meeting in Berlin that he was "not going to go to war with Russia!"

"For the last six years, I've personally tried to do everything I could to encourage friendship between the Soviet Union and Germany," Schulenburg finally answered Molotov. "But," he continued, resigned, "you can't stand in the way of destiny."

In hindsight their faith in the 1939 pact was spectacularly foolhardy. Warnings of the imminent blitzkrieg, code-named Operation Barbarossa—which in some cases were so accurate they included the exact date and timing of the attack—had been directed to Russia's attention for months. Stalin had willfully disregarded them all. When Britain and the United States shared credible intelligence reports with Russia, Stalin, wary of duplicitous misdirection from Winston Churchill and Franklin Roosevelt, remained unswayed. Not even when Stalin's own spies, operating undercover in Japan and Germany, sent reports of the German attack could the Russian leader be convinced. Soviet agents had wiretapped phone calls between German officers discussing their target's complete lack of awareness of the coming attack. For months, Red Army ground troops had sent reports of tell-tale abuses on the front line up the chain of command. By May, there were no fewer than seventy-one border violations committed by German forces under investigation. The signs were so apparent, even the Polish peasants appeared better informed than the Russian soldiers billeting in their midst. In the days just before the breach, local women were overheard calling to the soldiers across the river, "Soviets, Soviets, the war is coming! Soviets, the war will start in one week!"

Blindly confident that Russia's defenses could not be overrun, Stalin did nothing. Only on the evening of June 21 did he finally send word to troops to brace for possible battle. But it was much too late.

At 3:15 A.M. on June 22, the Wehrmacht soldiers cut through Russia's borderline defenses like scissors through string. The Luftwaffe, targeting strategic bases first, had demolished nearly a quarter of the Russian air force before Schulenburg had reached Molotov's office.

❧

As Molotov continued his public address, he steeled the people of the Soviet Union, reminding them that this would be a time for "discipline, organization, and self-denial worthy of real Soviet patriots," and encouraged listeners to remain steadfast and united around their "glorious Bolshevist party."

Moments before Molotov's broadcast ended, his voice broke from its steady pitch, suddenly growing loud and strong: "The enemy shall be defeated!" he cried. And then, in a final burst of volume: "Victory will be ours!"

The transmission cut out. Molotov's words hung in the air

around Novogrudek before the full weight of their meaning was understood. Earlier that morning, a number of planes had flown overhead. Anyone in and around the city who had heard or seen them assumed they were Russian. Now it was clear: the planes had been German.

While rousing, it's hard to imagine the foreign commissar's speech did much to put the Jews in the Soviet-occupied territories at ease, including those Rabinowitz family members currently in Novogrudek. On a pitch of bad luck, Morris's sister, Cherna, who just happened to be visiting with her young son, Simcha, not yet two years old, were stuck. They could not make the trip back to Zhetel now.

That night, Novogrudek went into a blackout. The street lights were not lit, curtains were drawn tight. Across the city, only the children managed sleep. There were rumors that the Soviets had received orders to leave the area. The few homes in possession of radios tuned in to broadcasts from Moscow or Minsk, but the reports of bombings and fighting provided little detail and even less comfort.

The mass evacuation of Russian occupiers began the very next day. Soviet officials in charge of everything from local factories to warehouses and municipal buildings did not show up to work. The streets were packed with cars and small buses; even bicycles were heaped with trunks and suitcases. All the city's core governing institutions, including members of the fire brigade and the police, were leaving or already gone. Even the teachers were clearing out of Novogrudek. They waved goodbye, calling out "See you soon!" to their Jewish students, who watched, confused, from the sidewalks. People were so desperate to get out of the city that they clung to the sides of wagons and trucks. Hoping to keep ahead of the invading German forces, the Soviets were fleeing east with their families to the safety of Russia's pre-1939 borders.

Their frantic departure incited a panic. People clamored around Novogrudek's main square, waiting for instructions on what they should do next. But with the city emptied of authority, none came.

That afternoon, small battalions of Russian troops passed through Novogrudek accompanied by military vehicles. They too were heading east toward Minsk. These soldiers still had their weapons and marched through Grodno Street in unit formation. Stray groups of soldiers soon followed—but these men were exhausted from battle, weaponless, and dirty. This was a retreat.

It was only the second day of the invasion. No one could believe the Russian defenses had been beaten down so easily.

❧

The citizens of Novogrudek were left to fend for themselves. Jews and gentiles alike scrambled to find any kind of transportation out of the city; some begged rides with their departing occupiers, but very few were offered passage.

Of those who opted to remain, many put their faith in Russia's military, holding on to their belief that Stalin would prevail over Hitler. Others argued that Novogrudek, which didn't intersect with any major route of travel and was some distance from larger rivers and bridges, offered little in the way of strategic importance and was therefore an unlikely target. Disturbed by warnings of Nazi violence from refugees who arrived in Novogrudek after fleeing the 1939 German occupation in the west, many Jews decided not to take their chances and prepared to leave the city. A number of families with the means to hire transport paid their Polish neighbors for safe passage. (Many were unwittingly cheated or outright robbed of their belongings and left stranded in the middle of nowhere.) It was mostly the young people who did not waste their time hand-wringing or deliberating their options, and hurried away from the city as fast as they could. In most cases, they set out on foot.

Some simply trusted that their new occupiers would maintain civility, unable to imagine that the disciplined, well-mannered German soldiers they had encountered during the Great War could perpetrate such heinous acts. The idea of a campaign of genocide was just too confounding to be believed. Others split the difference and entertained family separation in order to send the men—thought to be the most vulnerable to German internment and abuse—on their own to Minsk, convinced women and children would be spared.

However, many Novogrudek Jews refused to abandon their property and livelihoods, and the place that held their history and everything of value to them.

This was more or less Gutel Dworetsky's attitude, and any conversation Morris and Miriam had debating whether to chance the thirty-mile trip to the old border would have been unable to avoid it. This decision now involved more relatives than their group of four. Despite Luba's devotion to her sister and nieces, presumably her heart was anchored to Novogrudek with her fiancé. Perhaps Beryl Dworetsky and his new wife, Chana, could have been motivated to go, but Cherna's husband, Zalman, was back in Zhetel, as were Berl and Beyla. Fleeing Novogrudek would mean leaving all of them behind. The journey would no doubt be long and dangerous, especially with two young children: Rochel was still weeks away from her sixth birthday, and Tania had only just turned four.

In Novogrudek, they had a safe dwelling in Miriam's cousin's sizable home, where there was room for their entire family. Just next door, the neighbors had an underground bunker, a ready shelter where they were all welcome should an attack come. The risks were too risky; the unknowns too many, and the certainties too few.

And so, they stayed.

They could not have foreseen the sheer magnitude of what was advancing in their direction. If they had known what was coming, it's hard to imagine Morris and Miriam—or any Jew in Novogrudek—wouldn't have fled.

From the moment the first bombs fell, the German forces that had been gathering for months in preparation for Operation Barbarossa were spreading along and across the 1,800-mile border like a plague. Three and a half million German troops were approaching in a rolling groundswell, supported by 3,000 tanks and 2,500 planes. For months, Germany had positioned more than one hundred military divisions along the border, primed for the orders to launch their lightning war. Their element of surprise had been so profound that within a single day, the southern front (of its three-pronged assault) had pushed fifty miles into Soviet territory.

Already, Wehrmacht troops were triumphantly spilling into Soviet-occupied towns and villages, marking a new, more terrible turn in the war. These forces were operating under a mandate unlike any other in the history of modern warfare, one that violated all international laws and even Germany's own military norms. They were marching under the invisible flag of "total war" to stamp out Communism, an ideology believed to be so dangerous it had to be wiped out of existence. And the worst of its perpetrators—the enemy who deserved no mercy—were the Jews.

Following in the Wehrmacht's wake were the Einsatzgruppen, a shadow force of some three thousand men. Under the command of Chief of the SS Heinrich Himmler, these specialty task forces were mobile killing squads deployed with a singular directive: extermination.

Relative to the size of the infantry forces, their numbers were small, and yet they would be even deadlier.

ꕥ

At ten o'clock on Tuesday morning, June 24, 1941, nine planes flew low over Novogrudek. The first bomb dropped dead-center on Zamkova Street where the Russians had based their headquarters, leveling the building. The earth shuddered, registering the explosions; houses shook and windowpanes burst on impact. People scattered in all directions—some ran panicked back into their homes, while others headed to the hills in the direction of the castle ruins, away from the exploding city center.

Within minutes the skies were empty again. In the Jewish section of town, a giant crater smoked in the road. A woman and child lay dead beside it—the child still in his mother's arms. A wounded man sat off to the side against a building, stunned, holding his own dismembered leg. The square was mostly empty but for the bodies, which stayed unattended. No one was yet willing to risk removing them for burial. In something of a miracle, only thirty people were killed, though many more were wounded. The fires from the attack blazed for two more days.

No one in the Rabinowitz or the Dworetsky family had been injured in the raid, but all were shaken. Up until that point they had lived in separate places, but now Gutel, Beryl, and Chana joined Luba and the Rabinowitz family, where the nearby bomb shelter could accommodate them all.

It wasn't long before word reached the house that Luba's fiancé, the humble painter, had been killed. Luba sat at the kitchen table, crying. She brought her hands hard against her face and head, hitting herself over and over, beyond consolation. Rochel stared, caught between awe and fright; she couldn't tear her eyes away from her aunt's raging grief. Even then she understood that Luba's heart was breaking.

ঌ

Those next few days passed in suppressed distress. Fearful more attacks were imminent, Morris and Miriam would usher the children over to the neighbor's bunker in the morning, and the whole family would submerge themselves below ground for hours at a time, waiting out the worst-case scenario. Other families boarded up their homes and took off for the safety of the city's outskirts, trekking up to the hills and forest or traveling to nearby farms.

Emptied of any acting government authority, save the volunteers who made up the civil guard, Novogrudek was fast becoming a lawless place. It didn't take long for the looting to start: neighbors taking from neighbors, servants pillaging the homes of their former employers. Committing any theft, even in the attack's chaotic aftermath, was still a dangerous risk. The retreating Russian soldiers, coming from the front in steady droves and haphazardly passing through town, only stopped long enough to make an example of these thieves, first by shooting them and then hanging their bodies out in plain view to serve as a warning: *This is what happens to anyone who tries to steal what belongs to the Soviet Union.*

Elsewhere around eastern Poland, roads from the front were crowded with captured Russian soldiers, now prisoners of war. Their boots kicked up great clouds of dust as they walked sometimes as many as twelve across, forming jagged columns of men so long they stretched clear out of sight. Their faces were blackened with swipes of soot and mud, their untucked shirts filthy and crumpled. German soldiers on motorbikes rode alongside these men, corralling them west like cattle.

Those Russian soldiers who had managed to evade German capture came through Novogrudek in dragging, disjointed groups. These were beaten-down men, dirty and half-starved.

They walked without weapons or shoes; some were wounded and missing limbs. They had abandoned the fight and left everything in the fields, including their tanks and artillery. On their way back to Russia, they blew up bridges, scorched crop fields, and gouged the roads behind them with explosives. Now they hurried through the city, pressing ahead toward Minsk.

The residents of Novogrudek watched these soldiers fade out of sight, taking the last hopes of a German defeat with them.

❧

A period of calm followed. By Saturday, June 28, people were breathing easier. The weather was warm; the early summer sun flashed bright against a blue sky. A palpable relief settled over the afternoon.

Families who had boarded up their houses before taking short-term shelter in barns or in the woods were anxious to get home in time for the end of Shabbat and made their way back into town. Rumors were circulating that the Germans would be arriving any day, and a home without an owner present would be considered abandoned property.

The sun was still bright when the banshee wails of the Stuka dive-bombers sounded louder and louder as they dropped from the sky over the city, but the aircraft passed over just as quickly as they had come. When the high-pitched groans of their engines roared again, it was as if the planes were coming from every direction.

Bombs pounded down in a thunder of explosions. The planes' gunners sprayed the streets, jackhammering the ground with bullets. The tight-knit houses instantly lit up in flames, the fire catching from one wooden dwelling to the next—a ready chain of kindling.

Rushing into the shelter, the families squeezed together—Morris and Miriam, the girls and Luba, the neighbors, all packed into the dark underground space, the earth thudding as it registered each detonation.

This time the bombing went on for hours, coming in giant crushing tidal waves, one after the other. The first time the Nazis attacked, they hit known military locations and high-value Russian government buildings. Now it was as if they were trying to wrench the city off the face of the earth. From the hillside by the castle ruins, it looked as if all of Novogrudek was on fire.

The noise was deafening even as far as the Brecianka woods, a small grove off to the side of the city, to say nothing of the sounds reverberating off the walls inside the bunker. An explosion rocked the house next door. Everyone inside that bunker could be forgiven for believing they were about to be blasted out of existence.

The onslaught ended at dusk. When night fell, the city wouldn't go dark: the sky glowed red like a giant ember, reflecting the fires that still burned. Buildings groaned, their tin roofs twisted and buckled as the flames melted them, finally collapsing their frames to the ground. The choking cloud of smoke was said to have spread so far, the odor of the burning city permeated the air miles away.

When it was safe to emerge the next day, the family walked through the Jewish neighborhood toward Gutel's house. After a traumatic, teeth-rattling twenty-four hours, the whole family was sticking close together; everyone, including Gutel as well as Rochel and Tania, came out to survey the damage.

The synagogue had been leveled, its walls almost completely submerged in heaping piles of rubble. Bodies lay everywhere, some burned beyond recognition. The kosher butcher's corpse was on the road by the bus terminal, the wind lifting the hairs of his beard. The man who ran a hardware store and his daughter lay together, killed while trying to salvage their goods from the burning building.

The family finally reached Gutel's house. Or the place where Gutel's house had been. There was nothing to come back to, just a mess of charred beams and smoldering mortar, the crumbling chimney, and the brick cellar broken open to the sky.

All of Racelo Street had been incinerated. Not a single home was left standing.

In the first days of July, the Germans made their way into Novogrudek. Wehrmacht soldiers marched through the wreckage, high on their decisively swift victory. They occupied the larger homes that had survived the blast. If there was room, the residents were permitted to stay. One small group of soldiers commandeered accommodations at the Alter family's house on May Third Street. Whatever the family may have been expecting, it wasn't the polite, charming men who came into their home. Hardly the bloodthirsty marauders the families had feared, many of the soldiers behaved more like guests and ingratiated themselves with ease, telling jokes and singing songs. They shared their rations of soap and sardines, amiably passing bread from their table to the Jews in the house. Could these men really be the same monsters who loomed in the refugees' tales of vileness and cruelty?

This cordial entry was short-lived. The new invaders combed through the evacuated and ruined homes, searching for hiding Russians and items of value. This on its own was not alarming; it was war, after all. The Russians had perpetrated similar offenses if not worse ones during their invasion, and not everyone had been sorry to see them go. "Thank God, we got rid of Communists," one Jewish Novogrudek resident said. This was the price of being occupied and the kind of low-level degradation they fully expected to endure.

When a group of German soldiers came to the Dworetskys' house and banged on the door, Cherna answered. Where the others had dark, distinctly Jewish looks, Cherna, with her fair skin and blue eyes, could easily pass for a Christian Pole.

The men asked who owned the house. Cherna, holding Simcha, summoned her courage. "It's my house," she lied, and told them she was Polish. They demanded to know who the others were, and why they were there. "These are my neighbors," Cherna explained. "Their house was bombed, so they came here."

The soldiers on the doorstep took in Cherna's near-blond curls and the child in her arms. They either decided she was indeed the home's rightful gentile owner or saw nothing in the house worth taking, and left.

❧

While two of his children, a daughter-in-law, and three grandchildren cowered in an underground bunker in Novogrudek, some twenty miles away in Zhetel, Berl Rabinowitz was taking stock of the trouble he knew was coming, gauging its direction like an old sailor lifting a spit-slick finger to catch the wind.

The initial siege of the Nazi invasion might have bypassed the small town, but it had come close enough that Zhetelers saw the Luftwaffe planes on their way to drop their bombs in larger towns and cities, and heard their thunderous explosions. Fires could be seen burning in Lida some thirty miles away.

Newscasters gave radio reports of the late-June attacks and the nearby fighting that only confirmed what Zhetel residents had seen for themselves—the lines of retreating Russian soldiers and the abandoned tanks and weapons in the fields outside of town. Hitler's armies were maintaining the upper hand. As far as Berl was concerned, his children staying in Novogrudek—more centrally located with access to a rail line—couldn't have been a worse idea. Sensing there was little time to waste, he set off to retrieve his family.

As soon as Berl arrived in Novogrudek, he sat Morris down and pleaded with his son. The city was in ruins. Thousands of people had lost their homes during the bombings. Morris, Miriam, and the children could not stay here. Things would be easier in Zhetel, of this Berl was certain. There, the Rabinowitz family was not without influence or friends.

"Why are you just sitting here?" Berl insisted. "Let's go back to Zhetel."

Miriam was already worried they were running out of food. The Soviets' warehouses had been pillaged or destroyed, and supplies were scarce. It didn't take much convincing. A plan was set: Morris and Chaim Feldman, a wealthy friend eager to bring his own wife and two young sons to a safer location, would travel ahead of their families to secure places to stay and stores of food. The men hitched up Feldman's horse and wagon and left Novogrudek.

It was unfortunate that Morris and Chaim ran straight into the kind of trouble they'd hoped to avoid. The Wehrmacht presence had proliferated beyond the larger cities throughout the region, and soldiers on motorbikes were patrolling all the major routes of travel, hunting for Russian soldiers and refugees, stopping civilians and barking at them in German and Polish, "*Reisepass! Paszport!*"

It may have been under the pretense of searching for escaped POWs that the Nazi soldiers stopped Morris and Chaim. That they looked Jewish was likely reason enough for the encounter to turn violent. Morris took the brunt of the blows, one landing hard enough on the side of his face to burst a blood vessel in his left eye. The soldiers had their fill and left him lying in the road.

Chaim and Morris managed to get themselves to Zhetel without further interference. Morris's bruises healed, save a brilliant red mark that bloomed against the white of his eye. The spot would fade over time but never completely disappear.

A few days later, a Polish woman Morris had hired to ferry his family to Zhetel arrived in Novogrudek with a horse and buggy. The woman had also brought a pile of clothes for them to wear, something for Rochel and Tania, too, so they could blend in as peasants. After Morris and Chaim's roadside encounter, it was no longer safe for even women and children to be caught on the road. It was better to be poor and insignificant than a Jew or a Communist, or worse still—both.

Only Luba, Cherna, and baby Simcha would be joining them. Miriam and Luba tried to convince Gutel to go with them, but he refused to leave Novogrudek. Their brother Beryl and Chana, who was now pregnant, also decided to stay behind. As did Cousin Itka.

Before they left, Gutel pulled Miriam aside. He had collected the family heirlooms—a handful of silver cutlery, coins, and a few pieces of jewelry, including a necklace that had belonged to her mother, Rochel. Together, they buried the valuables under the brick chimney of the house. Once the dirt was smoothed back into place, Gutel turned to his oldest daughter: "Manya, remember where it is." She alone would bear the responsibility for this secret location, he told her, so one day their family would be able to retrieve what was theirs. "If somebody survives this."

If, he had said.

All her life Miriam had split the seasons between these two places—Novogrudek was for school, her father, and siblings; summers were spent in Zhetel with cousins and friends. She had always loved that when people asked her where she was going, no matter which direction she was traveling, Miriam could tell them: "Home, both ways." What a warm and comforting feeling it had been to know that no farewell was ever really goodbye.

Now she and Luba were leaving the shambling wreckage of their childhood home, as well as their family—their father and their brother, and Cousin Itka, the woman who had raised them. This wasn't a normal parting; it was a breaking apart. Home didn't belong to a place anymore, and wouldn't again for a very long time.

CHAPTER 5

Back to Zhetel

THE ROAD LEADING WEST INTO ZHETEL LAID BARE THE carnage the Nazis had perpetrated by way of announcing their arrival to Belorussia. The locals called this particular road Slonimer Street for the very simple reason that from Zhetel, it led east in the direction of Slonim. Now it looked as if a violent tornado had whipped its way across the surrounding fields, littered with overturned vehicles and bombed-out trucks blackened and burned from explosives. The charred corpses of the Russian soldiers lay strewn on the ground. German paratroopers had dropped from the sky to strategically position themselves between the retreating Red Army and the safety of the east. The Germans had ambushed the Soviets, trapping them on a length of backcountry road.

In sharp contrast to the prostrate bodies and scattered, dismembered limbs were five freshly dug graves lined up along the side of the road. Anyone traveling this way into Zhetel would have noticed the tidy mounds of dirt and likely understood the story they told. The Germans had only lost five of their own, and they had paid no regard for their enemy even in death.

The town of Zhetel may have been spared the aerial bombardments that kicked off Operation Barbarossa, but this scene on the road to Slonim served as a measuring stick of just how close the onslaught had come—a reprieve of mere miles.

In the very last days of June, the victorious German soldiers had been spotted marching on the main thoroughfares outside Zhetel in a parade of bikes and motorcars on their way toward Novogrudek and Minsk. One of the soldiers caught the eye of young Irving Abramowitz, and gestured with his thumb, hitching it back over his shoulder. It was a signal the boy understood: more Germans were coming.

The Wehrmacht finally came to Zhetel a few days later. These infantrymen, in town for a brief sojourn before moving farther east toward the front, presented a disarming introduction, just as they had in Novogrudek. They were friendly as they handed out candy to the children, Jewish and gentile alike, and seemed perfectly at ease engaging Zhetelers as they entered their homes to demand supplies, or even just as they met them on the street.

When a troop of soldiers came into the Senderowskis' home, they sat down with the couple's four teenage daughters, young black-haired beauties with ghostly gray eyes. When the soldiers asked the girls if they were Jewish, they answered them, yes. "*Shada, shada,*" the men chorused, shaking their heads. "It's a shame that you're Jewish," one told them, "because you're all going to die." Rather than feel alarm or fear, the girls were merely confused.

Arel Lazerowich, the son of the town's famous shoemaker, received a more pointed warning. While a group of German soldiers stopped to rest by his family's house, one broke away to speak to him. Seeing there wasn't much age between them, Arel might have ignored him, but the look of sympathy in the younger German's eyes appeared genuine. Now, it wasn't so bad, the soldier said, but "when the SS come, then it's going to start a lot of trouble for you."

Berl Rabinowitz's judgment—and his timing—had been impeccable. He had seized exactly the right moment to risk his trip to Novogrudek. Morris's skirmish aside, the family had managed to secure their safety between the Germans' first assault and their occupation of the city, and their eventual arrival in Zhetel. During those spare few days between the end of June and the start of July 1941, very little of anything happened in Novogrudek. It was a brief window of tranquility, like the eye of a hurricane. After ten days, the Wehrmacht left Novogrudek. Then the SS and the Einsatzgruppen arrived.

The Rabinowitz women had squeaked out of Novogrudek just in time. Their trip by horse and buggy stretched out the twenty-mile distance into nearly a full day. But in spite of their crawling pace, Miriam, Luba, Cherna, and the children disguised in their peasant garb made it safely back to Zhetel. They joined Morris in the middle of town, where he'd found lodging on Myetchansky Street. The family, including Luba, settled there together for a brief period. Troublingly, there was an empty seat at the Rabinowitzes' extended family table—Morris's brother, Solomon, had been conscripted to fight for the Red Army and had not returned; there hadn't been word from or about him for weeks. They did, however, have one welcome addition, though it's doubtful he was at all happy to be in Zhetel.

Issy Rabinowitz, the eldest son of Batsheva and Saul Rabinowitz—the wealthy aunt and uncle who had hosted Morris and Miriam's Vilna wedding—had been visiting when the war broke out. At sixteen, Issy had already grown into a man's build, with a formidable jawline, thick framing eyebrows, and a near copy of his father's steady, somber gaze. A sociable boy,

Issy had received a refined, upper-crust urban education: he'd studied Hebrew, had been active in the Betar (a Zionist youth movement that emphasized self-defense and making *aliyah* legally or otherwise), and even played the trumpet. As a gift for his graduation from the Tarbut gymnasium, a reputable Vilna high school, his parents treated Issy to a summer vacation. When Cherna and her husband, Zalman, had brought the baby to Vilna for a visit earlier that spring, Issy tagged along with them on their return trip to Zhetel. A few weeks later, the Nazis attacked. Now the Vilna teenager was stuck and separated from his parents and little brother, Simcha, to whom he was so close.

Little did Issy know it, but he was far safer in Zhetel. The Germans had devastated Vilna on the night of the invasion—bombs exploded just outside Batsheva and Saul's home—and troops entered the city the following day.

Soon enough, the stories of the brutality plaguing nearby towns, where the SS in their black uniforms had already arrived, leaked their way into Zhetel. In Łódź, a group of Jewish men were made to dig their own graves with spoons before being shot into the pits. In Bilitza, a rabbi was tied to a horse carriage and dragged through the streets until he died; there the SS also took turns with *Juden Spiel*, a twisted gauntlet run: they sent Jewish men down a line of Germans who stood waiting with sticks, boards with nails, or the butts of their rifles to deliver vicious beatings as the men ran past. In Baranovich, the Nazis set religious men's beards on fire in front of a crowd of jeering onlookers.

Zhetel may have been tucked out of the way, and more insignificant than either Vilna or Novogrudek, but that little window of good fortune was closing.

"We came back," Miriam said, "and then it started."

The Novogrudek region of the Weissruthenien, including the neighboring farming communities and small towns like Zhetel, was soon under the jurisdiction of *Gebietskommissar* Wilhelm Traub and his commissar of Jewish affairs, SS officer Wilhelm Reuter. They set up their SS headquarters in the former Polish governor's home, a villa Traub also used as his personal residence. Both men were fast building reputations for delighting in the violence they inflicted—Traub for a sadistic predilection to toy with victims before killing them, all while keeping hold of his pipe; and Reuter for the rubber whip he carried and for how frequently he expressed his distaste for Jews. He would not even strike a Jew without first pulling on a pair of white gloves.

When Traub's SS officers arrived in Zhetel on July 12, the new occupiers posted their first decree around the town: all Jews over the age of ten must wear a six-point star on the front and back of their outermost layer of clothing—the yellow *Juden* star. Other restrictions soon followed: Jews were not allowed to walk on sidewalks or permitted to travel on buses or by car.

Murmurs of worse danger for those living in the town center passed between Jewish families. Morris arranged for the five of them—Miriam, Rochel, Tania, and Luba—to leave the apartment on Myetchansky Street and return to the safety of the Belsky farm. They were not the only Jews to look to the farming community and trusted Christian friends who lived on Zhetel's outskirts, closer to the woods, for help. Jewish families sent their children away to the farms; their parents would bring them back and forth to establish a pattern of visits, preparing a ready cover story so that neighbors with prying eyes would believe the child was a visiting nephew or niece and not suspect that the other farmers were harboring Jews.

Some of these farmers sheltered their Jewish neighbors for payment, some out of kindness and friendship. A healthy portion of Zhetel's Christian population was ill at ease with this new regime and disturbed by the discriminatory rules it was putting into place. There was also more than a sliver of anti-Semitic Christian Poles and Belorussians who were happy to see the Germans push out the Russians, whom they believed had shown favoritism to the Jews during their two-year occupation of Zhetel, hoping that now the Nazis would give the Jews what they deserved.

On July 23, the SS sent word through Zhetel that all Jewish men between the ages of sixteen and seventy were to report to the market square. They were told a group was needed for a work detail and to bring provisions for a three-day journey. Hundreds of men filed into the center of town and spread out across the cobblestone. Some were accompanied by their wives and children. A crowd of gentile neighbors gathered along the sidelines waiting to see what would happen next.

As an SS officer read out a list of names, calling them one by one, a pattern began to emerge. These were the names of heads of households, but these men did not necessarily boast a natural build for hard labor, nor were they skilled tradesmen suited for factory work. They were lawyers and businessmen, teachers and rabbis, and the lone woman on this list, Shifra Dunyetz, was a nurse. The clear commonality was that these individuals accounted for Zhetel's most influential Jewish citizens.

When the name "Abramowitz" was called, nineteen-year-old Morris moved to join the others, but his father, Chaim Abramowitz, a *sofer* (Torah scribe), blocked his son from stepping forward with his hand. "Wait," he said. "You stay. I'll go." During the Great War, the elder Abramowitz had spent five years in a German POW camp, and knew better than to trust them now. "There were no nice Germans," Chaim had always said.

Chaim Abramowitz was directed into the center of the square with the others. The Einsatzgruppen closed in around them, shoulder to shoulder, two men deep. Once the list was finished,

119 men and Shifra Dunyetz were marched over to large military transport trucks with open beds and raised sideboards, and herded aboard.

Just then, one child ran into the square after his father. Of all Dovid Rozwaski's children, six-year-old Chaim, with a face like a woodland elf and wavy ink-black hair, was the most attached to his father and had followed Dovid to the square that morning. When the boy saw his father and uncle being pushed onto a truck, he felt the swell of emotion rise in his chest: his father was leaving without saying goodbye. Without thinking, Chaim darted into the crowd and reached the side of the truck just in time for Dovid to lean down and quickly kiss his cheek, before one of the SS officers pushed him away.

The German officers assured the anxious crowd not to worry. Their loved ones would be back; they were being taken to build a new road in Smolensk, a town not very far away. Many Zhetelers understood that wherever those trucks were taking these men, nothing good was waiting for them. Others took the Germans at their word, and for weeks would approach the SS officers with packages containing food, a pair of boots, or material for warmer clothing. The SS would assure them that the gifts would be delivered.

Chaim Rozwaski would wait for years for his father to come back, just as he was told. After the war, he would watch with longing as the parents of other children in his Displaced Persons (DP) camp would seem to materialize out of thin air to claim their otherwise presumed-orphaned children. Chaim would circle the camp, his hopes leaping at every corner, still looking for his father.

❧

As the trucks pulled away, the Nazis shouted to the rest of the men in the square whose names had not been called and forced them into lines. Led by the town's most visibly Orthodox men with their long beards—a rabbi and two men with dwarfism—the remaining three hundred or so men were marched through the streets of Zhetel and made to sing "Hatikvah," the Zionist anthem. The crowd watching from the sidewalks was encouraged to jeer and shout, laughing at the Jews forced to walk in this parade of humiliation.

The Jews of Zhetel were certain that list of names had not originated within its own community, and assumed instead that the Nazis had procured their information from either the local police or some other gentile source.

Neither Morris's nor Berl's name was on that list. It's possible their standing in town didn't fall into the category of intelligentsia that the Nazis were looking to eliminate, or that their roles at Kaplinsky's lumber mill held either a valued connection to the farming community or a certain functional usefulness, thereby securing their safety, if only temporarily. Whatever the reason, the omission was an early blessing for all but one member of the Rabinowitz family. Cherna's husband's name had been on that list. When the trucks left Zhetel that day, Zalman went with them.

❧

Only one man taken away from the market that July ever returned. Judeleh Edlach, a *sofer* and one of the men of small stature, was pulled from the march and packed onto a truck with the others. When he finally spoke about what he witnessed that day, it was more than a year later in the last waking hours of his life.

The 120 were taken to Novogrudek, brought to waiting pits behind some barracks, and shot. Just before they were killed, the SS made Judeleh collect their papers and passports and burn them, presumably destroying any official record of their existence. The

Gestapo who brought Judeleh back to town threatened him. "If you speak of this to anyone," they told him, "we will know," and they promised to find and kill him. For the next few months Judeleh swallowed down his fear and guilt with an endless stream of vodka.

The night he finally made his confession more than a year later, Judeleh went to the large barn where the Germans kept the hay for their horses, fell asleep perhaps with a less-burdened conscience, and never woke up. In hindsight, there would be something richly defiant in any Jew in Zhetel dying of his own accord in August 1942. At least by dying he stole the chance the Nazis had to kill him. Although, one might argue, he died at their hands all the same.

❧

For the remainder of the summer of 1941, the Nazis mostly left Zhetel undisturbed. Every once in a while, SS officers would come into town and demand supplies, large quantities of items that were already in dwindling supply—two hundred pounds of coffee, or outlandish sums of money. Each time, the pressure to produce the impossible stirred the town into a frenzy. It was a tactic predicated on the reliability of fear: demand what couldn't be given to incite terror so that the Jews wouldn't dare hold anything back for themselves.

The Rabinowitz family began to take some precautionary measures. Berl and Beyla buried their copper pots and pans in their backyard. Morris and Miriam hid a few gold coins and silverware behind the large white ceramic tiles of their kitchen stove. Morris received a work certificate to collect acorns for the Germans, and the paltry rations it provided were welcome as food sources were becoming more and more scarce.

At the end of August, a Judenrat—the proxy authority appointed by the Germans to relay their orders and do their bidding—was established in Zhetel. Twelve of the community's remaining prominent Jewish citizens were appointed to this council, including Berl Rabinowitz. During the German occupation, these councils were powerful entities and created a new hierarchy and power structure among the oppressed. For some towns and cities, the Judenrat would prove to be a problematic governing body—at worst prone to corruption, trading bribes for self-preservation, or simply placing too much trust in the Nazi contract and hoping that the utilitarianism of the Jewish people would be the saving grace for some, if not all.

In Zhetel, however, this would not be the case. Its Judenrat members were not profiteers, but men and women who vowed to protect their town. Soon after its creation, the council nominated a new leader, lawyer Alter Dvoretsky. During the July roundup of the 120, a few men plied the local police with money in exchange for the release of the rabbis and Dvoretsky before the others were taken away. The council's decision to appoint him as their leader and representative to the Nazis was calculating. All of Zhetel's special circumstances—the insulated community and its small-town unity, and now a brave council to represent them—were aligning in critical ways. For the Jews who lived there, this was a very fortunate thing.

On the first day of October 1941, the SS set up their official headquarters in the Zhetel *kino* in the town center. This time they did not leave.

At the end of November, on the last Friday of the month, the Nazis made all the registered Jews line up in front of their headquarters, arranged alphabetically by family surname. They had been told to bring all the gold, silver, and copper they had—flatware, jewelry—anything and everything that would help shore up the German war effort. Nothing, they were warned, should be held back. The very first person in line was a woman, a local business owner. She walked into the office to hand over her items, but within minutes the Nazis dragged her out again. One of the officers shouted to the crowd that they had discovered this woman had not turned everything over but in fact had concealed from them a ring, a wedding band that, of course, they found. And then, in front of everyone, they shot her dead.

The waiting line of people erupted in panic. Those representing their families in that line turned to their relatives waiting nearby, and sent them running home to unearth anything to which the Germans could assign value. The consequences of withholding had been clearly and effectively illustrated. The desperation was so strong it drove people to rip the fur off coat collars and hurry as fast as they could back to their relatives.

No one believed this woman had hidden her ring from the SS officers. It didn't matter if she had. On that day, a new fear cracked open in the hearts of all Jewish Zhetelers. But so did something else—resistance.

The copper pots in Berl and Beyla Rabinowitz's backyard would stay buried in the dirt. Just as the pieces of gold would remain tucked behind the white tiles of Miriam and Morris's stove. They were now a family growing accustomed—even willing—to taking risks.

The winter of 1941 was bitterly, brutally cold. In fact, it would be the coldest winter in the twentieth century. When the arctic winds blustered, they brought with them bone-rattling surface temperatures that averaged −4 degrees Fahrenheit, temperatures that would soon drop further, bottoming out at nearly 40 degrees below zero. For Morris and Miriam, one of the tremendous advantages of living at the Belskys' self-sustaining farm was its close proximity to the forest, where there was access to an endless supply of firewood. People living in town were quite literally taking axes to the beams of their homes so they had something to burn in their hearths and stoves.

It may have come as a small comfort, then, that the German troops were battling a formidable new enemy—General Winter, General Frost, and General Snow, all names attributed to this mercilessly cold season—and losing. The flimsy wool layers of Wehrmacht uniforms exposed just how woefully underprepared (and underdressed) the German army was for the long extension of Operation Barbarossa. The snow drifts rose so high they reached the horses' bellies, making it difficult for them to move. It was so cold that the gears of their vehicles and weapons froze into uselessness.

When reinforcements and warmer supplies didn't come, the German soldiers crunched up newspapers to layer underneath their coats and used straw to line their shoes. They even resorted to balling up their own anti-Russian propaganda leaflets to pad their leather boots, to no great effect. Some two hundred thousand Germans on the Barbarossa front line were plagued with blistering frostbite, and hundreds would require lifesaving amputations. Their skin fused to the metal of their guns, and the men who drifted into the numbing fingers of sleep lapsed into hypothermia and froze to the ground, dead. The Russians, long accustomed to their region's harsh winter cold, fared far better in their felt-lined helmets and quilted coats.

But Hitler's myopic gaze was locked on Moscow, and his own soldiers' suffering registered with seemingly no concern. When the commander in chief of the Army Group Center in Russia, *Generalfeldmarschall* Fedor von Bock, communicated the depths of their disadvantage on the front—perhaps attempting to more urgently convey the rate at which his men were succumbing to the frigid temperatures—the response he received was perfunctorily unsympathetic: "The Führer wants to know when Moscow will be captured."

With the Kremlin's windowpanes in their sights, the advancing German army got close to Moscow—twelve miles close. But on December 5, a surge of Soviet troops renewed their numbers at the front, pushing the Germans into a 150-mile retreat, and Hitler lost any hope of taking the Soviet capital.

In Belorussia, the coldest winter for one hundred years may have been literally freezing Hitler's troops to a halt, but elsewhere in those final weeks of 1941, critical developments of the war were picking up pace. On Sunday, December 7, 1941, Japan bombed Pearl Harbor, and on December 8, in a near unanimous vote—save one—the United States Congress sent America to war with Japan. Four days later, in a speech to the Reichstag, Hitler declared war on the United States, forcing America to abandon its long reluctance to join the Allied forces against him.

Novogrudek's own day of infamy would be December 8, 1941, or as its Jewish community would call it, Black Monday. This was the date of the Nazis' first large-scale massacre of the city's Jews.

After keeping 6,500 Jews of all ages locked in the city's courthouse buildings for three days—having already killed the community's elderly and infirm and all the children in the orphanage—the Gestapo agents and their helpers separated out 4,500 men, women, and children, loaded them onto trucks in groups of fifty, and drove them two miles away to waiting pits. They forced them to shed their clothes and line up in groups of ten before unleashing machine-gun fire across their bodies. Many were buried alive.

If anyone in the Dworetsky family had survived up until that point—Gutel and Itka, Beryl, Chana, and their baby—they would have been in those courthouse rooms, standing in temperatures that dipped to four below, while great downy flakes of snow fell from the night sky. Were they among the ones taken away for slaughter?

It would've been difficult for Miriam and Luba to convince themselves otherwise—Gutel was an older man with no artisanal skills; Itka, gentle and simpleminded, would not have had much by the way of protection. Nor would Chana and her young child. Perhaps Beryl, a man of working age and build, had a chance, but would he have wanted to go on, without them? Were they able to be together until the end? Miriam and Luba would never know.

Six weeks later, on January 20, 1942, in a mansion set along the Wannsee lake in an upper-crust Berlin suburb, fifteen high-ranking Nazi officials met to discuss what Hitler considered the Reich's—indeed all of Europe's—most pressing problem: the Jewish question. While sipping cognac, these men debated, in horrific detail, efficient methods for executing the Jews who were obstructing their way to completing the Führer's grand aim—lebensraum.

The plan and preparation for the mass executions of Europe's Jews had been in the works behind closed doors for some time. Before the end of 1941, the Einsatzgruppen had murdered some five hundred thousand Jews in the former Soviet-occupied territories alone. By the time this meeting took place, the Nazis' genocide against the Jews was well underway. Now it was Nazi policy—one that would continue unencumbered, with very little to stand in its way.

CHAPTER 6

The Ghetto

One day in mid-February 1942, farmer Belsky returned to the house with some grave news. Notices had been posted in Zhetel, and the Germans were handing out pamphlets around town: on February 22, all the Jews would have to move into a ghetto. They would be given six hours, from 8 A.M. that morning until 2 P.M. that afternoon, to vacate their homes and move whatever belongings they could carry into the sectioned-off parcel of town in which they would soon be interned. The postings had included a warning to anyone contemplating an escape: "Jews who leave their designated districts are subject to the penalty of death. The same penalty will be applied to persons who knowingly provide shelter for such Jews." And finally: any Jew found outside the ghetto after the designated time would be shot on sight.

All of Zhetel was aware of the gravity of this latest phase of the Nazi occupation. Shortly after word of the ghetto confinement made its way around town, one of Morris's farmer friends, a Pole by the name of Wallach, came to see him with an offer: he was willing to help his Jewish friend escape. Considering the risk involved, it was a generous show of fellowship, but Morris, afraid of what would happen to his wife and daughters without him, declined.

As they prepared to leave the Belsky home, Miriam and Morris decided to give away their possessions, things of value they couldn't carry into the ghetto or would have no use for there. Among these belongings was Miriam's sewing machine and her favorite dress, a navy-blue frock patterned with intricate white flowers and fine, delicate lace that collared the neck- and hemlines and circled the edges of its short sleeves. Luba had a dress exactly like it. The sisters had traveled all the way to a Vilna dressmaker to have them specially made. Morris and Miriam divvied up their personal effects among the farming families, all of whom promised to look after their Jewish friends' property. There was very little pretense or sugarcoating to the arrangement. "We'll want it back," Miriam explained, "if we live." If not, she said, brushing past the self-evident conclusion, "They're yours to keep."

There was snow on the streets the day Zhetel's Jews moved into the ghetto.

Encompassing roughly ten square blocks, including Myetchansky Street, Slonimer Street, and the main thoroughfare running along Shul Court, the ghetto fanned out from the center of town, around the synagogue and the Hebrew elementary school. The area's overall shape was more narrow than wide, a staggered corridor that barely ran the length of a single, haphazard mile. The fence that had been constructed around the space—open slats of wood loosely hooked together and topped with barbed wire—was hardly as tall as an average-sized man. A German guard stood watch as the families streamed through the ghetto entrance, which, oddly enough, led past the alley behind the Rabinowitzes' former house, the site of Miriam's old shop.

The Rabinowitzes' daughters had never wanted for much over the course of their young lives, but since the war, they had few remaining belongings of their own. In all of their moving around from temporary home to temporary home, Rochel had managed to hold onto a single toy, a doll. Over the past few months, her attachment to the doll—to its hard china-painted face and soft, stuffed body—had intensified. It had become an emotional pacifier, or perhaps something even deeper than that, a last anchor to childhood. The day they moved their things into the ghetto, that doll was tucked safely in Rochel's arms.

One of the very last to move into the ghetto was Chaim Rozwaski, the dark-haired boy who, on the day of the July roundup, had chased after his father in the market square. Earlier, while his family rushed to collect all their things, Chaim had stayed behind to watch his baby brother, who had been born shortly after their father was taken away. Now the six-year-old boy was pulling a heavy log behind him, dragging it through the snow. He knew his family was going to need more than clothes and blankets to make it through this winter in the ghetto.

The recent influx of refugees from other towns had inflated Zhetel's Jewish population by some 1,500 people. Roughly five thousand were packed into the ghetto, and it was crowded. Modest homes that had kept a family of four in stark comfort were now hosting twenty to thirty people. In the days before they ordered the Jews into the ghetto, the Nazis had evacuated this cordoned-off area of Zhetel and emptied the homes of their non-Jewish residents as well as any furnishings and remaining comforts. In their place, they had installed bunks, fashioning these homes into hastily arranged barracks. Those bunks were filled quickly, and the rest of the occupants had no choice but to share space on the floor.

Morris, Miriam, Luba, and both girls moved into a home that had belonged to a Christian family. Berl and Beyla, Cherna, little

Simcha, and Cousin Issy were placed in another part of the ghetto.

Once the Jews were squeezed together inside the ghetto, they faced new limitations on life's already difficult mundanities. The normal pace of the town's inner workings ground to a near-total halt, and a diminished daily life rose up in its place.

Most able-bodied men between the ages of sixteen and sixty were assigned work details outside the ghetto—clearing the roads of snow at night or cutting down trees in the forest for timber—for which they were given minuscule portions of bread, or sometimes a thin broth or water. Skilled workers in possession of a *schein,* a work certificate that was granted either by the Judenrat or the Nazis, went to work in the flour mill or continued their craft in special service to the Nazi officers. Zhetel's artisans, its seamstresses, and shoemakers, were some of the best in the region, and the Nazis took full advantage of their talents. These workers were the only ones permitted to leave the ghetto, getting up early in the morning and returning well after dark.

For those without labor assignments, securing work for pay or for rations, finding enough food for entire families, comfortable shelter—even a cup of coffee—became even harder. The Judenrat office inside the ghetto was flooded with people looking for jobs and something to eat—the basic necessities of life.

No one ever had enough to eat. Meager rations were disbursed to families; bits of cheese, margarine, and bread were meant to last for days or longer. Hunger was a constant ache.

It was strictly forbidden for the Christian Poles to have direct contact with the Jews in the ghetto, but many neighbors found ways to smuggle in food and supplies. Some of these deliveries were bartered—for jewelry, clothes, linens—or paid for in gold, but often enough food was just passed from friend to friend. Some locals constructed secret compartments in their wagons, or women would hide bread in their dresses and pass it through the gaping spaces in the slatted fence when the ghetto police were turned the other way. Often Morris would return from a hard day of labor with food from his farmer friends stuffed in his pockets or hidden inside his coat.

As conditions inside the ghetto deteriorated, the psychological toll of captivity manifested in a variety of ways. Some Jews daydreamed of a great uprising against the Nazis, and turned to literary contraband for inspiration, such as Franz Werfel's *The Forty Days of Musa Dagh,* based on the true events of the Armenian uprising against the Turkish genocide in 1915. The novel tells the story of one small coastal mountain community that bands together to fight slaughter and deportation. Werfel, who was of German-Jewish parentage, had written the book in response to Hitler's rise to power and very much intended for his readers to draw the obvious parallels to the Jewish persecution, hoping they would see the novel as a call to action. *The Forty Days of Musa Dagh,* which had been banned and burned in Nazi Germany as early as its publication in 1933, had become universally popular in Jewish ghettos, and well-worn copies made their way through the Zhetel ghetto.

When the close quarters and lack of hygiene brought on fast-spreading illnesses, including deadly ones like typhus, morale in the ghetto plummeted even further. Observant Jews stopped praying, while once-devoted secularists took up religion. People held seances and prevailed upon Ouija boards to divine answers to their troubles.

Miriam Rabinowitz had always been inclined toward superstition, and when the others in their shared ghetto home gathered around their large table to call upon the spirits, she and the girls joined them. Sitting side by side, they placed their hands on the table, palms down against the wood, while the adults took turns asking questions: "What does the future hold for us?"

and "When will the war be over?" They beseeched the spirits to reveal themselves, intoning, *"Habe sich, tischele!"* ("Lift yourself, little table!") and waited for the table to levitate in response. Even the nonbelievers pushed aside their doubts to make room for hope in the inconceivable. After all, what harm could it do?

Rochel and Tania thought these seances were just silly games. Like many children their age, the girls were caught between an underlying understanding of their grave new circumstances and the cushion of being young and so well loved and looked after. Morris and Miriam, with Luba's help, worked to keep their daughters shielded from the worst of what was unfolding around them. But with no makeshift school or coordinated activities of any kind in the Zhetel ghetto, the girls were largely left to their own devices and played outside in the ghetto yards. Not even the youngest children were oblivious to the ghetto's miseries: Hirsh Kaplinsky's little girl was observed calling after a kitten who had wedged its way through the barrier fence, "Kitty-cat, you can't do that! You don't have a *schein*!"

Each evening at dusk, swarms of crowing blackbirds would gather at one end of the ghetto in front of the Senderowski house. It was the very same house that had been visited by the Wehrmacht soldiers who had tsked over the fate of the family's beautiful gray-eyed daughters. Night after night, those blackbirds and their disturbing chorus kept Marsha Senderowski awake, their caws echoing in the settling dark. To the fifteen-year-old, their calls sounded like crying. She became convinced the birds were sending a warning, that somehow they knew something very bad was going to happen. She would never forget the sound—the scale of warbled notes imprinted a memory so lasting that for the rest of her life, the sight of a blackbird took her breath away.

&

That spring in 1942, Passover fell on the second day of April. While most of the men were shuttled out of the ghetto for manual labor—as they were day in and day out—the women gathered together to prepare the holiday matzah. This time, Miriam brought Rochel and Tania along to help.

The girls took turns rolling out the dough for the unleavened bread, standing next to their mother in the line of women working along the table. As they finished their second month in the ghetto, how could they not be struck by the weight of this ritual—preparing the same bread the Jews of Egypt baked in haste as they fled from their oppressors so they might be delivered out of slavery by Moses. The tradition of eating matzah at the Seder table is meant to serve as a literal reminder that Passover celebrants—unlike their long-suffering Jewish ancestors under Pharaoh—were free. What meaning did the matzah have now in the ghetto, where there was no freedom?

The ghetto was a nexus phase, the necessary middle part of the Nazis' plan to winnow down a race of people until it was ended. In this phase, the Jews were contained in a community of free labor in service to their oppressor. And all the while, the Nazis were whittling away at their strength—from body and spirit.

The Friday night before the Passover holiday began, Yoseph Rozwaski, young Chaim Rozwaski's grandfather, woke up in the middle of the night. The whole family—Chaim and his siblings, mother, aunt and uncle, and grandfather—shared the same tiny space. That night their room was warm, unusually bright with a contented light and a sense of calm. The old man had been disturbed by something, but when asked what was wrong, he replied that he felt perfectly fine. He drank a glass of warm water with a few sugar cubes, and got back into bed. In the morning, when the Rozwaski family got up to start the day, Yoseph could not be roused. He had died in his sleep.

Despite the Nazis' restrictions, the Rozwaski family was able to make arrangements to have Yoseph buried outside the ghetto in the Jewish cemetery. He wouldn't be the last Zhetel Jew to die in the ghetto—he would hardly be the last Zhetel Jew to die that April—but he would be the last Jew in the Zhetel ghetto to be buried in the Jewish cemetery. Indeed, it's highly likely that Yoseph Rozwaski was the last person to die in the peace and quiet of what still resembled a Jewish home in Zhetel.

Miriam's reputation running the patent medicine shop and her experience with prescriptions had earned her a *schein* as a nurse, and she had been charged with distributing medications in what accounted for the ghetto's convalescence facility and old age home.

When Miriam set out on her treatment rounds, she often left the girls behind to be looked after by Luba, or Beyla and Cherna. But one afternoon, Miriam brought Rochel along. Rochel trailed after her mother from bed to bed, but at some point, while Miriam was engaged with a patient, Rochel decided to explore and wandered off on her own.

One of the residents, an elderly woman, beckoned for Rochel's attention. "Come here," she said, extending her arm. Seeing the woman's kind face, Rochel didn't hesitate to go to her bedside. "Can I look at your hand?" she asked. Rochel nodded and the woman took the small fingers into hers, turning the child's palm open toward the ceiling. While tracing a crooked finger along the creases of Rochel's palm, the woman's lined face intensified in study. After a few moments she released Rochel's hand with a gentle pat.

"You are going to live for a very long time," she said, giving Rochel a smile. "You are going to have a full life and be safe."

The old woman could have been one of Zhetel's gypsy fortune-tellers, or maybe she fancied herself a clairvoyant. She wouldn't have needed the powers of foresight to predict the fate awaiting the residents in this home. Perhaps the woman saw a sweet-looking girl and took the opportunity to inspire a little hope, the kind she could no longer sensibly keep for herself.

In that moment, it didn't matter. Rochel gazed back at the old woman, this complete stranger, and believed her.

CHAPTER 7

The Resistance

LUBA HAD BEEN AWAY FOR DAYS. SHE WASN'T MISSING EXactly, and she had left of her own volition. Still, given her destination, Morris and Miriam had plenty of cause for alarm as her absence dragged on. All the family knew was that Luba was part of a small group planning to break out of the ghetto through the fence and make for the woods. Had they been caught by a Nazi guard or even the wrong member of the ghetto's Jewish police force, the family may well never see her again.

But Luba finally returned, and when she did she had good news for her sister and brother-in-law: rumors about the partisan army gathering strength and numbers in the forest were true. Not only was there a way to escape the ghetto, but there was a place to go once they did.

Miriam and Luba started packing knapsacks with scraps of food and the precious few items of value they still had, including one of Luba's nightgowns, an expensive negligee made of white silk. Once the bags were full, they sat ready to go at a moment's notice, brimming with a jittery possibility.

❧

As 1942 edged along, word of the partisan movement in the former Soviet-occupied territories was making its way to the hope-starved ears of Jews, some six hundred thousand of whom were interned in ghettos. Fifty miles from Zhetel, Jews in the Mir ghetto heard reports of the partisan fighters from the neighboring peasants. It didn't take long before those stray bits of information morphed into legend, the partisans' numbers greatly exaggerated. "We were like someone who is about to drown and tries to cling to anything that promised life," Esther Marchwinska would remember. "For us, however, the dream was important and not the reality. This dream told some of us that our salvation depended on the partisans."

For many Jews, it would. In the Lida ghetto, seventeen-year-old Riva Novoprudska had watched helplessly as her mother died slowly from a brain hemorrhage after a Nazi officer struck her while she sat in her own home.

When she and the other Jews of the Lida ghetto would return from a long day's work of cutting through the ice and snow on the road to the airfield, they had to pass beneath a balcony under the eyes of the *Gebietskommissar,* Hermann Hanweg. He was flanked by his notorious deputy Leopold Windisch on one side and SS officer Werner, with his massive German shepherd Donner, on the other. And then the game would begin.

"*Fang den Juden!*" "Catch the Jew!" Werner would shout. The dog would leap down into the crowd of returning workers, seize upon one—"whomever he caught, whoever was supposed to lose a life"—and maul the unfortunate victim in a bloody frenzy.

Riva would stare into the sky—the closest thing to freedom—and think, "God, why can't I turn into a bird?"

Over time, Riva began to notice that some of her friends, young men, were disappearing from the ghetto. There were rumors of an underground movement of partisans gathering in the woods. "That," she said, "was my dream. That was my only solution."

In Novogrudek, news reached the ghetto that Russian partisans had gotten close enough to the city to trade gunfire with the Germans. Those reports were confirmed when the Nazis ordered the area around *Gebietskommissar* Traub's headquarters to be reinforced and the trees surrounding the estate's garden cut down to eliminate the chances it would provide cover to intruders. The authorities' alarm sparked a ripple of hope for the rebellion in many Jewish hearts.

Across the whole region, thousands of Jews were gathering enough courage to run toward the dense forests of old Poland and Belorussia, where there was a chance, however slim, of survival. The Rabinowitz family, with their packed bags, were prepared and ready to join them.

It had been more than a year since Russian foreign minister Vyacheslav Molotov addressed the Soviet Union in the hours after Hitler launched his blitzkrieg on June 22, 1941. It took Joseph Stalin twelve more days before he made his own public speech. When his voice came over the radio waves on July 3, 1941, the Great Leader urged all those loyal to the Soviet Union to do everything in their power to upend the German enemy. He called for an insurgency, a partisan war to be launched from within.

"In areas occupied by the enemy, guerrilla units, mounted and on foot, must be formed; sabotage groups must be organized to combat enemy units, to foment guerrilla warfare everywhere, blow up bridges and roads, damage telephone and telegraph lines, set fire to forests, stores and transports." The enemy, Stalin said, must "be hounded and annihilated at every step, and all their measures frustrated."

Even at that time, the Soviet government was already laying the groundwork for coordinated action in the territories seized by Germany. The Communist Central Committee had issued a directive to the governing bodies and authorities in the regions threatened by the German invasion. They were to set up "partisan units and sabotage groups . . . to ignite a partisan war in every place and site."

It was here that Zhetel's Jews would find a way to join the fight in the war. Establishing contact with Russian partisans would be a critical part of the Zhetel ghetto resistance, an underground movement organized by one courageous and industrious individual—Alter Dvoretsky.

For a man about Zhetel, Dvoretsky was unconventionally worldly. A lawyer by trade, he had received a pedigreed education, having studied in both Vilna and Berlin, and conversed easily in multiple languages, including German. At a passing glance, the most noticeable thing about Dvoretsky was his spectacles, dense goggle-round lenses that magnified his dark eyes and gave the general impression of professorial restraint. Even his blond hair was combed so severely close to his scalp that it appeared as if it had been painted on his head. Set against his gladiator jawline and sturdy physique, these features combined in a perfect representation of the unlikely attributes he embodied—the bookish athlete. Dvoretsky's reputation in Zhetel was just as prominently stamped onto the local sports field as it was inside the town's political arena, where he'd earned a spot as a leading member of the Poale Zion, the Marxist-Zionist group. The young lawyer, who lived with his wife, young son, and his parents, was lively, honest, and immensely well liked across the town's social strata. In other words, where Alter Dvoretsky led, people were keen to follow.

As head of the Judenrat, the twelve-member council that included Berl Rabinowitz, Dvoretsky represented the Jewish population of Zhetel to its Nazi occupiers, who took an easy shine to the handsome, Aryan-looking lawyer conversant in their native tongue. "The Germans couldn't understand how he could be Jewish," remembered one Zheteler, because he "didn't look Jewish, according to their terminology." Careful not to disabuse them of this misperception, Dvoretsky exploited it, using his charms to remain in their good favor. It's hard to imagine that he would have been able to deceive them so completely otherwise. Perhaps it was his proximity to their cold indifference and cruelty, or his lawyer's pragmatic streak, but Dvoretsky was never under any illusions about the ultimate end of the Nazis' plan, nor did he ever harbor false hope that any amount of hard work or friendly exchange would lead to mercy or exception.

The *schein,* the little yellow piece of paper, had become a sought-after object in the ghettos. While it indeed held the power to determine fates, the reliability of its value was ultimately (and drastically) overestimated. Alter Dvoretsky believed the Nazis' dispensation of *scheins* and their deployment of workers to labor camps was a signal that worse abuses would soon follow. When his own mother begged him to get her a work permit, he refused: "The Germans didn't come here to employ us and help us earn a living. They came to kill each and every Jew." It was simply a matter of time.

Dvoretsky was hardly the only Judenrat leader to distrust the Nazis, but unlike many others, he wasted none of his time trying to operate within the Nazis' ghetto establishment. Rather, he moved quickly to work around it, taking every possible opportunity to argue for resistance. He quietly organized to gain the support of like-minded individuals. Distributing anti-Nazi materials to the townspeople and forging relationships with the Christian Poles, he also held surreptitious meetings with refugees new to Zhetel who had been leaders in their own towns. He counseled them all to keep their eyes open for signals that the Nazis were gathering their forces and preparing for a massacre. Last, he built a tenuous trust with a group of Soviet soldiers who had formed a partisan base in the woods not far from Zhetel. With networks primed inside the ghetto and out, all Dvoretsky needed was a Jewish army.

For this he turned to Zhetel's young people, tapping into a ready stream of restless men and women unencumbered by spouses and children and hungry to fight, all the consequences be damned. Dvoretsky harnessed their rage. His movement appealed to their impatience to strike down their Nazi oppressors; the offer to join his ranks was a rallying cry, an opportunity for which death would be a satisfying trade.

One of the first to join Dvoretsky's resistance was Arel Lazerowich, the twenty-something son of Zhetel's famous cobbler. He had small dark eyes, and dark hair that was cropped close around his already-balding forehead. Arel made no bones about what the resistance meant to him. "I am not trying to save my life," he said. "We are going to die anyway." What he wanted was to set his own fate, on his own terms. "I want to fight. I want to die in battle. I want to take a couple of Germans with me in the grave."

The underground's first meeting was a rushed encounter in November 1941, attended by just a handful of men. They convened in a Jewish house and there was no wish to linger. Everyone was afraid their gathering would be noticed; even Dvoretsky was on edge. The briefing was short and the directive perfunctory: they needed guns and ammunition. And eventually, fighters to wield them.

Before they went their separate ways, all the men pledged an oath of silence: they couldn't tell their families, their friends—no one. The fear that they would be discovered by their occupiers was constant. As the resistance grew, Dvoretsky established a number of fail-safes and internal measures of protection. Everyone in the underground had been sworn to secrecy, and its network—which eventually reached upward of sixty people—was broken down into smaller contact groups of three, so even its members' identities were kept anonymous from the group at large.

It wasn't just the Germans and their collaborators who posed a threat to the resistance, but others in the Jewish community who would view this activity as dangerous to the whole of the ghetto by tempting retribution from the Nazis. Many among Zhetel's Jews believed that if they followed the rules and gave the Nazis what they wanted, they could mitigate reprisals. Even news of executions in other ghettos did little to convince them; many rationalized away the dangers—*those* Jews had clearly done something to incite the Nazis. *We* can still avoid that fate if *we're* careful. It was this very mentality of fear, submission, and misplaced trust the Nazis had worked to cultivate.

A month later, when Dvoretsky heard about the December *aktion* (the German word that became synonymous with slaughter) in Novogrudek, he knew a massacre in Zhetel wasn't far behind. The lawyer and athlete began to strategize a final course of offensive action, convinced that the only way to save as many lives as possible was to launch an uprising and attack from within.

Every time Dvoretsky deployed his influence to further the resistance movement, he risked exposure. His was a delicate balance, a high-wire waltz between compliance and seduction. Dvoretsky executed all the orders the Nazis delivered, took money and property from the Jews of his town and then channeled those funds and the intel he gained to the resistance's advantage. He was the ultimate double agent—on one hand he was the Nazis' most trusted insider, while on the other he was spearheading the secret movement against them. The Robin Hood of the ghetto, disguised in a suit and glasses, he was funneling money out of their coffers—money the Nazis had stolen from Jews—to fund it.

After the ghetto was established in February 1942, Dvoretsky used his position to select sympathizers and others from within the resistance and appointed them to the Jewish police, clearing a path to smuggle weapons into the ghetto while smuggling fighters out. Meirim Dworetsky, Miriam's twenty-eight-year-old cousin, was one of the officers appointed to the ghetto police force, and he was primed to flee to the forest and join the partisans.

Soon weapons caches were tucked all over the ghetto—under floorboards and behind false walls; even the synagogue had weapons hidden in the ark—enough to outfit their army of some sixty men and women, all ready to fight their way out and to the woods where the Russian partisans were waiting.

The final phase of Dvoretsky's plan, coordinated to disrupt the Nazis as they initiated a ghetto liquidation, would culminate in a three-act diversion designed to draw the Nazi manpower away from the ghetto and give all its residents a chance to run to the woods. One contingent of fighters would begin by setting fire to the lumber mill, the other to the flour mill—two of the town's most valuable operations. The final group would surround two of the Nazi strongholds in Zhetel: the German police headquarters and the labor office, which housed their weapons.

It was a good plan, supported by months of careful preparation. By early spring the resistance was nearly ready. Who knows how many lives Dvoretsky's fighters would have saved if only they could have seen it through.

❧

Collecting arms was a dangerous task, but not a particularly difficult one. The retreating Russian soldiers had left plenty of firearms and artillery, even stray bullets, along the roads and in the fields outside Zhetel. It was just a matter of securing them without getting caught. Farmers who had been gathering the stray weapons were more than willing to sell them, or even trade them for clothes.

And this is how Dvoretsky's resistance members met the man called Vanya.

A former Russian pilot, Vanya was working inside the Zhetel ghetto but still maintained contact with the Russian partisans in the woods. When he reached out to resistance members in mid-April offering new weapons, Abraham Alpert, the ghetto's police commander and Dvoretsky's close confidant, had a bad feeling. He shared his suspicions with Dvoretsky, who agreed: something was amiss.

Not so easily deterred, Vanya tried another route to make his deal. And when he approached Arel Lazerowich and two of the other young fighters, Shalom Fiolon and Ohat Zukotun, with the same offer, they shared none of their leader's alarm and agreed to meet the man they considered their Russian ally.

On an April afternoon, they huddled in front of the ghetto slaughterhouse as Vanya briefed them on the deal: he had made contact with a villager who had weapons to sell, two revolvers and some grenades. It was a good deal, Vanya assessed, and worth the risk of leaving the ghetto. But, he said, "I want one of you to go with me."

Before any of them could volunteer, Vanya pointed at Shalom. "I want you to come," he told him.

Shalom, itching to play his part, didn't hesitate. "I'll go," he agreed.

Not even twenty years old, Shalom was the youngest among them. He was a slip of a boy with a face like a sparrow, with a wide mouth and gentle eyes. He had come to the Zhetel ghetto as a refugee without any family, and was perhaps more eager than the others to prove himself to the movement.

At the same time Shalom left the ghetto to meet Vanya, Arel's girlfriend, Irene, was in the Gestapo's headquarters sweeping where she and another Jewish girl had been assigned jobs cleaning the offices. As she went to the closet where they kept the mops, she saw a man leap out the window, and watched him hit the ground to break into a run, streaking away from the building. Irene immediately recognized the man's profile: it was Vanya. He had bolted as soon as he'd seen her. And that's when she knew he was working with the Germans. But while she was in the Gestapo building, there was nothing she could do to warn Arel or anyone else.

When Shalom arrived at their meeting point, Vanya was there waiting just as they'd planned. The older Russian handed the young fighter one of the villager's guns for inspection, and as soon as Shalom had the weapon in his hand, police officers appeared from hiding. Shalom tried to fire at them, but the gun jammed. It had been a trap. Vanya was working with the Nazis. Shalom was arrested and brought to the Gestapo jail.

The resistance network's mandate of anonymity had protected the majority of its members, but a few who had interacted with Vanya were now imperiled, most critically Dvoretsky himself. After Shalom was apprehended there was no word of Vanya's whereabouts or how much he had disclosed to the Nazis—perhaps he'd betrayed them all. Those at risk had no choice but to flee to the woods ahead of schedule.

Shalom was tortured for days. When the Nazis realized they couldn't beat information out of him, they started to cut him into pieces. In between the rounds of torment, he placed a note on his holding cell windowsill. Razinsky, the blacksmith, found the crumpled piece of paper and word of its contents spread around the ghetto. The message was inked in Shalom's blood. "Don't worry," he'd written. "I will not betray you."

After a few more days, the Nazis either exhausted the depth

of their torture tactics or the endurance of the human body, and killed Shalom. But they were no closer to breaking the resistance's ranks. The nineteen-year-old boy had not uttered a word against his friends.

❧

With the capture and arrest of Shalom Fiolon, Dvoretsky's great plan was abandoned.

On the night of April 28, 1942, Dvoretsky and four of his young compatriots snuck out of the ghetto and ran to the woods. Notably absent was Arel Lazerowich. He had planned to join them, but when his mother saw him packing, she became distraught. "How can you leave us in this moment?" she demanded. "We need you. How selfish can you be?" Racked with guilt, Arel couldn't bear to go, and the others went on without him.

When they arrived in the forest, Dvoretsky pleaded with the Soviet partisans to launch an attack on the ghetto, but they refused. Their goal was to upend the Germans, not to save Jews. They had been willing to join forces with young resisters, in spite of the fact that they were Jewish, because they brought arms as well as a revenge-fueled desire to kill Nazis. This may have been a partnership mandated by Stalin, but it was one of convenience, where loyalties and trust ranged from thin to nonexistent. Nothing Dvoretsky could say would engage their passions or their sympathy, and the last flame of the Zhetel resistance flickered and went out.

On April 29, Dvoretsky's wife and mother were arrested, as were the remaining leaders of the Judenrat, and a bounty of 25,000 marks was placed on his head.

That night, the Einsatzgruppen arrived. And as soundless as a coiling snake, they closed in around the ghetto.

CHAPTER 8

The First Selection and the Boy from Bilitza

PHILIP LAZOWSKI WAS WIDE AWAKE. EVER SINCE HIS FAMily had moved into the ghetto, they had been staying in Mr. Mirsky's house, which sat right by the ghetto entrance. As far as the eleven-year-old was concerned, that front gate wasn't a way out but the Nazis' way in, and that knowledge left him on permanent edge. What was keeping him awake on this particular night, however, was the light. The April stars were unusually bright, casting a glow so strong it reached all the way down from the sky to his window in Zhetel.

Their apartment was really just a single, still-under-construction room, and a miserably small one for their family of seven. Philip felt lost in this new town where the Lazowskis were refugees, where he was a stranger, and everything was unfamiliar. It had been five months since the Nazis emptied their small town, Bilitza, of all its Jews and sent them to the ghettos in Lida and Zhetel. The Lazowskis had loaded up their borrowed cart with food and family, then fell in line with the other horse-drawn wagons winding their way out of Bilitza. There were concerns that they might encounter trouble on the road, but the daylong journey had passed without violence. The worst they had to endure were the shouts and jeers of local gentile Poles who had come to watch the procession of the now homeless Jewish families, who they seemed to believe were getting their due. A light snow was falling as the Lazowskis approached Zhetel. The old farmers traded ominous whispers: the early cold snap that had downed tree branches with such heavy ice was a bad omen.

Small and remote, Bilitza had always seemed the kind of place where people were poor, but without ever knowing how much they were going without. Even in the 1930s, it was one of a few villages in Poland still without electricity and telephones. Joseph Lazowski, Philip's father, had made his living as a fisherman and his mother, Chaya, had owned a small fabric shop. They lived in a comfortable white house with a thatched roof under which the Sabbath was sacred and celebrated. His parents were religious and generous. Chaya, who was fond of quoting Proverbs, would make sumptuous meals of *kneidlach* soup, and Joseph often returned from synagogue with lonely congregation members in tow. Somehow, they always managed to find room at their already crowded table. It was a home in which love and order thrived in equal measure, where every one of the five children knew their place. Seating at their table was arranged by age—the youngest child next to their mother, and Philip, the eldest, took his chair by his father.

As a young boy he gravitated to books and religious studies, captivated by the Torah's teachings and the invigorating glow of piety. Philip was educated under the tutelage of old-school masters, men who relied on a code of discipline—the smack of a thin rod across the palm or kneeling on dried peas in the corner—to train their young male students to become not just scholars but respectable Jewish men. It was a punishing course of study, and Philip often worked well past the time the other children had come in from an afternoon of play and freedom.

He continued his study into the evenings, by the light of kerosene lamps.

Short and skinny, Philip had always been small for his age. But he was clever and quick on his feet. When Philip was told two of his teeth had to be pulled during a routine visit to the dentist, he managed to persuade his mother—and the dentist—to agree to a single tooth extraction, negotiating his pain in half. While enjoying the cool splash of water in the Neman River on a hot summer's day, he lost his footing in the current. He wriggled his hands and feet, mimicking the motions of the older boys in the river, and soon enough he was managing something more like swimming than drowning.

Philip hadn't experienced any kind of life outside his own, and yet he understood that what his family had was good.

On June 28, 1941, the Germans stormed into Bilitza on roaring trucks, guns ablaze. The hunt for Russians commenced on arrival, and without warning the attackers set the town on fire. The streets were engulfed in flames and chaos as people and farm animals fled in all directions. Holding hands, the Lazowski children followed Chaya to a clearing outside the village where the family stood with their neighbors watching the village burn, and with it their home.

The SS arrived a few days later and their torture of the Jews—public displays of humiliation and violence designed to spread fear and, with it, compliance—began. The threat was worse for the men, and Joseph and Philip's grandfather left to hide in nearby barns where, every few days, Philip would sneak away to bring them food. This was how the Lazowskis coped until November 9, when Bilitza's Jews were forced into two regional ghettos. The Lazowskis went to Zhetel.

Five months later, in the early morning hours of April 30, Philip, sleepless, gazed at the view from Mr. Mirsky's apartment window: the ghetto's barrier of wooden slats and barbed wire. But as the stars and nighttime darkness faded, and first light colored the sky, Philip could finally see what was waiting on the other side of that fence.

He ran to wake up his mother. There was barely enough time to warn her of what was coming before the attack began.

ॐ

The noise of it cut through the morning like rocks breaking on ice in a relentless storm of sound. The Gestapo and the Lithuanian officers were positioned around the ghetto, some mounted on rumbling trucks, wielding giant machine guns, shooting in from the outside—taking aim at nothing and everything. Their bullets ripped through house walls, waking people into a blind panic, sending them running into the streets from house to house with nowhere safe to go.

The ghetto's Jewish police officers shouted to the residents to come out of their houses. "Bring your papers," they called, pushing everyone to a clearing in the woods by the site of the old Jewish cemetery known to all the locals as the Marketplace. As the flood of people hurried in that direction, the Germans entered the ghetto, kicking their way into houses, pulling and shoving people along. "*Raus! Raus! Raus! Schnell! Schnell! Schnell!*" (Out! Out! Out! Fast! Fast! Fast!)

The Lazowskis rushed to the *skron*, the hiding place they had built inside the apartment walls. Having become acquainted with the Nazis' brutality in Bilitza, they started carving out their *skron* the moment they arrived in the Zhetel ghetto. It was only after they were inside that they remembered the chicken left sitting on the kitchen table. Jews were not allowed meat in the ghetto, and being discovered with contraband in the house was enough to warrant a death sentence. Thinking there was still time to hide the meat, Joseph and Chaya stepped cautiously into the room.

Philip followed his parents, moving past them to peek his head out the front door, and was met with the sound of thundering footsteps and shouting. Nazi guards were bursting into the adjacent apartments, looking to root out anyone who had decided to take their chances and hide.

Chaya and Joseph rushed back behind the wall, but Philip, certain he'd been seen, pushed the camouflaged door closed behind them, arranging the dirt to mask the entrance.

The apartment door banged open and a Gestapo guard came crashing into the room, rifle raised. He seemed surprised to find a boy by himself.

"Where is your family?" he demanded. "Why are you alone?"

Philip told him his family already went to the Marketplace. "I came back for my coat," he lied.

The man shouted at him to get out and swung his rifle butt down toward Philip's head. Small and quick, Philip dodged the blow and ran out the door and into the street.

He was one of the last to join the swarms of people.

❧

Thousands of Jews were corralled out of the ghetto beyond the fences toward the Marketplace. The throngs of families forced from their overcrowded ghetto dwellings were now surrounded by German soldiers and Belorussian police who stood with their bayonets drawn. The Jews called these militia men crows, because of their all-black uniforms; they were notorious for their drunken brutality. The Germans found the propensity of their coconspirators for drink so reprehensible and difficult to manage that they had even passed out pamphlets on the virtues of sobriety titled "A Reminder to the Belorussian Policeman." On this morning, the odor of alcohol was strong enough that it permeated the air around them like a haze.

Men and women, the elderly and small children, were all pushed together, funneled into long lines that moved toward a single point—a station where Novogrudek's *Gebietskommissar,* Wilhelm Traub, was sitting, gesturing to those standing before him to either side of his table.

As people trudged their way forward, pushing and shoving, the implication of Traub's gesture became clear: he waved the old, infirm, and unaccompanied children to the right, while able-bodied men and those holding *scheins* were sent to the left with their families. It was a selection: those who were sent to the right would be killed and those to the left would live. The dawning understanding incited a fresh wave of terror, turning the scene into barely contained pandemonium. Anyone who hesitated or intervened was shot on the spot.

As Traub made this decisive motion with his finger—to the right, to the left—the contrast of his steady demeanor against the human hysteria unfurling around him seemed almost irrational. His immaculate black boots, shining with polish, were the height of disregard.

Philip Lazowski stood in the midst of it all and could only stare as a Nazi sent the end of a bayonet into an infant as its mother held him in her arms, piercing the tiny body so the baby was lifted up into the air and tossed to the ground. A man and woman held onto each other, swaying back and forth. Perhaps they had accepted their fate and in doing so relinquished themselves to the bliss of oblivion, dancing to music only they could hear. The dead were getting trampled. The line to the front was getting shorter and shorter.

Fear overwhelmed Philip; he was all alone. Each passing moment sent him further into a kind of shock. He saw that the sun was shining; it was a beautiful spring day. He thought of his family, and realized that if they were not there, there was still hope they were safe. The understanding gave him comfort and suddenly it was as if he could hear his mother's voice: *Do not give up.*

The numbness vanished. Philip studied his surroundings with new purpose. Up at the front and off to the side was a woman Philip recognized. He made his way to where she was standing with her family, and tried to sidle up alongside her, but she spotted him coming and shooed him away. "Don't stand next to us," she hissed. "You don't belong in this group." When he hesitated, she threatened to call the Germans.

Rebuffed, Philip scanned the line again. He noticed that exceptions were being made for people with working papers. This time his gaze landed on a woman standing with her two young daughters; the girls were frightened and clutching her sides. This woman's face was kind. Philip saw that in her hand she was holding a yellow *schein*.

He was looking at Miriam Rabinowitz.

❧

At the sound of gunfire and the barking calls to evacuate the ghetto, Morris and Miriam had dressed quickly and then hurried Rochel and Tania into clothes. Once they were in the street, the Jewish police officers had assured the anxious crowd that this was a gathering to check papers.

Morris and Miriam allowed themselves to feel the smallest relief; each of them possessed a work certificate, and those pieces of paper held all the promise of a talisman. That confidence would have surely wavered when they arrived at the Marketplace. There was no sign of Berl or Beyla, Cherna and Simcha, or Cousin Issy.

At the entry to the cemetery stood a large SS officer, towering in his black leather trench coat, a giant dog leashed at his side. As they joined the line, the force of the crowd had been too strong, and like a great undertow, the jostling bodies pulled Morris away from his family. Luba too, got swept up in the crowd. Miriam caught hold of Rochel and Tania and didn't dare let go.

Already at a height disadvantage to orient herself in the pulsating mass of bodies, she would have had to strain to raise her head above the shoulders around her, scanning the crowds desperately for Morris's wave of black hair. But there was no sign of him. She and her daughters were on their own. Miriam placed Tania between herself and Rochel, as each of them gripped the littlest one's hands.

Philip walked up to Miriam and got her attention. "Please," he begged. "I don't have anyone here. Will you take me as your son?"

Miriam looked at the young boy, taking in his thick shock of hair and desperate eyes. It took her but a moment to decide.

"If the Nazis let me live with two children," she told him, "they'll let me live with three." She offered the boy her free hand and Philip, relieved, gripped it tight.

All around the Marketplace, families with and without work certificates were being ripped apart. One man was sent to the left, but when his wife was pushed to the right, he ran after her and was shot in the head. Bodies began to pile up; blood colored the ground.

Seventeen-year-old Sara Raznow was quick to figure out what these separate lines meant. She and her sister were pulled into the good line while their parents, fifteen-year-old brother, and their elderly grandmother were sent to the other. Sara knew her father had a work certificate and in the mass of shouting chaos, Sara broke out of the line and ran up to one of the SS officers. A man who understood what she was doing called to her in Yiddish as she rushed past him, "If you don't watch out, you will get killed because of your parents."

Sara didn't stop, and called to the SS officer, "My father has a *schein*." Her young face was plain but her shining brown eyes were sweet and when the officer turned to her, he only asked, "Who is your father?" At that, the men standing in the line around them shouted at Sara in Yiddish, "Tell him, I'm your father! Tell him, I'm your father!" The SS officer pulled Sara's parents out of line along with her younger brother. Everyone but her grandmother. When the elderly woman saw that her family was leaving without her, she couldn't understand why and held on to her grandchildren.

A policeman grabbed her arm and started to pull her away. But she resisted, begging, "*Ich bin nur eine Großmutter!*" (I'm only a grandmother!) When she became hysterical, the policemen beat her to death in full view of her family.

As the crowd inched forward, Miriam, Rochel, Tania, and now Philip moved closer and closer to the front. Miriam looked down and saw that Philip's yellow Star of David was torn, the cloth patch hanging askew from his shirt. If one of the guards saw it, she knew it would draw attention and the boy would be beaten, or worse. She reached into her pocket and hastily pulled out a safety pin and did her best to smooth the star back into place.

Finally, just as they approached the head of the line, Miriam caught sight of Morris, who was already through and standing to the left. Their eyes locked and she called out to the officers in front of them, "*Das ist mein Mann!*" pointing to Morris, who shouted back, "*Das ist meine Frau!*" *Gebietskommissar* Traub glanced down his spotless round spectacles at Morris, and motioned Miriam to the table. He took her certificate and looked it over. He pointed to the left.

Miriam rushed all three children toward her husband and threw herself into his arms. Philip was so relieved that he ran from the Marketplace as fast as he could, not stopping to turn and thank the woman who had just saved his life. It wasn't until later that he realized he never asked for her name.

❧

Philip Lazowski rushed back to the ghetto. But as soon as Mr. Mirsky's house was in view, he stopped dead in his tracks. There were four bodies lying in the street. He had barely finished the thought that it might be his family before a dizzying wave hit him and he fainted. The first thing Philip would see when he was roused a few moments later was his mother's eyes looking back at his.

The day the Nazis burned down his home in Bilitza had marked the end of Philip's childhood, but the day of the selection was when he leapt across that divide from boy to an age that doesn't come with just the passing of years, or show the markings of time. His features were still soft, his wild hair and thick, high-arching eyebrows would still knit an impish expression across his face. But like one of Peter Pan's Lost Boys, the look of youth was just a veneer. Something deep inside was now all grown up and would never be the same again. It was also the day when Philip Lazowski proved himself a survivor, showing that the will to live can go a long way when the legs, however small, are strong enough to carry it.

As those who had been spared shuffled back to the ghetto, those who were sent to the right that day—men, women, and many children, nearly 1,200 people in all—were marched a mile into the woods. Bashe Rozwaski and her children were in this unfortunate group. She was the wife of Dovid Rozwaski, who had been taken away with the first roundup of 119 Jewish men (and one woman) in July 1941. Bashe had been pregnant at the time, and now she held that baby boy in her arms; her seven-year-old son Chaim and two young daughters were by her side. With no husband and no papers, her family had not made it through the selection in the Marketplace.

German officers corralled the Jews into a long column and

then forced them to sit down on the ground alongside the road. Bit by bit, people were pulled from the head of the line and marched into the woods. Each group's departure was followed by a ringing chorus of gunshots. Everyone collected on that road understood what was waiting for them. Some began to shift toward the back of the line. Others, feeling that all was lost, dropped their identification cards on the ground and stayed where they were, having accepted their fate.

Suddenly, a car drove up and out stepped *Gebietskommissar* Traub. Soon he and the other officers began to review people's papers, conducting yet another selection. The horrible process was repeated again, but Traub began to motion some people away to the side of the line—in the direction of safety. The chance for a reprieve awakened the Jews in line with new hope, and this time the pushing and shoving was a competition to live.

Bashe and her children were standing with her sister and brother-in-law, who both had papers. Her brother-in-law planned to say Bashe was his wife so they could divide the safety of the two *scheins* to cover both families. But when it was time to stand in front of the officers, there was a rush of chaos and confusion, and the family was tossed apart in the thrust of the crowd. A few moments later, Bashe's children had made it through the line with their aunt and uncle without her.

Bashe and her baby, and the rest of the Jews who hadn't passed through the second selection, were sent to the edge of three gaping pits. They were forced to strip off their clothes and file into lines. In groups of twenty they were brought to the ditches' edges, where they were mowed down by machine-gun fire. Some were killed instantly, others were just gravely wounded, pushed into the mass graves still alive. The limp bodies of babies and toddlers who'd been silenced as their skulls were crushed against tree trunks were tossed onto the pile before the Nazis doused the pits with bleach and threw grenades in at random to make sure none were left alive.

Bashe Rozwaski was still holding her infant son when the force of bullets pitched her body into the trench.

As the Jews were marched from the woods back to the ghetto, the local peasants and Christian Poles had gathered along the road and stood there watching. Chaim Rozwaski saw them staring and he couldn't understand what these people had come to see. When Chaim looked back again, he noticed one old woman crying silently, the tears streaming down her face.

Later, someone brought the Rozwaski family a shawl they'd found on the ground. Black with embroidered flowers, the initials sewn in red thread on the corner of the fabric belonged to Bashe. She had wrapped it around herself and the baby earlier that morning. In all the twisting of the crowd, it must have been pulled from her shoulders.

A few people in town claimed they could hear the gunshots, while others weren't certain of what happened until later, when eyewitness accounts eventually reached the ghetto. During the last moments of the massacre, for no discernible reason, those at the very end of the line for those pits were offered a reprieve and sent back to town.

After the four hours it took to slaughter more than one thousand people, the Nazis had run out of ammunition.

❧

That night, one of the women brought to slaughter in the wooded area outside Zhetel opened her eyes. The Nazi bullets had missed Judith Moszkowski, but she'd fallen into the grave with the others. She had lain there all day, in a disassociated state of shock. When she came back to a clearer consciousness, it took her hours to understand that she was, in fact, still alive.

This is what it must feel like to be dead, she had thought. In the middle of the night she realized that she could not stay where she was. Somehow, she untangled herself from the bodies and climbed out of that hole. She walked through the field and to a farmer's house, where the family that opened their door to her couldn't have been anything other than stunned to see a naked young woman covered in blood standing there. But they took her in and gave her clothes. The farmer helped direct her to safety, pointing her toward the place where the Jews were gathering in the forest.

Over the next few days the Germans consolidated the ghetto, pulling in its borders to make for an even smaller, more confined space. The Rabinowitz family moved into a new house belonging to the Cooperman family and located on the far end of the ghetto just inside the fence. It was the last place in Zhetel they would ever call home.

They had just received devastating news. A Polish farmer got word to Morris that his father was dead. After Alter Dvoretsky disappeared, the SS commanders rounded up the remaining eleven members of the Judenrat and interrogated them, Berl Rabinowitz included. It's not clear what exactly they wanted from him—information about Dvoretsky's resistance, or assistance corralling the Jews for selection. Whatever it was, Berl Rabinowitz had refused. The Nazis rewarded him with a swift and gruesome execution—beheading by ax.

If Morris hadn't decided already, his father's death would've woken him to the understanding that there was no more room for hope of exception; work papers would not keep them safe forever. The Nazis were not going to stop killing until all the Jews were dead.

Together, he, Miriam, and Luba decided that the next time the

Nazis called for a gathering of any kind, the Rabinowitz family would not answer. Alter Dvoretsky's plan may not have been fully realized, but the way out of the ghetto had not changed; there was still a chance they could make it to the woods, it was just a matter of timing. But until then, they would need a place to hide.

Under the cover of night, while the children were sleeping, the adults began to dig.

CHAPTER 9

The Escape

Sometime in the late spring of 1942, little Tania Rabinowitz developed a fascination with the piles of sand that had started to appear in the Coopermans' yard. It didn't escape the eyes of this precocious five-year-old that the richly colored earth arrived in the morning against the side of the garage where it had not been the night before. When Tania asked what it was doing there, her parents brushed away the question. "Don't be silly," they said, the dirt had always been right where it was. When Tania insisted the sand that she saw looked *clean,* Morris and Miriam directed her to the weather, suggesting a heavy night's rainfall had washed the sand into the yard, an explanation that did little to quash her suspicions. Finally, Tania's interrogations became so probing that she was forbidden from discussing the topic.

The Rabinowitzes were fortunate to be living with the Coopermans. Before the war, they had been one of the town's wealthiest families, and their large house, which offered such luxuries as a private water pump, had plenty of room to accommodate the motley collection currently setting up residence there: Mr. and

Mrs. Cooperman, their son, his wife, and their baby, and a few of their extended family members including Ola the dentist. There were also three others who had managed to evade the first selection—an older deaf man named Mr. Kaplinsky, who had come with his daughter and sister-in-law, a young man in a wheelchair, and a girl on her own who was just a few years older than Rochel. Together they made a small but adequate force, able to manage the clandestine labor they would endeavor together.

The group understood that when the next raid occurred, they couldn't simply lie low in the root cellar or under the floor and expect to survive. And so they set to work on a far more elaborate and clever design, utilizing the Coopermans' garage, which was separate from the house. In the back of the garage they constructed a long narrow room behind a wall. It was a space designed to look hastily built, complete with all the visual hints of a *skron*—outfitted with stools and benches, and even a bucket by the farthest wall to suggest a makeshift latrine. When the Nazis came to search for hiding Jews, they would undoubtedly be on the lookout for attic hideouts and basement bunkers. If all went according to plan, the Nazis would find this first *skron* empty and end their search.

The real hiding place was under the bench on the left side of the room, down through a trapdoor that blended into the floor. Night after night, the group had worked for weeks to carve out a space underground able to accommodate more than two dozen people. Longer and wider than it was tall, there would only be room for the adults to sit, crouch, or lie down.

It wasn't a guaranteed way out of the ghetto, but with the Coopermans' house located by its outermost fence near the woods, far away from the main entrance, it was enough to provide a modicum of hope for escape. And the Zhetel ghetto was running very low on hope.

Nearly a third of Zhetel's Jews had been killed on that April afternoon, and many of those who returned from the selection were racked with guilt at having lived when their relatives and friends had not. Some even professed envy of those who'd been killed and entertained fantasies of suicide. There were deliberations over which obtainable poison might provide a quick and painless end.

In May, more despairing news came to the Zhetel ghetto. Alter Dvoretsky was dead. He'd been killed by the same Russian partisans whose alliance he had worked so hard to procure. For all the Zhetelers who had pinned their fates on the resistance—who had prayed Dvoretsky and his underground forces would lead the partisans back to Zhetel to save them—word of his death dealt the ghetto another mournful blow.

There was very little doubt that another *selektion* was coming, and people throughout the ghetto braced for it, however futile their preparations. The fear that their youngest offspring would be taken away prompted mothers to dress their children in clothes from more grown-up wardrobes, while women who dreaded being thought too old to be useful, or aged beyond appeal, traded their longer locks for cropped cuts in the hopes of acquiring a more youthful appearance. These grasping attempts at subterfuge had little to no hope of saving anyone.

Even the youngest Zhetelers absorbed the gloom, and new games broke out among the children still left in the ghetto; they performed macabre reenactments of the *selektion*. One child would play the role of *Gebietskommissar* Traub, ready to pantomime the dreaded signal—pointing to the left or right. The little thespians playing victims approached the "SS officer." "*Mein Herr,* let me live," they pleaded. "I am still so young." Even in their game there was no room for mercy, and with his tiny finger, "the Nazi" sent his friends to execution.

There wasn't much for the children to do during the day. The Coopermans' young relative who was relegated to a wheelchair had a disarming and gentle nature, and he delighted the Rabinowitz girls by performing an assortment of magic tricks. Tania especially grew fond of him. Otherwise, Rochel and Tania spent most of their time outdoors in the Coopermans' yard. But not before their parents issued stern warnings about what terrible things would happen to them if they were tempted by those boundaries so close to their house and made any move to go beyond them.

One day, while Rochel and Tania were playing outside with a group of ghetto kids, some local children gathered nearby, watching the Jewish kids from the other side of the fence. One Polish girl crawled under the wood and wire and made her way to Rochel, who had her doll cradled in her arms. As soon as she got close, the girl reached out, snatched the doll from Rochel's grasp, and ran away. Stunned, Rochel could only watch the girl retreat with her beloved toy back under the fence to a place where Rochel would not dare to follow. Tania stood next to Rochel, keeping near while her sister cried.

For days, Rochel was inconsolable over her lost doll. The tears seemed endless. Morris and Miriam soon had enough of what they called "her carrying on," very likely preoccupied with more urgent concerns and unable to fully appreciate the psychological toll this was taking on their oldest daughter.

"You shed more tears for that doll than you did for your grandfather," Morris admonished his daughter.

In any other circumstance, seven-year-old Rochel would be nearing the age where young girls typically put aside toys like dolls for other interests. But in the ghetto, after all that had happened, this was the final wresting away of a childhood Rochel might never reclaim. Her doll wasn't lost, it had been taken by another little girl—the Polish girl outside the ghetto—who represented everything Rochel—the Jewish girl inside the ghetto—could not have, and everything she would never be able to be.

ॐ

Not all the events of those spring and summer months would prove so dispiriting for the Rabinowitz family. One day, Tania began to complain of ear pain, the reoccurring affliction that had plagued her since the day she pulled the pot of hot soup from the stove. Despite Miriam's pharmacy experience and her medicinal knowledge, she wasn't able to alleviate Tania's discomfort. It just so happened that while they were on their way see a physician who treated families in the ghetto, Philip Lazowski was looking out his window. He immediately recognized the woman from the Marketplace and yelled for his mother, Chaya.

"Ma, come here quickly," Philip called. "I see the woman who saved my life!"

They hurried out the front door but only just in time to see Miriam and Tania disappearing into the doctor's house, so Philip and Chaya waited for them in the street. When the Lazowskis introduced themselves, Miriam was relieved to see that the boy she'd looked after during the *selektion* was safely back with his mother. Chaya thanked Miriam for saving her son, offering her Hebrew blessing after blessing before the women parted ways.

Miriam had never been a religious woman, but in that moment, she felt a sense of protection. She couldn't have known how soon Chaya's blessings would be needed.

ॐ

In the still dark of Thursday morning, August 6, 1942, Morris and Miriam roused their two sleeping daughters, ushering them out of their shared bed and through the house. "We have to go to the *skron,*" they told Rochel and Tania in hurried voices. It was time to go into the hiding place, just as they'd rehearsed, and they must not make a sound. Miriam's cousin, Meirim, the guard in the ghetto's Jewish Police Force, had seen the Gestapo and SS assembling outside the fence and took off running to the Coopermans' house to warn them: the Germans had the ghetto surrounded. The family had bided their time for the right window to escape the ghetto and missed.

SS officers, and the Lithuanian and Belorussian police officers with them, were shouting, "*Juden raus!*" They were shooting at anyone who made a rush to the fence in an attempt to push through its wide-gaped boards. The sound of rapid gunfire and the screams that followed echoed around the ghetto.

Everyone in the Cooperman house filed out the back door before they could be seen, hustling across the yard and into the garage through the first room, and down the trapdoor to the bunker.

Only Morris hung back. His mother, Beyla, sister Cherna, and nephew Simcha didn't have a hiding place or *scheins*. And, now, after Berl's murder, without a man at the head of the household, Morris knew they were both vulnerable to another *selektion*. He'd made it through the first *aktion* with his work certificate; maybe by pretending Cherna was his wife, he could keep them safe from this one, too. He had to try.

Miriam, meanwhile, would stay to hide with the girls and Luba, as they'd planned all along.

"When it's safe to come out, we'll find each other," Morris said, reassuring his wife. A forester, one of his most trusted Christian friends, lived in the woods on the outskirts of town—a remote place they both knew. "Find the forester," Morris told Miriam, "and I will find you."

Morris waited while everyone climbed down into the bunker before closing the trapdoor behind them, doing his best to camouflage the entrance from sight. A loudspeaker bleated out a call across the ghetto for all the Jews to report to the cemetery. Morris left the Coopermans' yard and made his way to the Marketplace alone.

❧

Morris joined the nine hundred people in the Marketplace by Zhetel's old cemetery. Men, women, and children were then herded south along Kastrychnitskaia Street, past the town boundary toward the wide-expanding meadows and the unbroken green of the surrounding woods. They marched along the dirt road worn by decades of wagon-wheel tread, until they reached the new cemetery. To the east was a small field. To the west was the close edge of the forest, a wall of shrubbery and bottle-brush pine.

The SS officers ordered them all to lie face down, pressed flat against the grass and dirt. An impenetrable ring of German officers, Gestapo, and Belorussian police encircled the field three times over.

Morris was lying beside his sister, Cherna. He had found her in the crowd with Simcha, and his mother, Beyla, before the Nazis marched them to the field. Whatever hopes Morris had that his *schein* was going to save them must have crumbled in a sickening realization as the Nazis and their police henchmen began to shout over their prostrate forms, warning them not to lift their heads, to look at nothing but the ground. This was not like the last time—there were no lines, no scrutiny of work certificates. It seemed that no one would be spared.

Suddenly, the Germans started calling for workers: *Schneider!* (Tailor!) *Schuster!* (Shoemaker!) And then, *Tischler!* the German word for carpenter. Morris, unable to make out what they were saying, lifted his head. A German officer barked again, "Carpenters, come here!" Cherna nudged him. "Go," she whispered. "Maybe you'll be saved." When still he didn't move, Cherna turned to her brother, blue eyes imploring. "*Go*."

Morris raised his hand. An SS officer came over, looked him up and down, and without asking for a *schein,* ordered him off to the side of the field. When others realized that this call for workers was likely translating into safety, men started to send their hands in the air, calling out to be picked. Then the Nazis began to ask for papers. When most of the men couldn't produce them, they were shoved back down to the ground.

When they called for shoemakers, Arel Lazerowich raised his hand, and he and his father, favored by the SS officers for the work he did personally on their boots, were also pulled to the side. When Arel looked back, he saw his mother raise her head from the ground to watch them walk away. When they locked eyes, she lifted her hand and waved.

If Morris had the chance to look back at his mother, sister, and young nephew, hopefully he took it. It was the last time he would ever see them.

In short order, the Nazis pulled roughly two hundred tradesmen from the group and hauled them a short distance away, then had them lie back down on the ground, shouting again for them to place their heads down into the crooks of their arms. Blinded to what was happening around them, they could hear the faint cries and whimpers of children still lying in the grass, and the thudding sound of boots and rifle butts that followed as the guards silenced anyone disrupting the quiet. The tension mounted as they braced for the shots and machine-gun fire they expected to hear. But none came.

The men, women, and children whose lives held no further value for the Nazis were put on trucks and driven away. Morris Rabinowitz and the rest of the workers whose lives had been spared were marched back to the ghetto, where the Nazis pushed them into the old movie theater and locked the door.

❧

The men and women crowded into the two-story building, filling it from wall to wall. There were no facilities, no water, and all the windows were closed and covered with heavy fabric. In addition to the workers pulled from the cemetery, the Nazis continued to add a rolling haul of men, women, and children discovered hiding in the ghetto.

Well prepared for their near-final phase of liquidating the ghetto—the clean sweep, a *Judenrein*—the Nazis, of course, had anticipated that many Jews would go to ground. The SS tactics to unearth them ranged from barbaric, door-busting invasions to more steadied, patient approaches akin to a hunting cat waiting for its prey to expose themselves. After Thursday's roundup and massacre, the SS and Gestapo guards walked through the ghetto streets, assuming the voice of a friend or family member, calling out: "It's over! It's safe to come out now."

Both approaches yielded results, but the Einsatzgruppen were nothing if not thorough.

That evening, SS officer Wilhelm Reuter walked into the crowded *kino,* where people anxiously waited for what was to come next. A tall man with round glasses, Reuter was the architect of the brutality inflicted on the Jews in the Novogrudek region; the liquidations were carried out under his command. Now he spoke to a room of mostly men, and a few women, with coaxing practicality, reassuring them that they were "the saved," the valuable exceptions. "Who has relatives hiding?" Reuter asked. "Go ahead and bring them out, and we'll make a new ghetto, a smaller one," he promised. "And all of you will continue to work."

Reuter's announcement prompted a wave of tentative relief among some of the men. If they were to be saved, then why not their families? It had been the case before, why shouldn't it be true now? Some left the *kino* to retrieve their hiding loved ones, in a hurry to reunite with them and to deliver the good news.

Morris Rabinowitz would not take this bait. After Reuter left, a man Morris knew from town maneuvered his way to Morris's side of the crowd. The two men were well enough acquainted as to be familiar with the other's families, and this man had noticed that earlier in the day, Morris arrived at the Marketplace without his wife and children.

"Maeshke," he said. "I didn't see your family this morning." Now that Morris was going to be sent to the labor camp in Novogrudek, both he and his family could be saved. Why not bring them to the *kino*, the man suggested.

Morris tried to side-step the man's questions. As his probing grew insistent, Morris, sensing a trap, played his one and only gambit.

"My family was killed already," Morris told him, concocting a story about how Miriam and the girls had been discovered in their *skron*, describing the dupe hideout in the Coopermans' garage. The man appeared to accept this information and offered condolences, before disappearing back into the crowd.

As the hours passed, more families caught in hiding were brought into the *kino*. Soon the theater was so full, the SS opened a second building to house the latest captives.

What else could Morris do but wait, agonizing as the moments passed, knowing that he had just directed these murderers to the room right above the space where his family was hiding?

There was nothing left to do but pray that his misdirection had just enough truth in it to fool them, and that they would find only what he had intended for them to find—an empty room.

❧

After Morris closed the trapdoor behind them that morning, time had metered out at an imperceptible pace in the darkness of the *skron*. More than twenty anxious people squeezed together in the narrow, neck-bending space under the Coopermans' garage.

Hours had passed. The discordant strain of gunshots and cries played over and over, reaching all ends of the ghetto. Soon enough, they heard shouts in German and the thumping of boots on the floor above them—the Nazis had found the first hiding place. The adults in the bunker went rigid. Rochel and Tania huddled together, holding their breath.

"Jews were here," one voice said, clearly surveying the benches against the garage wall in the decoy room. "Someone must've found them already." The next voice was imperceptible, but the exchange between the Germans was brief and the tunneled sound of their voices faded and the noise above retreated, moving farther away.

Maybe it was hunger or the building anxiety surrounding him, but in that moment the Coopermans' baby stirred, fussing and twisting in his mother's arms. Both parents moved to hush him, but the child was inconsolable, and his whimper broke into a wail, rising louder and louder. In a single motion, one of the men took the child from his mother and put a hand over his mouth and nose, holding fast until the small body went still.

In the breath-held silence, they waited, straining for any indication that the Germans had heard the child. But the moment passed and there was nothing. It seemed, for the time being, their hideout was secure.

As soon as the Coopermans' daughter-in-law realized what happened to her baby, she went wild, screaming and crying. The others rushed to quiet her, covering her mouth with their hands.

Her hysteria scared the girls. Rochel, who understood the sacrifice that had just transpired, turned to Tania, their faces close together in the dark. "We better be quiet," she whispered, "or we'll be next."

❦

All over the Zhetel ghetto, people crowded with their families and neighbors in basements, attics, and backyard sheds. They stood pin-straight behind walls, laid themselves flat underneath floorboards, and squatted in the cramped range of root cellars, spaces never intended to hold anything larger than a season's haul of potatoes. When there was no *skron* to share, people squirreled themselves away wherever they could, like the pair of young women who stood chest deep in the foul pond of waste under the ghetto's shared latrines.

As the hours stretched on, the challenge of staying put was punishing. The houses were so close together that those in their hiding places could hear the moans and crying as their unlucky neighbors were pulled from safety and forced onto trucks. The steaming August temperatures rose as the sun climbed in the sky, and the heat became unbearable and the air in attics and bunkers grew stifling. People were forced to relieve themselves where they were, and over the hours human waste pooled in the space around them. Few of these hiding spots had windows or ready ventilation. Within a day's time, the air was putrid. One mother watched as the clothes on her infant son disintegrated off his body. Another dabbed urine on her children's parched lips, letting them lick a sugar cube in turns, as there was nothing else to eat or drink.

On the second day of hiding in an underground *skron*, nineteen-year-old Sonia Berenshtein could no longer tolerate the heat or the sounds of her father gasping as he slowly suffocated from lack of air. When Sonia decided she would rather take her chances against a German bullet than languish any longer in the stench and tried to leave, the others hiding with her beat and clawed at her skin, drawing blood, ready to kill her rather than allow her to exit the bunker and expose the rest of them.

At the first sound of the shouting loudspeaker, the Raznow family quickly divvied up, scattering between the three hiding places they had prepared in their shared two-family house. When the older Raznow daughters, Sara and Mira, saw that a woman with a baby was descending into the root-cellar *skron* with their parents, they shifted direction, agreeing that the narrow space between the chicken coop walls was safer than hiding with so young a child. When the Nazis searched the house, the child, not even one year old, began to yowl. One moment he was crying, and the next he wasn't. The mother had muffled him with her hands until he no longer drew breath, to keep them from being discovered.

In another ghetto house, a collective of families stowed themselves under the wooden floorboards where they had dug away at the earth of a small cellar used for storing wine and root vegetables. In the group of two dozen people hiding in this space was a woman with a six-month-old baby. When the baby started to cry, the others pushed her to take the child elsewhere. So, the woman went out into the house to nurse her child, but then she saw through the window that the Germans were coming so she left the baby on the bed and fled back to the hiding spot. Even before the hideaway door was closed safely behind her, the others could see the Germans come in, suspicious and bewildered to come across a baby alone. Searching the house, they found no one else. When they left, they took the child with them.

A young mother from Bilitza, separated from her large family and husband, hid in a friend's house where they had dug a tunnel. The group of women and children stayed submerged in the underground cavern for five long days, waiting out the massacre, and—whether it was to save them from pain or an inevitable, slower death, or to preserve themselves and others from discovery—two mothers in that tunnel suffocated their babies.

In the suspense of the ghetto hunt, children, especially infants who were unable to comprehend the need for endless quiet and submit to snap-sure obedience, were the ultimate liability. But as the days wore on, it wasn't only the endurance of the young that wavered.

Ten-year-old Samuel Kaminsky was hiding with about eighteen others—his mother and his siblings, cousins, and grandmother—in a space under the neighbors' house. As the air quality worsened, two elderly people struggled to breathe. In time, the sound of their choking gasps became too loud to ignore. It was one of the neighbors who took matters into his own hands. In the limited space, it might have been difficult to understand what the shuffle of movement and those sounds meant, but Samuel was fully aware of what was happening to his grandmother and cousin. "We knew. We knew," Samuel remembered. His mother, sitting next to him, began to cry. "You could not give out the whole group." They had to stop the noise. And so, in an act of self-preservation and mercy, they "put them to sleep."

❧

By Friday, the second day in the *kino*, the crowd of people bulged even further, body packed against body. There was not even room to sit. There were no toilets, or even a space designated for relief; the floors were soon covered in excrement and urine.

Morris Rabinowitz would have had little recourse, other

than to scan the crowd for a friendly face or hope to catch the eye of a trusted acquaintance who might have some news of Miriam, the children, or anyone else staying in the Coopermans' house.

Finally, the man who'd probed Morris so insistently about Miriam and the girls' whereabouts came back. "You were right," he told Morris. "The Germans couldn't find anyone at your house."

As he walked away, Morris expelled his contempt, muttering a Yiddish curse under his breath. "I'll have you in hell," he swore at the man's back.

Even as this surely came as a relief to Morris—it meant Miriam and the girls were likely still alive—his own predicament was only getting worse. The number of Jews saved from the field had more than doubled during the second day of the liquidation, and there was no reason to believe the Nazis would let them all live. And if Morris was carted off to a labor camp—as far away as Dvorets or Novogrudek—what then? Getting to the woods to find his family from there would undoubtedly prove more difficult, if not impossible.

But even in the doomed space of the *kino*, Morris was not without friends. In an auspicious moment, a woman he knew came up alongside him with a long-shot hope small enough to fit in her pocket.

"Maeshke, I have a way to get into the attic," she told him in a low voice. She had worked for the SS officers who had set up their headquarters in this very building. When the chance presented, she had taken the key to the locked upstairs room—and she had that key with her now.

It would be a risk to try and break away from this tightly packed group, like fish leaping from a barrel without making a splash. But there was hardly a better offer on hand, and he seized at it with both of his. "Let's hide there," Morris urged. "Maybe we can escape."

Morris, the woman with the key, and two others quietly peeled away from the crowd and made their way up the stairs to the building's top floor. If their absence was noted, no one came looking for them. Perhaps this woman had the only key, perhaps the attic had already been searched. One more reprieve had found its way to Morris. The night passed and they were not disturbed.

Early the following day, on Saturday morning, there was another *selektion*; the remaining workers and the families who had been wrenched or tricked out of their hiding places were separated again to the left and to the right. The final two hundred workers were loaded into trucks and driven to the train station, where they waited for the rail cars that would take them to the labor camp in Novogrudek. All the others were killed.

That night, when dark and silence fell over the movie theater, Morris Rabinowitz and his small group from the attic stole out of the building and escaped the ghetto, heading in the direction of the forest at last.

*

After hearing how close the Germans had been to their *skron*, Miriam, Luba, and the others agreed that leaving the Coopermans' garage was much too dangerous. They would have to wait.

They stayed in the bunker through that first night and then another day. All the while, periods of quiet were upset by sounds of shouting and shooting.

There was only one pot for them all to use to relieve themselves, and soon the stench overwhelmed the space, already stifled by the summer heat. Rochel and Tania were finding it difficult to breathe. Miriam helped her daughters undress to keep them cool, but even stripped down to their underwear the girls found no comfort.

On the evening on the second day, they heard the unmistakable commotion of people moving in the room above them. This time it wasn't German voices, but Polish, rising above the din of scraping and banging of wood on wood—the sounds of furniture being overturned. It was looters who, knowing the Jews had endured another slaughter, had come to pillage their homes.

"Rich Jews lived here," they heard one man say. The rumbling of voices continued and they were able to make out bits of conversation as the scavengers discussed a plan to return in the morning to dig around the yard for hidden valuables.

An understanding settled in the bunker: If there were looters moving freely through the ghetto, it meant the Germans weren't patrolling. And if the looters were indeed going to return, they could not still be in the Coopermans' garage when they did. They would have to leave soon while it was dark. "We better get out now," one of the other adults said.

But afraid of what they might encounter once they opened the trapdoor, no one wanted to be the first to leave. While they hesitated, a thumping, almost like footsteps moving back and forth across the floorboards, sounded overhead.

"Maybe they left someone behind to stand guard," a man said. It could be a Pole, or worse, a Nazi. There was an exchange of harsh whispers and it was decided the only way to get out was for someone to go above and attempt to bribe whoever was up there. Still, no one made a move—they were too scared.

It was Luba who volunteered to leave the bunker to check. She went out first, followed by cousin Meirim. Down in the dark, the rest waited until finally they heard Luba's voice. "Manya, lift up the kids," she called down to Miriam. The coast was clear.

Outside, it was unusually dark. There was no moonlight or starlight to illuminate their surroundings. They all began to exit the bunker, splintering off in pairs and small groups. The younger people left first, then the Cooperman family. Rochel and Tania heard a cracking noise and started, but it was only an animal—a stray cat or dog—moving through the yard.

Another noise shuffled close by, but this time it was a man, one of the young resistance members who, months ago, had been with Luba on their expedition to navigate a way to the woods. It was by pure coincidence they were meeting now, escaping the ghetto at the same time. He was glad to see Luba and seemed ready to join them, but when he noticed Rochel and Tania he balked. "I'm not going with her and the children," he said, nodding at Miriam, and urged Luba to leave the ghetto with him instead. She rebuffed him without a moment's hesitation, and the man took off, disappearing into the night.

Together with the girls, Miriam, Luba, and Meirim began to pick their way along in the dark through the Coopermans' yard. With no lights in the ghetto, they could barely keep track of one another.

Suddenly there was shouting nearby. Someone in their group called out *Deutsche!* There was a rush of bumping bodies. Frightened that the Germans were coming, Rochel turned back to the garage and jumped down into the hideout.

The noise of voices only propelled Miriam to move faster, and she pulled Tania by the hand while Luba and Meirim hurried to keep up. They made it all the way to the barbed wire barrier and were safely on the other side before Miriam realized Rochel wasn't with them.

"Where is *Rocheleh*?" she asked Luba, who stared back at her. "I thought you had her," Luba said.

"I have to go back," Miriam said, moving toward the fence. "I'm not leaving without her." She turned to Luba, gesturing them into the cornstalks to hide. "If I'm not here in twenty minutes," she told her sister, "go on without me."

Miriam navigated a path over the broken glass, dishes, and wires. She found her way back to the Cooperman house and stopped. The air was bitterly cold for a summer night. They had very few supplies, no food, and the girls had left their clothes in the bunker. In an abrupt decision she ran into the house to see if there was anything she could salvage. Each room had been ransacked; what little of the Coopermans' furniture had been left was overturned and emptied, their scant belongings scattered. Miriam rifled through the things on the floor, feeling around until she pulled up a large black coat.

Back in the bunker, Rochel stood under the trapdoor, holding off panic. No one else in her family had come back down with her. There were still a few others left in the hiding place, the older people who had hesitated to leave with the rest of them. One woman turned to her. "Your mother left you. She's not coming back." Her words filled Rochel with dread, but then came a defiant spark of anger. "I'm not afraid. My mother would never leave me," she retorted. "She will come back for me."

But after a few minutes, Rochel's confidence wavered again. What if her mother didn't return? What would she do? Then she heard rustling above and Miriam's voice calling her name. "*Rocheleh,* where are you?"

"I'm here, Mama," Rochel yelled back, relief flooding through her.

Miriam yanked the trapdoor open, and reached down for her daughter. But as Rochel reached back, she felt hands grabbing her legs and ankles, pulling her down. It was Mr. Kaplinsky's sister-in-law.

"What are you doing?" Miriam cried. "Let her go!"

The woman called up as her grip on Rochel tightened, "Take us with you and we'll let her go."

Aware that this urgent window held precious little time for them to escape the ghetto unnoticed, Miriam had no choice. "Alright," she relented. "You can come with us. But," she warned, "I don't really know where we're going."

It didn't matter to the few still left in the bunker; escaping the ghetto with a directionless group was better than being left behind.

One by one, the rest of the hiding-place dwellers emerged, all except the elderly deaf man, Mr. Kaplinsky. He was so paralyzed with fear he refused to leave the *skron,* and there was nothing to do but go on without him.

❧

It had taken three long, merciless days for the Nazis to complete their *Judenrein*. In a rough calculation, some three thousand people were rounded up from the Zhetel ghetto and murdered over the course of August 6 to 8, 1942—nearly three times the number of Jews the Germans had killed in April.

After being separated from her in-laws in the dark, Sonia Minuskin still managed to escape the ghetto with her two young sons, leaving town by its southern road, which brought them past the still-fresh mass graves. "I could hear the weak and feeble; moaning, gasping, and rasping sounds of dying people," she would remember.

Sonia knew that these were the cries of her neighbors, possibly her friends. *Forgive me,* she thought, as she pressed on without stopping, every instinct in her body shouting her forward.

❧

Miriam held on to Rochel with one hand and the black coat with the other, and led their new followers to the broken space in the fence and barbed wire where Luba, Meirim, and Tania were waiting on the other side. There was little time to explain the addition to their party; they had to get to the woods.

Miriam and Luba walked quickly, anxious to put the ghetto behind them. Miriam did not possess her husband's knowledge of the land and was navigating blind. Even if they'd had a map to follow, sorting out their direction in the dark would have been difficult. They walked through the entire night but the forester's house wasn't in sight. They had now gone more than two days without food and clean water and Miriam knew they could not continue much longer. The children were exhausted. Meirim lifted Tania onto his shoulders and carried her, while Rochel trailed just behind. Dawn was coming and as soon as it was light, they would have to hide again.

In time, a humble little farmhouse came into view. It was a risk, but they had no idea where they were. They would have to knock on the door and ask for help. While the others stayed out of sight, Miriam, accompanied by Meirim, walked up to the front door and rapped her knuckles against the wood.

An elderly man opened the door. It was clear he understood where they had come from and that he was scared—to shelter a Jew at this moment was possibly more dangerous than ever. But when Miriam implored him for help, he invited them inside. They didn't have very much to offer but the man's wife gave them some food. When Miriam told her that she had children who had not eaten in days, the old woman brought her two loaves of bread and a jar of pickle brine. Surely Miriam's courage flagged when the old couple told her that they were just two miles outside of town. They had gone in a circle, wasting a night's worth of safety while getting nowhere nearer to their destination, and nowhere nearer to finding Morris.

When she told the old couple they wanted to get to Lipiczany Forest, the old man talked her through the directions on how to take the road to the woods. Miriam thanked the couple for their kindness, then she and Meirim brought the food back to the others waiting on the road. Meirim broke off pieces of bread for Rochel and Tania, while they relayed to the others what the couple had said. Gray morning light began to crown over the trees. They couldn't stay in the open much longer; they would have to find a place to hide for the day. They risked continuing along the main road as long as they could, walking until they crossed a wide field thick with stalks of corn. Together the group waded deep into the silken husks to lie flat and still on the ground, where they stayed after the summer sun burned off the cool morning air, well into the afternoon.

For a while, all was quiet. But soon they heard the clip-clops and creaking rattles of a horse-drawn wagon. It was a farmer riding down the road.

At just that moment Rochel saw the dog. It sniffed the air moving toward their spot in the corn. It came closer and stopped, lowering its head in their direction after having either picked up their scent or the sense that there was someone lurking nearby. The dog began to bark in sharp, alarmed snaps, sending a silent, wild panic through both girls' chests.

Just as the dog was nearly on top of them, another horse-drawn cart pulled onto the road, its wheels clanking along under the sound of men talking. The cart was piled high with furniture and household items. They were scavengers, local farmers or just Polish peasants, who were clearly returning from stripping the Jewish homes in the emptied ghetto. The dog, distracted by the new arrival, turned and chased after the rambling wagon instead, barking at its wheels.

They stayed in the cornfield, waiting for the sun to set before picking up and walking, more confidently this time, behind Miriam and Meirim, following the old man's directions to the forester's home.

After a few hours, they found the right house. Miriam surely steeled herself before she knocked on another unfamiliar door.

The forester answered. The man was glad to see his friend's wife, but he had no news of Morris to share. All he could do was offer Miriam some food and promise that if he saw Morris, he would tell him she had been by with the children.

Returning to their small group, Miriam did not despair in front of her daughters. The adults convened and made a decision: they could not wait for Morris. Going deeper into the woods was their only choice. Perhaps they could navigate their way to the place Luba had ventured months ago, where the remnants of the partisan group Alter Dvoretsky had started were rumored to still be banded together.

As they moved on, it began to rain, the drops falling light and steady. Miriam, seeing her daughters' fatigue, decided they should rest. Their group took cover under some trees where she and Luba arranged a space on the ground for the girls to lie down, covering them both with the black coat.

After a few hours, Miriam raised her head sharply, alert to a familiar sound.

"Maeshke," she breathed, and then shouted his name into the darkness. Luba clamped a hand over Miriam's mouth, her eyes wide. "Manya, are you crazy?" she hissed.

Miriam pushed her sister's hand away. "I hear Maeshke's voice."

Miriam called for him again. The others traded alarmed looks, murmuring in hushed voices, "My God, she's lost her mind."

Luba listened but heard nothing, and gave her sister a dubious look. But Miriam was certain. "Maeshke!" she called into the night.

A few seconds later Morris's voice rang back and finally his silhouette became distinguishable in the dark. Husband and wife had scraped past death once again to find each other, pushing the limits of how much joy and relief a single moment could hold. Behind them was the unimaginable trial they had just barely escaped; ahead of them was another.

As Morris would say later, "If I had known what was waiting for us in the woods, I would never have gone in."

PART III

The Forest

CHAPTER 10

The First Winter

THE BIAŁOWIEŻA FOREST WAS AN ANCIENT PLACE, A uniquely undisturbed stretch of land and one of the earth's last remaining primeval woodlands. A vast expanse that covered some 580 square miles across the borders of Belorussia and Poland, it was hauntingly beautiful, from its natural arbors to its sticky peat bogs. The little-tracked underbrush was occasionally interrupted by small streams and creeks that sometimes opened to wider river valleys. But far more often it was the forest's plentiful swamps that encroached on the woods, where deceptively deep waters stranded oaks and old alder trees onto small orphaned islands in a maze of intractable marshland.

Its mighty trees stretched their formidable branches to touch the sky. The tallest among them were the slender-trunked spruces, their piney tufted tops rising some 180 feet above the forest floor. The oldest oaks had lived for half a millennium, their boles as wide as six feet in diameter. The forest's elder tree trunks had deeply ridged hides, wrapped in wizened bark or covered in a lush fur of verdant moss or spackled with flaking patches of lichen. There were spiky-leafed maples and petal-leafed hornbeams. There were groves of Norway spruce standing shoulder to shoulder like proud herds of Christmas trees, their full-bottomed limbs heavy with rosetted pine cones. Some tree trunks were bent, as if midway through life they had decided to head in the other direction, trading the sky for the earth. Their branches grew over each other along the ground in a twisted mess of limbs as thick as barrels. In the summer, the leaves of the living trees would form a canopy of green so complete, it would obscure even a hawk's eye from seeing the forest floor.

The woods were home to a wide array of creatures, both large and small—bison and elk, wolves and lynx, otters, frogs, and a diverse congregation of birds and insects that provided a near constant chirping chorus of sound, a steady clicking hum of life.

At various points over the centuries, long before the Great War, the ruling monarchs of the region had claimed these woods for themselves. In the early 1400s, the Polish monarchy cordoned off the forested area from public use, and more than three hundred years later this royal remit extended under the Russian czars, who, beginning in the late 1700s, banned all hunting on their land for the next two hundred years. Though it was mostly for their own feudal indulgences—the czars hosted exclusive hunting parties and erected a lavish mansion on the grounds for their infrequent sojourns—this privatization of the land would eventually establish them as something of inadvertent conservationists. Because the forest was so long closed to nearly all other outsiders, it had been left alone to continue growing wild, and therefore was almost entirely preserved.

That the forest had not one single river or waterway with the berth to accommodate a robust logging trade only further helped to safeguard it. Aside from a few small-scale lumber operations and their surveyors, as well as the foresters and the small population of surrounding farmers, recent decades before the war had seen very few man-made intrusions on these woods. Save a few uneven roads and walking paths, hive hollows left by stray beekeepers, and ancient burial grounds, human imprints of any kind were few and far between.

It might seem quite natural then to assume that a few thousand Jews who escaped their ghettos in the spring and summer months of 1942—running from towns like Bilitza, Dvoretz, Novogrudek, Deretchin, Baranovich, and Zhetel—could hide here and reasonably expect to be left alone. To be sure, they were trading one certain danger for another, putting their lives at the mercy of Mother Nature. But presumably in the forest, they could wait out the war removed from its immediate chaos and direct torments.

The forest, however, would not be exempt from the war's brutalities or the bare-knuckled survival required to endure it. Nor would it provide ample shield for the Jews or the partisans—Russian and Jewish alike—who had taken shelter here and set up their outposts in its wilds, no matter how dark or deep. The farther they went and the safer they were, the more determined their hunters became to root them out.

The edge of the forest closest to Zhetel lay immediately west, a mere few miles outside the village boundary, from which point it rolled on hundreds of acres deep. This particular area of the woods nearest the town was known to all the locals as *Lipichanska pushcha*.

Since the early weeks of spring 1942, members of Alter Dvoretsky's resistance had made the inhospitable forest their home and headquarters, and welcomed the trickling stream of refugees to their hastily arranged campsites. In the first days after the ghetto's August liquidation, those numbers multiplied as survivors straggled into the woods in broken groups—children without parents, wives without husbands, fathers without families.

As close as it was to Zhetel, getting to the forest was no easy feat. They may have torn the yellow *Juden* stars from their backs and arms, but the ghetto escapees were marked from the moment they fled. Even if their features weren't typically Semitic, they could not hide their gaunt and drawn expressions, or their shadow-beaten eyes—even their hanging, threadbare clothes betrayed the starved figures underneath. It was easy to spot a Jew on the run.

Often it was that last stretch to safety that was the most perilous, when there was no other option but to run into the fields between the village and the forest, where, exposed, they were picked off by gunfire or discovered hiding in cornfields and bushes, only to be dragged back to Zhetel by the Nazis and their collaborators to join their massacred neighbors in the still-open graves.

Some tried to bypass the woods and sought shelter on nearby farms and in surrounding villages. If they were lucky, they found their gentile friends and neighbors still loyal, or chanced upon sympathetic strangers who would not betray them. Many of the local Polish farmers and Belorussian peasants, horrified by the massacres in their town, set themselves firmly against the Germans and worked in careful and secret opposition to undermine them, keeping tabs on their forest activity and sharing that information with the refugee Jews and partisans.

But not all were welcoming or willing to help. After walking out of the ghetto in the middle of the night with her two young boys, Sonia Minuskin went to see an old acquaintance, a devout Christian woman who Sonia believed would help them. When the Polish woman opened the door to find the Jewish mother and her young children on her step, she crossed herself and cried at the state of them. She gave them some soup with milk and hid them in the attic. While Sonia and her boys slept, this woman learned what the Nazis were doing to anyone harboring Jews and her pity was wiped away by fear. She pulled Sonia down from the attic by her feet, wielding a pitchfork, and shouted at the young mother to leave. In that moment, Sonia's reserves gave out and, crying, she sank to the floor in an exhausted heap. Her host dragged her out of the house by her hair, while the woman's son pulled Sonia's children along by the nape of their necks, leaving them in a field.

There were worse betrayals. Many Jews who were promised safe haven by gentile neighbors were turned in to local police while they were sleeping. There were locals who took matters into their own hands and robbed, beat, or killed the Jews they encountered.

For those families who made it to the woods, some kissed the dirt in thanks while others collapsed with bitter relief, drawing in what must have felt like their first breath of freedom since the Germans invaded more than a year earlier in June 1941. A few walked into the woods to the happy realization that family from whom they'd been separated were still alive, or they were met by familiar faces, friends and neighbors already sitting around campfires and eating blueberries. For others, the absence of their loved ones was likely the dreaded confirmation that they had perished in the slaughter.

These escapees would soon fall into two groups—the small collections of mismatched family camps or the growing army of fugitive Jews who, untrained and unprepared, were rising up throughout the forest alongside the Russian partisans. Membership to either kind of group was often contingent on harsh criteria under which the most vulnerable—the weak, the young, and the old—were wholly undesirable.

By the end of that August, some eight hundred Jews from Zhetel, Novogrudek, and Dvoretz had found their way into the woods and gradually to each other, congregating in a more or less central location in Lipiczany Forest. After a while, with so many Jews in one place, the area came to be known among its dwellers as a Jewish haven.

They called it Tel Aviv.

The Rabinowitzes arrived in the forest better off than most. Morris and Miriam had managed to keep their family together, reuniting before they reached the woods.

Just a few short hours after Miriam had left the forester's house, Morris arrived on his doorstep hoping for news of his family. When Morris heard from his friend that his wife and children had just passed through and were looking for him, he didn't stop to rest, but rushed out into the night, determined to catch up with them.

What words, if any, would've been necessary when Miriam and Luba saw that Morris came to them alone—without Cherna or the baby, without Beyla. There would have been little time to dwell on anything at all—not their relief that Morris was alive, or to explain how they had escaped the bunker, let alone mourn the family they'd just lost. They needed food and fresh clothes. Tania and Rochel were still in their underwear, which, after days in the putrid air of the bunker followed by two days walking on the hot dusty roads and hiding in the fields, were soiled through.

Once it was dark, Morris and Miriam set off together through the woods to the Wallach farm, leaving the girls with Luba and Meirim. Now that Miriam was with Morris, there was no danger of getting lost and they returned the next day without trouble. Miriam was wearing clothes Mrs. Wallach had given her, garments that provided more than just cover but costume; now when they traveled in and out of the forest to get supplies, an onlooker would see a Polish farmer's wife and not a Jew. They brought boiled potatoes, a jar of sour milk, and clothes for the girls, rough garments stitched together out of grain and potato sacks.

It was fortunate that it was summer, the forest's most hospitable season. The warmer temperatures and soft ground were a blessing for those without shoes on their feet or thick layers on their backs. The nearby bushes were heavy with berries, and the damp soil in crooks of tree roots revealed an array of edible mushrooms, a welcome supplement to a sparse food supply. The vegetation around them was lush, the trees' full leaves providing a trellis roof against the rain, under which the family put together teepee-like structures held up by scavenged branches. Rochel and Tania helped, working their fingertips against the large-trunked birch trees to peel away broad strips of its paper-like bark, which they hung like sheets to cover their improvised tents.

In a reunion that would define their forest circumstances, Morris Rabinowitz discovered that Chaim Feldman—the friend with whom he'd made that harrowing journey from Novogrudek to Zhetel in the aftermath of the German invasion just one year earlier—was also in the woods with his family. A man of great financial means, Chaim had taken costly measures to ensure that he and his wife, Leah, and their two young sons, Motel and Samuel, not only escaped their ghetto but did so with lavish reinforcements. Somehow, he'd arrived with a wagon full of necessities, including pots and pans, tools, and even blankets, items that, in the woods, were more precious than gold—and he had plenty of that as well.

If Chaim Feldman and his wagon arrived with obvious advantages, Morris Rabinowitz possessed something even more valuable—his knowledge of the woods. "Rabinovich was a woodsman, he knows every corner, every swamp, every creek," said one member of their group, surmising, "He had maps in his head."

Indeed, he had. Having spent long years scouting these

woods and working with the local farmers, Morris had cultivated a cartographer's orientation of the forest, and a ready network of Polish friends. And so, Feldman and Rabinowitz, bankroller and navigator, formed a mutually beneficial and amiable partnership, making for something of an extended family, and set up camp together.

The girls were glad for the company. The Feldmans' boys were almost exactly the same age as Rochel and Tania—Motel was seven and Samuel was nearly five. The forest was wide and wild, but all their curiosity was stifled by the fear that Nazis and their local hunting parties were lurking around every brush and tree. New restrictive rules mandated quiet, and their parents issued a ban on all exploring.

Another addition soon joined their camp. In the early days of their time in the forest, Luba began to keep company with a man named Beryl Sakier. Nearly ten years her senior, he was tall with wide, sloping shoulders and large hands. His forehead was heavily lined and his face was dominated by a long-bridged nose that lay flat as if it had been pressed with an iron. Beryl had survived the ghetto massacre but had lost his wife and children, and he walked into the woods a man without a family.

The romances forged in the forest were often driven by impulses that would have been foreign to these couples anywhere else. In the aftermath of so much loss, people experienced a desperate need for human connection and closeness. That loneliness was only compounded by the harsh realities of the woods. As one woman described her feelings: "You don't belong to anybody; there is nobody who would miss you, whether you were there or disappeared from this earth like a bit of dust, without even leaving a mark."

For many women who were on their own in the woods without male relatives to protect them, partnering with a man, especially a partisan fighter, was a critical means of survival and one of the surest ways to avoid rape, a menacing and prevalent threat. The old social lanes melted and the once desirable qualities for a good mate were turned on their head—roughnecks paired with educated women of society's upper crust. The expectations that had burdened courtship in another life were shed, as were the prudish guidelines that had once defined respectable relationships. None of it mattered here. These matches were considered forest marriages and were accepted without judgment.

The Rabinowitz girls took a shine to the man now attached to their lovely aunt, and they were soon calling him Uncle Beryl. Perhaps his own instincts as a father lent himself naturally to the role, however painful or bittersweet it may have been to engage with such young children after losing his own. Rochel and Tania, and Motie and Muley (as they called the Feldman boys), loved his bedtime stories. An enchanting weaver of tales, Beryl would regale the children with Old Testament dramas while they sat around him captivated, bathed in firelight.

It was an advantage to have another strong set of arms in their group, as there was plenty of hard labor to go around. As the summer warmth faded in September, the natural camouflage of the forest wilted and crackled away, exposing the teepee-like tents. The families began to set up more permanent camps with sturdier shelters, ones that would not only ward off the coming cold but serve as ready-made hiding places. They called these dwellings *zemlyanki*.

Dug into the ground at least four feet deep, *zemlyanki* were built into the earth and their dirt walls were supported by felled branches and found wood. Their slightly raised roofs were covered with patchworked tarps, which they concealed with brush cover. An entryway peeked out through the forest floor. The more sophisticated *zemlyanki* were large enough to host a dozen people or more, with long bunks installed against the walls, and small stoves for cooking and heating. When they were distinguishable from the forest floor, it looked as if a great storm had dredged up a tidal wave of moss, dirt, and brush that crashed over a congregation of crude log cabins, driving them down into the ground.

The Rabinowitz-Feldman *zemlyanka* housed the two families of four, as well as Luba and Beryl. Rochel and Tania shared a bunk that was arranged head-to-toe with the other beds running along the walls of the dugout shelter. Morris had procured hay and wool blankets for them and at night the girls would snuggle into each other—limbs crossing limbs, feet on top of feet—to keep warm. When they needed light, they lit a branch, a version of a very fast burning candle; before it went out, they replaced it with another, and then another.

But in the woods, any feeling of security was foolhardy, even dangerous. Most of the Jews hiding there were not familiar with the forest. The people from large towns and cities, who had no closeness to small rural communities like Zhetel, found it especially hard to adapt to the raw elements and had little sense of how to fend for themselves. People made simple, and sometimes fatal, mistakes—singing songs or lighting fires during the day—inadvertently providing beacons for the Nazis and their hunting parties to find them.

Not far from where the Rabinowitz and Feldman families had settled in the Lipiczany Forest, there was a campsite known as *Mayak*. This group had arranged themselves into the leveled slope beside a hill on top of which was a tall wooden tower or what the locals called a *mayak*. These towers provided the land surveyors and foresters a scouting view of the area, like an eagle's nest on the mast of a ship. Gathering roughly ten *zemlyanki* around such a prominent landmark for any length of time was tempting obvious disaster. One young man who took brief shelter there, baffled by their decision to build a camp right under the tower, described it as "the worst give away in the woods." His apprehension was prescient. A year later, the camp would be discovered and wiped out by the Nazis.

Such vulnerabilities could not have escaped Morris's attention. The group from the *skron*—the ones who had initially trailed after Miriam from the ghetto—made Morris uneasy. Since their arrival in the woods, the number of people who were keen to hitch their fates to his had only grown. Now there were some thirty-five people in all. He knew that ultimately safety would not come in numbers; in fact, the more people together, the greater the threat they were to one another.

As the fall of 1942 began, there were very few forest refugees who could reliably claim to know the woods well enough to find their way around without trouble. And even fewer who could gauge which vegetation provided safe sustenance. Not only was Morris Rabinowitz such a man, as one of the young men in their camp put it to fine point, "Rabinovich was the man to follow."

And follow him, they did. Even as he begged them not to. "Please, let's separate," Morris would implore, appealing to their sense of reason. "It's not safe like this to be in such a large group. You'll be better off on your own, away from us."

The others were not so easily convinced. Even if the Rabinowitz and Feldman families did not share their resources, the benefits of hovering close were self-evident.

As those first weeks in the woods turned into months, the Jews in the forest were at risk of discovery by the Nazis as well as their proxy hunting parties. In some areas, the advertised reward for information on the partisans or hiding Jews was a single cup of sugar. This was either a reflection of the paltry value of a Jewish life, or the peasants' depth of desperation. Whether they were active or just passive humanitarians in considering the Jews' plight, these locals were more often than not caught between the partisans' threat of execution and stolen property, or the German threat of violence and cut rations. The war between the partisans and the Nazis was erupting right into their yards and barns. To help one side over the other was not just a moral quandary but a gamble of one's life, family, and livelihood.

When Abraham Salutski fled to the Lipiczany Forest with his wife and four children after escaping the Deretchin ghetto liquidation in July 1942, they ran to the woods and right into a group of Soviet partisans. Unsure he could trust them, Abraham spoke directly to their commander, Pavel Bulak. "What should we do now?" he asked.

"You're going to fight with us," Bulak replied.

Concerned, Abraham asked, "but what about my family?" No one would be excluded, the commander reassured him. "We are going to protect you."

Then the Russian leaned his head back and looked up to the sky. "Here," Bulak said, "everything is ours."

As escaped Jews from the surrounding ghettos arrived in the forest throughout the summer of 1942, many—like Miriam and Luba's cousin Meirim Dworetsky—came ready to pick up the mantle of Alter Dvoretsky's resistance and join the fight.

Men like Morris Rabinowitz and Chaim Feldman, however, would simply endeavor to stay hidden, using the forest as a refuge. The others made the forest their ally, weaponizing its most unforgiving qualities. To them survival was not the point—or, at the very least, it was secondary. Theirs was a righteous crusade with an unwavering mission: to add a river of Nazi blood to the forest floor.

❧

The Zheteler partisans who had begun coalescing in some form in the Lipiczany Forest from the early months of 1942 under

Alter Dvoretsky's leadership had reconvened under his successor and resistance partner in the underground ghetto movement, Hirsh Kaplinsky.

Before the war, Kaplinsky had the look of a banker, sporting a collared dress shirt with a high-knotted tie. In the forest, he wore a Mauser C96 semiautomatic pistol tucked against his hip and a belt of grenades around his waist. His thick, rippling hair pulled back to reveal a generous forehead over a square and determined face, cut hard at the jawline.

Kaplinsky had been a soldier in the Polish army and, like his predecessor, was a respected leader of Zhetel's Zionist movement, two sets of experiences that made him a productive organizer of the Zhetelers' burgeoning partisan army. That he'd lost his entire family to the massacres made him a passionate leader of a battalion built solely to kill Nazis.

The partisan ranks provided purpose and a way to siphon all the pain and anger into action: revenge. These newly arrived refugees—homeless, orphaned, alone—ventured to the edge of the partisans' campsites because they had nowhere else to go. To be alone in the woods was a death sentence. The partisans—organized, galvanized, and armed—offered safety, shelter, and food, and above all, a place to belong.

In town, these men may have been tradesmen, merchants, or religious scholars, useful, even prodigious, in their professions. But in the woods the measure of a man was appreciated on entirely different terms than it had been before the war, or even as it had been weighed inside the ghetto hierarchy. Education, status, wealth, possession of a *schein*—none of it meant anything in the forest. Here, a weapon was the golden ticket for entry into the partisans' league; without it, a man (or a woman) was just another mouth to feed.

Kaplinsky took the would-be Zheteler fighters—more than 150 members in all—under his wing and broke them into three separate units, each with its own individual operating base. All the men and women under his command had a role. He procured weapons and supplies for his fighters and built field kitchens and food stores, nursing stations, laundry services, even a bakery. It was Kaplinsky's men who protected Tel Aviv.

In the forest, Soviets had the ruling jurisdiction over all the partisans' efforts, and Kaplinsky operated under the command of Russian officer Nikolai Vakhonin, known as Kolya, while Jewish partisan leader Dr. Yehezkel Atlas and another Zheteler, named Eliyahu Kowienski, were part of the *otriad* (military detachment) led by Pavel Bulak and Boris Bulat. Their relationships with the Russians were strained at best. The majority of Soviet partisans had no interest in saving Jews or fighting alongside them. Their anti-Semitism was as rampant as it was blatant. Still, neither side could deny the advantages to their combined numbers.

At its core, the partisans' mission was one of disruption—to handicap the Germans at all costs and at every opportunity. They attacked German forces and local police stations. A slew of early successful skirmishes buoyed the Zheteler partisans' spirits. In August, they overtook a German garrison and blew up a bridge on the Neman River. In September, they tangled with Nazi forces at Kozlovschina, and overtook a German plane after forcing it to make an emergency landing. In October the Jewish partisans in the Lipiczany Forest would hit the peak of their efforts when, together with the Russian Orlanski battalion, they attacked a German stronghold in the town of Ruda Yavorska—taking the lives of at least fifty Germans, capturing ten POWs, and destroying the outpost.

The men under Kaplinsky's command, native Zhetelers like Pinyeh Green and Shalom Gerling, earned reputations throughout the woods for their bravery, quickly becoming heroes among the pines. "These men were absolutely fearless," one fighter noted with admiration. They "inspired us to battle."

On one of their riskier October missions, Kaplinsky's partisans were sent to Mirovschina, where a group of Lithuanian collaborators were stationed in an enemy garrison. Their objective was to render the road impassable, but in order to do that, they would have to immobilize the men guarding the intersection. In the dark, the partisans moved through the woods toward their target and waited for the signal. As soon as a red rocket flared in the sky, their attack was on—a barrage of bullets and gunfire sparked light against dark until finally it seemed the courtyard had emptied.

Then in a moment of daring, the youngest among them broke away from the safety of their line. The first to dash across the breach, he shouted back to the others that the enemy was in retreat. "Comrades, forward!" he cried. "They have fled!"

It was a daredevil display, and not atypical of this particular young partisan, Issy Rabinowitz.

What a joyous event it would have been, the day Morris and Miriam discovered that their cousin Issy, who had been in their family's care since the German invasion in June 1941, was not lost to the Nazis. The sixteen-year-old had found his way back to his relatives, and to their camp in the forest. Rochel and Tania were overjoyed to be anywhere near their handsome older cousin, and he was happy to dote on them.

But even the girls' attention couldn't settle him; restless and withdrawn, Issy was only in their camp for a short while before his patience cracked. He had convinced himself that his family—Batsheva, Saul, and Simcha—were dead. If this is what the Nazis had done to the Jews in Zhetel, how could his parents and little brother have survived the onslaught in Vilna? He eyed the partisans, and a new idea took hold. He was going to join them.

As soon as Morris and Miriam caught wind of his plans, they tried to talk him out of them. "Issy, stay with us," they said. "You're too young to fight." The partisans, it seemed, agreed with this assessment, and the battalion commander repeatedly turned him away. But Issy knew that if he had a weapon, they couldn't refuse him, and he put all his frustrated energies into finding a gun.

Given Issy's determination, Morris shouldn't have been surprised that the boy eventually got what he wanted. When Issy came to their camp to show them his gun, Morris became desperate. "Please, don't go," Morris begged. Issy was family, and as far as he and Miriam were concerned, as good as their own son, and their responsibility. Issy was not to be dissuaded. "The Germans killed my entire family," he said. "I have a duty to avenge their blood."

It was exactly what Jewish partisan leaders like Kaplinsky, and especially Dr. Atlas, wanted to hear. When any man or woman approached Atlas to join his battalion, he would ask: "What do you want?" The only acceptable answer was: "To die fighting the enemy." Earlier that summer, when the partisan camp learned of the Deretchin ghetto liquidation, he delivered a rousing speech to his troops. Atlas told them that July 24, 1942, the day of that massacre, was the day their lives ended as well. Every single moment they continued to breathe air on this earth no longer belonged to them, but "to your murdered families," he said. Vengeance was all that mattered.

When Issy went back to the partisan commander, this time with a gun in hand, never mind how rusted or antiquated the weapon was, the tenacious boy was finally accepted into their ranks.

If only he'd known that his mother and eight-year-old brother, Batsheva and Simcha Rabinowitz, were still safe in the Vilna ghetto—hell-bent on keeping each other alive.

Miriam Dworetsky, pictured in the first row, second from right, circa 1926.

Tania and Rochel, ages two and four, at their home in Zhetel, 1939.

Rochel (middle row, fourth from left) and her kindergarten class in Zhetel, 1938.

Rochel, Tania, and a friend on the front stoop of Miriam's patent medicine shop, Zhetel, 1939.

Madame Troolaloo, Rochel, Miriam, Tania, and a friend just after liberation in Poland, 1945.

Luba and Rochel in Santa Maria di Leuca, 1946.

Yolanda Bencianowski and Rochel in Santa Maria di Leuca, 1946.

Rochel and Tania in Italy.

Beryl Sakier, Tania, Miriam, Rochel, Morris, and Luba soon after arriving in Santa Maria di Leuca, Italy. Miriam and Luba are in their matching dresses from Vilna.

Rochel and Tania (fourth and fifth from left) with other refugee children at their Hebrew school camp in Santa Maria di Leuca, Italy, 1946.

Dora and Joseph Kogan with Tania, cousin Solomon, Rochel, Morris, and Miriam in Santa Maria di Leuca, 1946.

Rochel as Queen Vashti in the Purim play. With Tania and her best friend, Gloria Koslowski, in Italy.

Rochel, Tania, and friends in Santa Maria di Leuca.

Morris and Miriam in Santa Maria di Leuca.

Luba.

Beryl, Luba, and baby Gita
in Italy.

Tania, Rochel, and baby Gita
in Rome, Italy.

Rochel, Morris, and Tania in Rome, Italy.

Rochel, Miriam, Morris, Tania, and cousins Solomon and Genia at the Titus Gate in Rome, May 1948.

Toby is crowned Miss Hillel at UConn in 1957.

Rochel, who by this point had long been called Ruth, at UConn.

Philip Lazowski with Ruth in New York at his graduation from Yeshiva University, 1954.

Ruth and Philip in the Catskills,
Labor Day weekend, 1954.

Ruth and Philip at Ocean Beach, 1955.

Miriam, "Mr. Morris," and Philip at the lumber mill in Canaan, New Hampshire.

Ruth and Philip at their wedding, December 1955.

Morris and Miriam and their family pose together circa 1970.

Miriam and Morris with their grandchildren in New Hampshire.

Miriam with her granddaughter, Toni.

Toby and ten-year-old Toni.

Issy became a partisan just as the worst battles the war would bring to the forest were about to begin.

⁂

The partisan movement had been growing in numbers, coordination, and sophistication since Joseph Stalin's address on July 3, 1941, when he instructed his soldiers in all occupied areas to "foment guerrilla warfare everywhere." It was a call that had not gone unanswered. In the final months of 1942, it's estimated that there were upward of 150,000 partisans operating in the Belorussian forests, including a few thousand Jewish fighters. Their forces were gaining ground and momentum, proving to be much more than just a thorn in the Nazis' side. Their pinpointed attacks had grounded many German operations across the east to a halt. The Davids were hammering away at Goliath's defenses.

In fact, this comparatively small band of fighters had so unnerved leaders in the Third Reich that they would insist on diverting legions of troops away from the pursuit of Moscow and an insecure front line to the edge of the woods, hundreds of miles away, to battle an army of mere thousands of men and women, many of whom had never had military training. These forest fighters were quickly provoking the ire and consternation of Hitler himself, and he would send a hellfire of retribution to the forest. As one historian would later observe, it was under Hitler that the tenants of *Bandenbekämpfung*—Germany's military policy for meeting wartime resistance at the rear—would become "the soulmate of *lebensraum*." It was in the name of *Bandenbekämpfung* that the Nazis waged their war against the partisans, who had long been a fixation and source of frustration inside the Nazi regime, and that Hitler seized the opportunity he felt had been so richly delivered by Stalin. "This partisan war again has some advantage for us; it enables us to eradicate everyone who opposes us," he said, adding that the "best solution was to shoot anyone who looked sideways."

❧

It was in late November 1942 that the Luftwaffe planes started their sweeps over the forest. The summer canopy of green was gone, exposing the forest and all its activities. In the first days of December, German troops drove their tanks and a force of some thirty thousand to fifty thousand men up to the forest's edge and launched Operation Hamburg.

When news of the onslaught reached Russian Command, they sent word that all partisans had to report to the front. All fighters, Kaplinsky and Atlas's men included, were ordered to rush to the edge of the forest. They were not to let the Nazis infiltrate their stronghold in the woods. But hundreds of partisans armed with rifles and automatic weapons were no match for the thousands of approaching Germans fully armed with machine guns and tanks.

Just days after the Nazis invaded the forest, Kaplinsky's partisans responded with one of their most ambitious reprisals and attacked a Nazi stronghold in the village of Wielka Wola. During the fighting both Atlas and Kaplinsky were shot—Atlas died quickly in the arms of Zheteler partisan Eliyahu Kowienski. Kaplinsky noticed a machine gun dropped to the ground, and despite his injuries, he dragged himself through the explosions and gunfire to retrieve the abandoned weapon and hauled it to the safety of a nearby barn. Once inside, two Russian fighters, seeing Kaplinsky was gravely wounded, tried to take the gun from him even though they were fighting on the same side. When he refused to let go, they killed him.

Later rumors reached Kaplinsky's battalion that their leader had been shot in the back.

❧

For two more long weeks that December, the Nazis and their collaborators—small bands of local Poles, Lithuanians, and

Ukrainians—continued to patrol the area. Unlike the German troops, who were strangers to these woods, these groups were accustomed to the cold and the forest and were therefore at a clear advantage. Eager to kill Jews and partisans, they rained terror on the family camps throughout the forest, and in the area known as Tel Aviv.

With the Nazis in the forest, the risks Morris and Miriam were taking to get food had become even more dangerous. But the alternative was to slowly starve, so Morris went out at night to the Belskys' or the Wallachs'. While the girls slept, he took their winter shoes—which was just the felt lining of boots that didn't stay warm for long in the wet snow—and made his way through the dark forest to the farmer's house where he would replenish their supplies and dry the fabric on his friend's hearth. It was during these nighttime visits that Morris would glean as much information as possible about where the Nazis and their hunting parties were staying, and how close they were to their camp. When it seemed like they were in danger of being discovered, Morris would instruct everyone in their camp to gather their things, and off they would go in a new direction or deeper into the woods.

Word didn't always come in time. One winter day, the cracking shots of rifles sent people in the Rabinowitz-Feldman family camp running in all directions. Morris picked up Tania, her small legs wrapped under his arms as he ran carrying her on his shoulders. For the first time since they'd been in the woods, since the war had started, Tania absorbed with a cold clarity the danger she was in and thought to herself: *I might die.*

There wouldn't have been time for Morris to worry that he was leaving a trail behind him in the heavy powder. Those who ran didn't stop until they found places to hide, under bushes and underbrush or until they found the parts of the forest that were so dense and disorienting, the Nazis wouldn't pursue them there. Others held back, paralyzed or forcing themselves to stay put, trusting in the cover of their *zemlyanka* to keep them hidden and safe from the fray.

They waited, hours or longer, until the din of artillery quieted, feeling that if the Nazis believed they'd killed all—or enough—of the Jews, it was safe enough to go back to their *zemlyanki*.

Fifteen-year-old Morris Raznow, the boy from Zhetel whose grandmother was beaten to death in the April selection, had been just outside his family's *zemlyanka* when one of the Hamburg raids crashed into his family camp in Tel Aviv. He took off at the first sound of gunfire—and ran and ran until he couldn't run anymore. It turned out no one was chasing him. As he slowly made his way back through the woods to their camp, he came across some color in the snow and immediately recognized what he saw; it was his mother's shoe. He bent down and picked it up, and thought, *I'll bring it to her*. When he got back to his family camp, he discovered that she'd been killed, shot by the Germans. His father had seen her fallen body in the snow. They had to leave her there with the others.

With every passing December day, the situation worsened for all the Jews hiding in the Lipiczany Forest—family camps and partisans alike. Kaplinsky and Atlas were dead and the number of their Jewish forces had been drastically depleted. Their food stores were ruined, and it was much too dangerous to risk leaving the woods to get more.

One Russian partisan took mournful stock of the devastation: "Many of the camps fell into the hands of the murderers. The others wandered, hungry, ragged, and exhausted, through the forest, with small children in their arms. . . . People dropped in the forest, but we were unable to help them, because partisan command forbade us to visit the sick, fearing that they would pass on diseases to the partisans. . . . A horrible picture unfolded before my eyes: not far from the bunkers, there had appeared a cemetery for the children and their parents, who had died of sickness and starvation."

British intelligence intercepted a cable sent to chief of *Ordnungspolizei* (Order Police) Heinrich Himmler, dated December 20, 1942, detailing the outcome of Operation Hamburg.

As the summary stated, the operation led by *SS-Brigadeführer* Curt von Gottberg had been a resounding success. It claimed only seven German sergeants were lost, and fewer than twenty men wounded. Not only had their forces secured "large amounts of booty," including "four tanks, artillery pieces, and guns," but the ultimate measure of their victory was the number of kills, which by their count totaled 6,172. Of that tally, the report claimed, "1,674 were 'bandits' killed in action, 1,510 were executed suspects, and 2,988 were bandit 'sympathizers' also executed." Of course, "sympathizers" meant innocent civilians: men, women, and children.

Not one of the original Zheteler leaders had survived. The cold was bitter, down to 25 degrees below zero or lower—to dig into the frozen ground would've been like cutting into cement. The Jews in the forest should have lost the will to continue, but rather than despair, the remaining partisans set about making a new camp. Arel Lazerowich, one of Alter Dvoretsky's original resistance members, would later remember that winter and wonder, "Why did we want to live, we were supposed to commit suicide. And yet we had the strength and the will to dig in and we made new bunkers under the ground."

With the bitter winter of 1941—which had devastated the Nazi troops with its punishing cold and frostbite—still nightmarishly fresh in the Reich leadership's memory, the Nazis packed up as the end of December drew near and left the forest just in time for Christmas. In the end, departing the forest and suspending the hunt proved a more reliable tactic. The winter, silent and merciless, would do their killing for them.

The most pervasive threat in the woods turned out to be even more unrelenting than the Nazis and their henchmen, and far more deadly. Come midwinter it would find its way into the Rabinowitz-Feldman *zemlyanka* as well.

❧

Smaller than a grain of rice, about the size of a sesame seed, the *Pediculus humanus corporis*, or body louse, infiltrated in three forms—the egg, the nymph, and the adult—but it was the latter two that were lethal.

The forest camps' cramped quarters and lack of hygiene provided the ultimate setting for the spread of lice. They were everywhere—uninvited and unrelenting. A nearly invisible wildfire, they moved through each group, sweeping from one warm body to the next, ravaging each new host in turn, crawling all over their skin and making themselves at home in the lining of their clothes. The fight against their infestation was a constant and losing battle. The best way to rid them was to strip off and boil the clothes. But in the winter, where most people only had the clothes on their back and lighting open fires was often too dangerous during the day, this was a challenging technique.

Rochel and Tania, driven mad by the itching rashes, took pleasure in running their fingertips along the seams of their clothes and feeling the tiny bursts when the lice snapped and popped under their pinches. It was far more satisfying than removing their clothes to shiver in the cold, shake them out, and listen as the lice dropped like little pebbles against the ice.

It was impossible to completely eradicate the lice; their nips were terrible and people were covered in the resulting red rash outbreaks. With every bite came an irrepressible itch, and it was the itch that began the trouble—for with every scratch and rubbing came a microscopic break of skin that opened the bloodstream to the intruder's waste and, with it, *Rickettsia prowazekii*, the bacterial agent that causes typhus. In the beginning there were headaches and body aches; then a brain-frying fever would take hold followed by stomach pains, retching, and vomiting. There was delirium and grips of hysteria and hallucinations.

As the winter temperatures sank below −20 degrees, the season's storms brought torrents of snow landing waist-high around the forest, and conditions in the camps—both family and partisans—worsened. Frostbite was another ever-lurking concern. Few people had proper shoes—no winter boots or lined footwear of any kind. The feet were the most vulnerable extremities, and without proper nutrition and proximity to constant warmth, frostbite spread, and spread quickly. The skin blistered into flaky purples and blues and then burst; infection would race like poison through blood and tissue, turning into gangrene.

On the backs of lice, typhus swept through the camps of Tel Aviv, and soon people everywhere began to get ill. They were dying so quickly in the family camps, and the ground was so cold, there wasn't the strength or time to bury them: they were just covered and left where they were. As one member of the Rabinowitz family camp said, "I noticed people are passing out into a coma, disappear. They sleep forever. Some wake up, some don't."

Death was becoming so commonplace, there was hardly a morning where they didn't wake up to find a body, someone who had succumbed in the night—to the cold, to exposure, to starvation. Even Rochel and Tania were no longer fazed by the sight of a corpse.

Then one day, Miriam came down with a fever.

Morris immediately took charge of his wife's care, setting up a vigil alongside her log bunk. Without real medicine, Morris searched for any remedy he could find. Believing the sunlight would help to heal her, he would bundle her up against the frigid temperatures and carry her outside. He did this day in and day out.

Despite Morris's best efforts, Miriam wasn't improving. Already a slight woman, the weight just seemed to slip off her body. Her eyes settled deeper into her face; her hair thinned and fell from her temples like molting feathers. Morris only broke his vigil to get her food, leaving Rochel and Tania with Luba until he returned with the most nutrient-rich items he could get his hands on—eggs, bits of meat, and milk—to hand-feed Miriam.

They hadn't the luxury of quarantine, so everyone stayed together in the same *zemlyanka,* and the girls were told to keep their distance. One day when Miriam was coming in and out of a lucid state, she caught sight of her younger daughter. "Taibeleh," she called. When Tania stared back at her mother's bed, she didn't recognize the wasted woman lying there; the weak voice sounded unfamiliar and strange. When Miriam reached out her hand, Tania shrank back, afraid.

Morris did his best to keep everyone in the family safe while so closely monitoring Miriam's care, but the threats of the forest that winter were near relentless. The bulk of Nazi forces may have left the forest, but local bands of Poles and Lithuanians had not. *Oblavas*—raids on the partisan camps and the family camps in close proximity—often came without warning and their perpetrators weren't looking to take prisoners. These attacks were quick-fire massacres.

One afternoon while Miriam was ill, Morris came running into the *zemlyanka* and called out that an *oblava* was coming. Miriam, still bedridden, was too weak to be moved, so along with Luba and Tania, Morris rushed her into the only hiding place in their bunker, a small carved-out space barely large enough for two people. He squeezed them inside and called for Rochel. Together the pair of them hurried out of the *zemlyanka.*

Morris grabbed his older daughter by the hand and they took off running into the woods, where they hid for hours. Not until it was dark did they emerge and make their way back to camp. Luba, Miriam, and Tania were all fine. The raiders hadn't found their *zemlyanki*.

With Miriam being so sick, there were fewer eyes on the girls. Both Morris and Luba were distracted, and so Rochel and Tania found themselves with slightly more freedom than they'd had before, and the others in the camp took note. They were aware of Feldman's wagonful of supplies, and knew that because of Morris's connections the Rabinowitzes almost certainly had more food.

One of the women in the camp caught Tania's attention and motioned her close. "If you give me some food, I have a special pin I will give to you." The woman must've seen the hungry curiosity in Tania's eyes because she continued, describing its beautiful glittering stones. It didn't take long before Tania was captivated, and her heart was filled with a yearning for that pin. She went to Morris and told him that she was hungry, and he gave her some bread and butter. But instead of eating it, Tania tucked it away out of sight. When her father was busy, she retrieved the food and left it in a tree, just as the woman had instructed her to do.

The next time Tania saw her, the woman apologized. "I wasn't able to find the pin," she told her. "But don't worry," she promised, "if you bring me something else to eat tomorrow, I'll give it to you then."

Thus began Tania's covert operation to secure that little pin. She thought about it all the time, how shiny and pretty it would be, and while she squirreled away the food her father gave her, as Morris was busy focusing his attention on an ailing Miriam, the image of that pin grew lovelier with each passing day.

The next time Tania, holding on to a few potatoes, snuck away and met the woman a short distance from camp by a tree, the woman still did not have the piece of jewelry. She assured Tania that she would have it the next day. And again, with the pin just out of her reach, Tania went back to her father to procure more food, another payment on the guarantee of her coming treasure. Morris, who had finally noticed his youngest's outsized appetite, was growing concerned, briefly wondering, *how could this child still be so hungry?*

This woman may have thought nothing of taking food away from such a trusting girl whose belly was full enough that she would so eagerly trade her rations for the promise of a trinket. It might have angered an adult with nothing to eat that this child could be so well fed. The balance of fortune was not any kinder or more equitable here in the woods than it had been in the ghetto. Some people would have enough to satiate their hunger, while others would starve. That the Rabinowitz and Feldman families had so much to begin with likely made them the object of envy and ire in the woods.

The days passed and still no pin. Each delivery of food was met with another one of the woman's excuses, and the fantasy of the pin drifted further away. And then Tania knew—there was no pin. The woman had tricked her.

The disappointment was terrible. It left Tania with a ringing, hollow feeling of guilt and shame so great that she finally confessed what she'd done to her father. Morris was furious. "To give away all that food when we have so little, and with your mother so ill!"

How could just the mere hope for something so small have meant so much to her? And yet for that time, the dream of possessing that pin had meant everything.

❧

As it got colder, the distress in their *zemlyanka* intensified as Miriam's condition worsened. She had lost all of her hair and could no longer see.

Finally, they sent for the doctor.

There were a handful of practiced physicians and a spare few others with medical training scattered among the Jews in the woods, but perhaps the most capable among them was a renowned gastric surgeon from Warsaw, Dr. Chaim Miasnik.

Dr. Miasnik, his wife Bronka, and their young daughter Miriam had been spared multiple rounds of slaughter in the Lida ghetto because the Nazis wanted to keep the surgeon in their service; he was often pulled out of the ghetto in the middle of the night to operate on wounded Germans. His reputation and value had spread beyond the ghetto and one day in November 1941, partisans from the Lipiczany Forest broke into the Lida ghetto and approached him with an offer—they would rescue the doctor and his family, if he would come to the woods and work for the partisan fighters. He agreed. And by mid-December Miasnik and his family were in the woods.

That winter the partisans kept him busy, and though Soviet command had strictly forbidden him from providing aid to anyone other than their fighters, Miasnik would visit the Jewish family camps on his forest rounds, to share stores of food and administer care.

Dr. Miasnik examined Miriam in the *zemlyanka,* where she lay on her bed of straw and rags. By now she had grown very weak. There wasn't much he could do.

Medical supplies of any kind were in direly short supply. Dr. Miasnik carried a small satchel of boiled operating tools and strips of cloth, but he had few if any medications and was without proper anesthetics for the operations he would perform. Vodka became the all-purpose medicinal implement—the doctor used it to sterilize his tools and to anesthetize his patients and manage their pain. Gastric surgeries were performed not with a surgeon's blade but with any available knife; amputations were conducted with wood saws.

When he was finished with his examination, the doctor stepped away from Miriam and turned to Morris; whether he saw a desperate husband consumed by his own futile resolve to save his wife, he did not mince his words.

"It's not worth it," Miasnik said, speaking in Polish. "All this effort," he told Morris, "is not going to help your wife." And then, perhaps to head off any last desperate pleas or false hopes, he said, "She is going to die."

Morris refused to accept the doctor's prognosis. He continued his regimen of sun and vigilance, and remained glued to Miriam's side. When infection pooled in her mouth and small growths sprouted like mushrooms on her tongue, Morris would take hold of her small face with one hand to gently open her mouth. With the other, he used the flat edge of a spoon handle to scrape the bacteria off the surface of her tongue. It was the closest he could come to ousting the sickness from her body with his bare hands.

Whether it was by Morris's sheer force of will, or yet another remarkable stroke of family good fortune, Miriam's fever finally broke.

So too did winter's raw hold over the forest. The air steadily warmed under a more present sun. The drifts of snow began to thaw; the melting ice flooded the camps and turned the *zemlyanki* floors into swamps.

The winter had been a costly one for the Jews of the forest. The members of the Rabinowitz family were alive and accounted for, all except one. In February, Miriam and Luba received news that their cousin Meirim Dworetsky, who had been a devoted part of Alter Dvoretsky's Zhetel resistance and a police guard in the ghetto, had been killed.

After the deaths of Kaplinsky and Atlas, the Soviet partisans disbanded the all-Jewish battalions and divided their fighters among the Russian *otriady.* In the absence of united Jewish numbers and solidarity, the barely contained anti-Semitism that festered inside the Soviet partisan movement raged rampant. But Meirim, like the many other Zheteler partisans, joined a Soviet battalion.

In February, Meirim was on a mission with three other Jewish partisans—two men and a woman. They met up with two Russians from another *otriad.* At first the meeting was friendly, the five partisans sitting together by the fire, but it wasn't long before the Russians had pistols to their heads and demanded their weapons and supplies. With no available advantage, Meirim and the others set down their guns, but that wasn't the end of it. As the Russian partisans marched them onto the road, Meirim and the others made a run for it, and a spray of bullets soon followed. Meirim was shot, then quickly hit again. One of the other Jewish fighters took a bullet to the hand but managed to escape. Their attackers grabbed their female compatriot, Sara Alpert, and dragged her deeper into the woods, where they raped her in turn before they shot and killed her, leaving her body in a potato pit.

Meirim died from his wounds shortly after. The mission—incomplete and violent—had been his last.

It was with exhausted hearts that the Rabinowitz family—and all the Jews of Zhetel—closed out that first winter in the woods.

Whether they were the fittest or the luckiest, those who survived the carnage and the disease, the cold and the hunger, had developed a harsh utilitarian edge. Life in the forest may have been communal, but resources were scarce. Sympathy was in short supply and goodwill toward neighbors stretched only so far. In the forest, there were far fewer saints than survivors.

However, among the Zhetelers who had endured that first winter, there were men and women who would manage to be both. Morris Rabinowitz was one of them.

It's hard to imagine Morris, the gregarious gambler, the cigar-smoking carouser, a businessman who wore his small-town suit as comfortably as a second skin, relished any part of being a war-time survivalist. His former vocation had introduced him to the forest, but even if the woods had once been his professional habitat, he'd always been the dealmaker, never the outdoorsman.

There was little question about where his most heartfelt efforts were directed—his family came first. But while he may have encouraged their troupe of tagalongs to leave, he never pushed them away. Ultimately, begrudgingly, he had accepted responsibility for them as well.

In the forest, Morris found new purpose and a previously undiscovered resolve that, in the course of a relatively undisturbed life, would never have been tested. Rather than be broken, he was made.

As February 1943 came to a close, Morris took stock of their situation. Miriam had recovered much of her strength, and with spring on its way, the Nazi raids were sure to begin again. It wasn't safe to stay where they were.

It was time to leave Tel Aviv.

CHAPTER 11

The Second Summer and the Boy with the Frozen Feet

OF ALL THE BETS MORRIS RABINOWITZ MADE IN THE FOREST, this was by far the most daring.

It was as if the great rising trees had been abruptly drawn back, whisked away like a large curtain to reveal a clearing, a huge expanse of open space. A thick wall of forest stood to each side, and an impenetrable swamp stretched out far and wide behind it. The road that ran along the other open edge of the clearing was one of the main thoroughfares the Germans used to ride their tanks back and forth.

It was unthinkable that anyone would choose to hide here—madness even to try.

What Morris saw in this clearing was the genius in its potential—that, in fact, its drawbacks accounted for its greatest assets. It was because of their impassable sucking trenches of mud and muck—and the waters that so often appeared shallow but would instead lead into a sudden drop deep enough to submerge a tall man to his waist—that these difficult-to-navigate swamps were avoided by the Nazis at all costs. The flanking woods were shielded corridors to the world beyond, a way in and a way out. The theory hinged on the gamble that a Nazi brigade or a band of Jew-hunting locals traveling this road would see an empty field and carry right along without giving a passing thought to searching the area.

There would be no hiding in plainer sight. If there was any hope of finding real security anywhere in this forest, Morris had a hunch this was the spot.

After the Rabinowitz-Feldman group left Tel Aviv in March, they'd wandered from place to place for months. Their first stop was on a remote plot of swampland. From its stench to the relentless mosquitoes, it was a miserable place to settle but an early test of Morris's theory—the more undesirable and difficult the conditions, the higher the guarantee that they would be left alone. He was quickly proved both right and wrong. They had only been there a few weeks when a couple of partisans paid their group a visit. It seemed the Rabinowitz-Feldman group had set up their camp near the Soviet partisans' secret hospital run by Dr. Miasnik. Their presence compromised its security. The men had been dispatched to encourage them to seek shelter elsewhere.

After being shooed away from the swamps, they traveled to Nakrishki forest, the wooded area just outside a village bearing the same name. Shortly after arriving, they discovered the Germans had set up a headquarters there and the group quickly set off again. It was just after Nakrishki that, determined to keep a distance from any local village, the Rabinowitz-Feldman camp set down stakes between the clearing and the swamp.

Morris, Chaim Feldman, and Beryl Sakier built their new *zemlyanka* bigger than before, ready to invest for the entire winter. They dug some five feet deep into the ground, making it twelve feet wide and nearly thirty feet long. The walls were lined with scavenged wood boards and cut logs, giving the earthen bunker sturdy support. Its roof, also cobbled together from wood and doors stolen from nearby factories or barns, was slightly raised above the ground, allowing for a small, drop-down entrance at one end and space for a stovepipe to pop up through the ground at the other. Inside they built a sturdy oven out of bricks pulled from chimneys of houses in the surrounding villages that had been destroyed in the fighting.

If any of the others balked at this location, they had survived the forest so far by keeping close to Morris Rabinowitz, and weren't going to change course now. They set to work building their own shelters, scattering around in the wooded area. In the space of a few square acres, they built a small forest community, an underground village.

In another, smaller *zemlyanka* close by was a farmer from Ruda Yavorska by the name of Elyashiv. A large burly man, he had escaped to the woods with his wife, his sister, and his elderly mother, the oldest person in their camp. Though the elder Elyashiv woman had proven her mettle by surviving that first winter, she was very frail. Whenever they moved from camp to camp, her son would hoist her onto his shoulders to carry her over logs and underbrush as handily as a sack of potatoes.

There were Mr. and Mrs. Charney, a couple on their own, and an unsmiling woman named Grunia. And farthest away, some two hundred feet, an older woman and her two grown daughters took shelter in an abandoned *zemlyanka*—unsettling evidence that another group's attempt to hide in the area had not been successful. The sisters were an interesting pair. One was a vivacious dark-haired beauty whose voluptuous figure had not diminished in the forest. The other, who'd experienced an injury or illness that left her with a permanent limp, was more retiring.

There was one hanger-on whose presence was so odious, so unwanted that for weeks the men in the camp had done everything they could think of to get rid of him. But much to their chagrin, Nioma Weinstein had instructed his son and nephew to dig their bunker no more than ten feet away and directly across from the Feldman-Rabinowitzes' own *zemlyanka*. It was an audacious move, but an undeniably savvy one. It ensured that if the rest of the group was ever going to leave—whether running from the Nazis or a Polish gang—they wouldn't be able to sneak away without Weinstein.

Their efforts to expel him had ranged from gruff to violent. Beryl Sakier had even threated the man's life, vowing to "chop off his head!" But Nioma remained indifferent to it all—the blatant animosity, the harassment—and he pushed and prodded his two children, Maishel and Faigel, and his nephew Tuvya, to keep up with the Rabinowitz-Feldman family group. They had been tagging along for some four months since leaving the area known as Tel Aviv in the cold, still-melting winter damp of March 1943.

If Weinstein himself wasn't deterred by the threats, they made thirteen-year-old Tuvya terribly uneasy. This group's resentment was just another troubling complication to an already miserable set of circumstances. As they made their way through the uncut wilderness, over broken branches and sharp twigs, each step was a painful reminder that they were choosing an unwelcome road. Tuvya's bare feet were blistered and raw, fat and purple from frostbite and too swollen now for his only pair of shoes.

Nioma Weinstein was accustomed to being not just disliked, but spectacularly despised by most everyone who knew him. Still, his determination to keep after this particular group was fueled by more than a boorish stubborn streak or a tin ear for menacing comminations. During all his growing-up years in Deretchin, there had been one boy against whom young Nioma had measured all his own successes and failures. In Weinstein's mind, all he had ever gone without and all he could ever want was represented by the divined good fortune of another boy—Chaim Feldman.

When Weinstein heard Feldman was in the woods, a flash of self-inspired brilliance hit him—in order to survive, all he needed to do was to find Feldman. The idea took hold with a fever pitch, and when finally he got word that Feldman and Rabinowitz were packing up their families and leaving Tel Aviv, Weinstein hurried the children together so they could follow, casting an invisible line to their heels.

Tuvya knew his uncle was willfully provoking the group's anger, but he'd run out of options of his own. Tuvya understood as well as his uncle that to be left behind was not an option.

When they'd arrived in the clearing, Weinstein took no part in building their *zemlyanka,* letting his son and nephew manage the hard labor. The boys paid very careful attention to Morris, Chaim, and Beryl while they worked on their *zemlyanka*. And when Tuvya and Maishel asked Morris if they could use their tools, Morris handed over his saw and ax to the boys. If the animosity directed at the Weinstein family had not diminished, it seemed their presence was at least, and at last, accepted.

Being so young and naïve, Rochel and Tania were either unaware or unconcerned by the tension this new family ignited among the adults. Instead, they were immediately curious about the new children—the girl, Faigel, was only a few years older than the sisters. And they also took notice of the older boy, who came to their part of the woods without shoes. Before they knew his name, they became captivated by "the boy with the frozen feet."

ꕥ

Tuvya Weinstein had a gentle face with delicate features—a long nose, and elfin ears and chin. His eyes, clear and bright, were framed by a bold set of eyebrows as thick as his dark, curly hair.

Before the war, Tuvya lived an observant Jewish life in the Polish town of Baranovich with his parents and younger brother, where his father, David Weinstein, was a wholesale textile dealer. The family lived in a comfortable but modest four-room house that rather than shrink when overwhelmed with visiting relatives, somehow expanded to accommodate them all. They spent happy summers at their country dacha, where there was a small creek for swimming and a steady stream of cousins who trailed after them on vacation.

Tuvya had always been an industrious child with a keen mind for scales and numbers, making him a natural for math and music. When the Germans invaded, he stowed his academic medals in the roof of the outhouse and carefully hid his violin in the barn. Prized possessions he would, of course, never see again.

After the Nazis' first display of violence, the family left Baranovich and went to Dvoretz, the ghetto with the labor camp, considered by many to be a safe haven.

One of Tuvya's cousins who had escaped to the woods arrived in Dvoretz sick with typhus and covered in a rash that they called *kretz.* Tuvya's mother Rywa nursed the girl for three weeks and while she was recovering, she told them about the forest, where Jewish partisans from Zhetel were gathering and how she had been in the care of their Uncle Nioma. But he'd been so difficult and mean that she decided a ghetto was better than the woods with him. Tuvya thought her a rather spoiled sort of girl—she was from a wealthier family, and clearly ill-suited for the rough life of the woods—but still he listened closely to her stories of their uncle. Whether he was conscious of it or not, his naturally calculating mind began building a registry of locations, plotting out a small map of his own—one for which he would very soon be grateful.

One cold morning in December 1942, Tuvya got up early for his shift as the yard supervisor's assistant. He helped manage the booth, keeping it clean and recording the wagons that came in and out of the camp. The supervisor, a Christian Pole, had plucked Tuvya from his original work assignment, saving him from hard labor of the rock pile. The supervisor's wife had been a close childhood friend of Tuvya's mother, Rywa.

The day had barely begun when a call went out that everyone in the camp had to report back to the ghetto. But Tuvya, who knew he had to clean up the booth before he could leave, lingered behind. By the time he was done, there were only a handful of workers left, and all of them were too afraid to walk back to the ghetto. So Tuvya approached the supervisor, who had shown him some kindness, and asked him, "What do we do?"

In a calm and careful voice, the man spoke to Tuvya in Polish: "Run to the woods."

This reply was confusing but when Tuvya asked him what he meant, the man reared back and with a single shove of his foot to the seat of Tuvya's pants sent the boy flying. "I told you," he bellowed, pointing away from the camp. "*Run to the woods!*"

After that, Tuvya didn't hesitate. He and a few others ran away from the camp, but instead of going all the way to the forest, they stood in a little wooded area nearby waiting to see what would happen. For a long time, nothing did. So Tuvya and another young man started to walk back to the ghetto. They saw SS officers and all their vehicles outside the ghetto, but all was very quiet. They hesitated, wondering if it was safe to return.

Then, like a wave gathering to slam into the shore, there was a rush of sound as a wall of people charged the barbed wire fence as if they could run right through it, under the eruption of gunfire. At the crackle of shots, Tuvya thought they'd been seen and the Germans were firing at them, so the boys rushed back to the cover of the woods.

That day, December 28, 1942, was the day the Nazis liquidated the Dvoretz camp. As many as three thousand Jews were brought to the woods and killed. They were put in the backs of trucks and gassed before their bodies were piled into mass graves. Tuvya never saw his parents or brother again.

From the moment Tuvya ran to the fields, he wouldn't stop long enough to catch his breath for weeks. He bumped up against death at seemingly every possible turn only to slip past it just in time, whether by luck or by accident, like an alley cat with lives to spare. While he was chased by Nazis, bands of Jew-hunting locals, and even a wild dog, Tuvya was chasing after anyone who might be willing to help him. And then he remembered that his Uncle Nioma was in the woods and decided to try and find him.

Eventually he made his way to *Mayak,* the little camp by the big tower, where a cousin of his father's found him. By that time, he'd contracted typhus. The woman took one look at him and put a hand to his temple, and knew immediately Tuvya was not well. She was willing to help him, she explained, only she had nothing to help him with. When he told her that his father had hidden a gold coin in the heel of his shoe, she scoffed. "You're already hallucinating," she told him. But Tuvya insisted. The last thing he would remember was the feel of a painful yank as she tugged the boots off his swollen, frostbitten feet. When he emerged weeks later from his typhus-fever delirium, his older cousin was still there. She had found his gold piece and used it to purchase a large sack of flour, and true to her word, she'd nursed him through the weeks of sickness.

The typhus infection was finally leaving his system, but the frostbite on his feet remained a problem. During a visit to the area, Dr. Miasnik examined Tuvya and must have seen the first signals of gangrene on his feet—when the skin hardens and discolors to black, and the tissue underneath begins to rot. He told the boy that his left foot would have to go. But having seen the young amputees in the camp warming themselves around the baking ovens, Tuvya knew that if they weren't already dying, without both feet they were as good as dead. Tuvya begged the doctor to leave his foot where it was. The line of the sick was long, and Dr. Miasnik left without trying to change his mind.

As winter was coming to an end, Tuvya, who still had both his feet, found his uncle Nioma.

On another man, Nioma Weinstein's full cheeks and middle-aged paunch would seem jolly, but even his expression was sour. Still, in a somewhat confusing contradiction, when the occasion had called for it, Nioma had shown flashes of sharp judgment and real courage. During the Deretchin ghetto massacre, Nioma had singlehandedly rescued his own children and his nieces and nephews from being slaughtered by the Nazis. The bullet that struck him during their escape was still lodged in his heel.

It may have been with reluctance, but Nioma took his nephew Tuvya with them, accepting from that point on that he was no longer just a father of two children, but three. What may have mattered a good deal more than the kindness and affection, which he would never show his nephew, was that Nioma Weinstein was a survivor. From the moment he entered the woods he had no intention of submitting to any scenario where he didn't make it back out of the forest the same way he came in—alive.

❧

It happened most every day that summer. Rochel and Tania would dig into the dirt until the springing bubble of fresh water would rise up to meet them, and they would cup the water into a dish and carry it over to old Mrs. Elyashiv, who trusted no one but the children in their camp to deliver her daily water.

Not only was Mrs. Elyashiv the oldest person in their camp, she was the most stubborn as well. While most of the other kosher-adherent Jews who came into the woods had put their culinary observances to the wayside in exchange for even partly full bellies, Mrs. Elyashiv would not allow a crumb that wasn't kosher to pass her lips. She refused any and all of the meat they were able to get, and instead subsisted on broth and foraged vegetables. She wouldn't drink a sip of water out of dishes or cups that had been tainted. Her family and the other camp members were exasperated by her rigid religious observances in the woods, where everything was a struggle. Which is why she turned to the camp's children, trusting that they, unlike the adults, would never try and trick her. The Rabinowitz girls were certainly always happy to have an important mission.

In the woods, the main preoccupations were procuring food and hiding, which left little room for the activities of children. It might have seemed natural for Luba, a teacher, to direct the girls' attentions with lessons, but there was no schooling of any kind. Rochel and Tania, now eight and six years old, contributed in a variety of ways that helped them pass the idle hours.

Morris had taught his daughters about foraging in the forest for food and would take them out on walks to collect berries and mushrooms that were safe to eat. Sometimes he made a game for the girls, challenging them to find the largest mushrooms possible. When Tania unearthed an unusually overgrown and meaty specimen, Morris made a show of how it was so enormous even his hat wasn't large enough to carry it. When they returned to their camp, Tania paraded ahead, proudly wielding her bounty. The whole family celebrated with mushroom soup.

While Miriam was making the soup, Grunia came over to their campfire. She was a generally sour and humorless woman with a thick bosom and wide hips, and from their early days in the camp Tania, who had never possessed her sister's deference toward adults, felt no compunction in dubbing her Madame Troolaloo. Tania used this cheeky nickname without reservation, even when Morris and Miriam scolded her rude behavior—as they did whenever she called Grunia Madame Troolaloo, which was often enough.

As Grunia passed by, she commented on how good the soup smelled, and at that very moment the water in the pot surged and boiled over. Exasperated, Miriam muttered in Yiddish, "She gave it a *kinehora*"—in effect, calling the woman a jinx. Both Rochel and Tania were tickled by their mother's outburst.

Every once in a while, the Rabinowitz-Feldman camp would have visitors from other family groups. The Charney couple occasionally hosted their seventeen-year-old nephew, Lova. And from time to time, a teenage boy named Chaim Weinstein would come to see Tuvya. A survivor of both Zhetel massacres, young Chaim was one of the fortunate few who escaped the April selection when the Nazis exhausted their supply of bullets. When Chaim visited, he would stay with the older sisters—the brunette with the shapely figure and the quiet one who walked with a limp—who had taken up residence in the abandoned *zemlyanka* with their mother a little further away from main campsite. Chaim did odd jobs for the women in return for the safety and shelter of their *zemlyanka*.

It was known throughout the camp that the sisters in this *zemlyanka* entertained male guests. The livelier of the two women had a relationship with a Russian partisan, an older man who would always arrive with gifts for her.

On afternoons that summer, Rochel and Tania took note of the men who would come to the camp to visit the sisters. They'd watch the couples disappear into their summer tent, and wait until the tarp and branch cover would jerk and flap, movements that were accompanied by a mix of huffing and grunts. The children would linger, not quite understanding what was transpiring inside, but delighting in the whispered shock of knowing that it was something risqué. A prurient curiosity awakened.

When one of the younger women in their camp became pregnant, Tania fixated on her changing shape and form, noting the woman's ballooning belly and waiting for the baby to come. Then one day she saw the woman and the bump was gone, but there was no baby to be seen.

Tania, ceaselessly curious, ran to Miriam. "Where is the baby?" she wanted to know.

Miriam couldn't—or wouldn't—bring herself to tell her six-year-old daughter what really became of the newborn. "A cat came and took the baby," she told her.

The forest was an even less hospitable environment for infants than the ghetto; their chances of surviving were slim, and no one wanted a crying newborn in their camp. When babies were born, most weren't given the chance to survive—they were smothered or left out in the cold where the frigid temperatures would make quick work of a terrible but necessary business. The partisan hospital and the other physicians operating in the woods regularly performed abortions. Whether by choice, by necessity, or against their will, sex fell in with the other harsh realities of the forest. Any judgment reserved for such decisions was discarded at the edge of the forest. All was permissible when the alternative was death.

Life in the woods was always about survival.

While the Rabinowitz family had done a better job than most in removing themselves from harm's way and the fighting in the woods, the war between the Nazis and the partisans raged on. By the time they settled in their camp in the clearing, things in the realm of the partisans' woods had begun to change.

The Soviet partisan operations had coalesced under new leadership. By all accounts they were more organized and better supported. The Central Partisan Committee based in Moscow was sending planes to the area twice a week to parachute necessities—medical supplies, food, Russian propaganda leaflets—and when it was safe, the planes even landed to pick up the wounded.

This new leadership, aware of the anti-Semitism and discord and abuses it inspired in the partisans' batallions, acknowledged the issue by making it clear to their ranks that anyone who perpetrated violence against their Jewish combatants in arms (or against the Jewish refugees in the woods) would be prosecuted. For some Jewish fighters, this increased morale. But as partisan Sulia Rubin noted, "Moscow was far away and the Jews were near and hated. The more of us killed, the better." Any Jew who continued to fight with the Soviets "had to be twice as cautious, smart and alert."

Rather than join Soviet brigades after Kaplinsky and Atlas were killed during the winter of 1942, many of the Jewish fighters left their camps in Lipiczany Forest to join the one Jewish partisan group still operating in the woods. It was under the command of the Bielski brothers, who were known to be large as bears and fearsome fighters. Originally from a small village near Novogrudek, the four brothers—Tuvia, Zus, Asael, and Aaron—were the only surviving members of their family of twelve. Their siblings and parents had been killed by the Nazis on Black Monday in the Novogrudek ghetto. When the brothers arrived in the woods, they quickly found weapons and formed their own *otriad*. By 1943, Tuvia Bielski had 700 fighters under his command.

That spring there was also an exodus of Jews who left their small encampments in the Lipiczany Forest to join the family camps under the protection of the Bielskis' partisans. Unlike the revenge campaigns launched under Atlas and Kaplinsky, the Bielski brothers' ethos was to preserve Jewish life at all costs. "I would rather save one old Jewish woman than kill ten Nazi soldiers," Tuvia once said, a comment that would later become Bielski gospel. Their camp welcomed all, and by 1943, the brothers had some 1,200 Jews under their protection—nearly three-fourths were elderly, women, and children. They put the skills of their residents to good use by setting up a makeshift hospital, a bakery, even a tannery. Their camp was more than just a safe haven, it was a small city in the marshlands, located off the northernmost point of the Neman River, to the east in the direction of Minsk, in the even more remote Naliboki Forest.

It was even larger than the kind of encampments Morris Rabinowitz had worked so hard to avoid. Wise they were to stay away.

Almost as soon as the Rabinowitz-Feldman group settled into their campsite in the clearing, the next wave of *Bandenbekämpfung* began. By mid-July 1943, the Nazis were coming straight for the heart of the partisans' stronghold in the Naliboki woods. For those Jews who survived it, the raid would be known as "The Big Hunt."

❧

The telltale whistle—the hiss-sizzle of the falling bombs—cut through the sky, giving mere seconds of warning before their thudding explosions hit the ground. The braying motors of Luftwaffe airplanes roared overhead, relentless, while the partisans in their camps packed up their tents and hurried to evacuate their camp in Naliboki woods.

Word of a pending attack had been circulating around the forest. The Nazis were preparing their biggest effort yet to push back the partisan forces in the Belorussian woods. This would be no passing *oblava,* but a massive assault supported by sixty-five thousand troops. In addition to Luftwaffe air support, Operation Hermann deployed SD (*Sicherheitsdienst*) commando units from the Nazis' intelligence agency, rifleman regiments and a sharpshooter unit, and reinforcements from the Lithuanian police.

In the first wave of attacks, the Nazis set fire to villages surrounding the forest area, burning them to the ground. The flames filled the woods with smoke so thick the partisans and the panicked villagers fleeing to the swamp had to repeatedly submerge their faces in water to clear the stinging from their eyes.

All around the woods partisan groups were evacuating to the swamp, and the call from Command had come through: they were not to engage. Dr. Miasnik's hospital, the one hidden deep in the marshes—where only weeks earlier the Rabinowitzes and the Feldmans had set up camp—was ordered by the Russian partisans to evacuate. The swamp waters that made their location impenetrable made it equally difficult to leave, and the hospital workers—men and women alike—collected their patients and carried them out of the building on their backs. Even the Bielskis instructed their camp's fighters and families to grab what food they could stuff in their pockets and leave everything else behind—even their livestock, and all that they'd worked so long and hard to build.

Among the units enlisted in Operation Hermann was the *SS-Sonderkommando* led by *Obersturmbannführer* Oskar Dirlewanger. The Dirlewanger unit was a squad outfitted with what the Nazis identified as "poachers." It included rapists, murderers, and psychotic deviants. Among these men, Dirlewanger was in like company; he himself had been convicted of having sex with a minor in 1934, and received a two-year sentence that was expunged after he rejoined the Nazi Party in 1940.

Even the look of Dirlewanger was sinister. His gaunt face might well have been drawn off the pages of a Grimm fairy tale. There was a bruising color around his sunken eyes, and the sallow skin of his face pulled tight over his cheeks as if there was no flesh beneath, merely skull and bone. A trim toothbrush mustache bristled above his thin mouth. Jews called him "the butcher." The litany of his crimes was so heinous that he would later be described as "the most evil man in the SS."

Other Nazi killing squad commanders were so disturbed by Dirlewanger's sadistic behavior, often fueled by drunken tirades, that they called for his removal. A series of secure dispatches exchanged between SS higher-ups expressed alarm over what was only ever referred to as the "whipping scene at Minsk." (The omission of further explanation suggests the details were too gruesome to put down on paper.) An investigation was launched and the presiding Nazi judge recommended his dismissal. Even Himmler called Dirlewanger an "oddity" and noted the medieval tactics of the unit. But the Nazi leadership allowed him to continue virtually unfettered, believing that *SS-Obersturmbannführer* Dirlewanger was an effective, even excellent leader. The Dirlewangers, as the men under his command were known, shredded their way through Belorussia under the *Bandenbekämpfung* banner. They raped, pillaged, and burned villages, taking more than ten thousand lives in the first months of 1943 alone.

Each of the participating SS units had to submit a ledger of their successes and losses—number of artillery pieces claimed, POWs captured, number of partisans killed. During the summer onslaught, which lasted for almost an entire month, July 13 to August 11, 1943, the tally of "bandits" slaughtered—which of course by direct command included unaffiliated civilians—numbered 4,199. They took more than 2,000 people prisoner, and another 5,500 men and women were captured and listed as having been arrested and designated for labor camps. Not surprisingly, the Dirlewangers boasted the highest number of kills and captures, including hundreds of women and children (Jewish as well as local civilians).

The Rabinowitz-Feldman clan and their followers survived the monthlong onslaught safe in their new campsite on the edge of a clearing, outside the fray.

They were only halfway to the end. And the nearer they got, the harder it would be to make it out alive.

❦

As they entered their second autumn, and with it, their second year in the woods, the Rabinowitz family had learned a thing or two about surviving there.

To manage the lice, cropped hair was not nearly as good as a shaved head, but it helped to keep the vermin at bay. Some managed to get their hands on a coarse kind of soap, others used ham fat, or even kerosene. From her time working with home remedies at the patent shop, Miriam knew that undiluted pine oil, with its strong aroma, was a natural repellent for lice and mosquitoes. After hearing this, Nioma Weinstein became fixated on getting his hands on some, and when they learned there was a village nearby that made pine oil, he sent Tuvya out to steal some. Tuvya returned with a bucketful of the stuff, and Nioma covered the children in it. As it turned out, the powerful odor repelled humans as well. The peasants from whom they begged food could detect the stench from a distance. "Get away!" they'd cry. "I can't stand the smell!"

As hard as it had become for some to get food, Morris's connections to his farmer friends held steady. Others in the camp would travel two or three villages over from wherever they were staying just in case someone saw them or decided to try to turn them over to the authorities. Both Morris and Miriam went in search of food, going either to the Wallachs' farm or back to the forester, and to a handful of other farmers who'd remained friendly. The arrangement was certainly mutually beneficial; food stores and fabrics were bartered for money or other items the Rabinowitz family still possessed. The things Miriam and Luba had packed away in their knapsack while they were still at the Coopermans' proved valuable after all. Luba's silk nightgown was traded to a farmer whose daughter needed a wedding dress.

Often, Miriam would don her peasant's clothes and make her way through the woods alone. Once she returned with an entire bag of flour, which they dined on for weeks. She would melt snow in a pot over the fire and mix the hot water with the flour to make little pancakes.

They might have had more food than most, but the family never had full stomachs. When one of the local farmers told Morris that a dead horse had been left in a field after a partisan skirmish, he made up his mind to go investigate. He packed a knife and left the camp, telling Miriam and the children that he would see if there was any meat to salvage. But when he got there, the animal's carcass was covered with flies and maggots. "I just couldn't risk it," he explained when he saw their disappointed faces. Even this ache of hunger was not worth the sickness that would come from eating spoiled meat.

Forest life had deprived them of all the comforts and little luxuries of their former lives. To pass the time the men hunted for a tobacco substitute, trying out various leaves for something that might produce a similar taste. They would scour the forest searching for leaves to dry out, to bake away the damp and moisture in the sunlight, and eventually wrap them into makeshift cigarettes. The taste was never right, but maybe the act of re-creating even the smallest indulgence—to feel the roll of paper between their fingers, to close their eyes and to drag in the puff of smoke—was to inhale themselves away to somewhere else, if only for a moment.

The men shaved off thick slices of bark and whittled them down into rough-shaped rectangles, fashioning a deck of playing cards. Watching the adults play games, some children decided they wanted cards as well, so they were given a penknife to fashion their own.

Stories of the partisans capturing Germans made their way around the woods, passing from family camp to family camp. The details were grisly. One such account told of a captured German officer who, just before his execution, made a final request: that the man who took his life not be a Jew. Out of the assembled partisans, one man approached the Nazi and bound his hands. But before he took an ax to the man's neck and beheaded him, he made sure the German officer knew that he was Jewish. Another Jewish partisan tied a captured German officer to a tree. The partisan's entire family had perished at the hands of the Nazis. After gagging the prisoner, he took a sharpened blade and hacked away, each slice of flesh payment for a murdered loved one—one for his mother, one for his wife, two for his children. He counted down the tax in Yiddish, calling out their names until the debt was paid.

Doubtless the children in the Rabinowitz-Feldman camp overheard these tales in all their horrific glory. At some point they began to play a new, sinister game. Rochel and Tania, Motie and Muley, would dance around the fire and challenge each other to come up with even more terrible plans for vengeance. *What would you do if you caught a German?* "I would hang him from a tree!" *What would you do if you captured Hitler?* "I would cut little pieces from his flesh and rub the wounds with salt!" While she stared at the fire, Rochel could feel a little catch in her chest, where a tiny knot of hate was burning.

The girls attempted to engage the Weinstein children in their games, and always hoped Tuvya might join them. Maybe they thought he would be like Issy, another older boy who paid them special attention. But as hard as they tried, Tuvya wanted nothing to do with them.

He could see they were sweet girls, but it was clear that they didn't perceive the tension between the adults or the drastic difference in their circumstances, differences he couldn't ignore—how much they had to eat while he had so little, and how much better equipped they were in their *zemlyanka,* with blankets and loving parents. In the woods they were the haves, and he was the have not.

One time, Tania saw Tuvya and she reached out to tickle him. He pushed her aside. His gruffness surprised Tania, and she walked away from the encounter feeling confused and upset. But it baffled Tuvya that the girls would want to play games. *How,* Tuvya wondered, *could anyone play in such misery?*

Somehow, Rocheleh and Taibeleh's innocence held. Or more likely it teetered back and forth. They were still charming little girls who managed to maintain a remarkable amount of childlike wonder in this bleak forest reality. It was a quality that won them affection from many of the adults living around them. Rochel, eight, was the shy one. Her large brown eyes cast her with a timidity, and some in the woods had taken to calling her the "girl with the round face." Tania was the fair-haired imp, and as the youngest of the group she was the most indulged.

It was one of the great ironies of their life in the woods that a place so vast and wild required so much hushed confinement. And it didn't matter where they were—in the clearing, in the swamps—the laws of the forest remained hard and fast: they always had to be quiet, they were never to go running off or stray far from the camp. But where one sister's inclination was to abide by the rules, the other's was to bend and break them.

Back in Zhetel, before the war, it had been Rochel who galloped along the street, racing back and forth from their house and Miriam's shop to Beyla and Berl's brick home. That world had been a safe world. Here in the woods, Rochel had absorbed the adults' worries and their fears, and she never dared to take such risks.

It was remarkably out of place here in the forest—where running was often prompted by terror, providing the only means of escape—for a child to run for pleasure. But Tania did. Knowing that the sensation of the wind whipping against her face was generated by the push and pull of her own limbs was exhilarating. She loved the thrill of speed as she charged through the trees and leapt over logs and branches. There's only one thing that could give Tania the feeling of safety required to experience this kind of freedom in these woods, to experience any kind of joy in the forest.

It's hard to imagine that there was another child still alive and hiding in the forest who felt anything remotely like it.

❧

From the moment Rose Salman ran to the woods, she felt unwanted. Her family had been killed in Zhetel by the Nazis. An orphan at thirteen, the only thing that helped Rose keep the fear and sadness at bay was the will to live. Small as it was, it remained rooted, resolute, deep inside her, overruling all her other instincts to relent and give up. She was in the Dvoretz labor camp in the fall of 1942 when she heard older teenagers talking about how they were going to run to the woods to join the partisans. Rose and a friend decided that when this group ran away, they would follow.

As Rose and her friend hurried along after the escapees toward the woods, the older teens saw they were being tailed and called out in hoarse whispers for the younger girls to turn back.

When that didn't work, the older kids threatened to harm the two girls and tried to chase them away. But Rose refused to budge. "I'd rather die from you than from Hitler," she told them.

When they made it to Lipiczany Forest, she tried to join the partisans like the others, but being so young, and hardly what anyone would call sturdy, they had no interest in taking her. Eventually, Rose found a family camp where a few of the adults had known her parents in Zhetel, and she was permitted to stay. But none in the group would allow her to sleep in their *zemlyanki,* so at night she curled up on the ground outside. The pity they took on her soon ran thin. When the group moved camps to avoid being discovered, they tried to leave her behind. Rose would wake up on the cold ground to find the group had gone while she was sleeping.

She was frightened about what would happen to her if the Germans came and captured her alive; she'd heard stories of torture and abuse. Her despair brought her to thoughts of suicide but she saw no feasible way to take her own life. Rose would seek out the tallest tree she could find, following its branches to where they seemed to touch the sky. "Please, God," she would pray, "take me away." To die would be better than to be found alone.

Someone in the group would inevitably return to collect whatever belongings they couldn't carry to the new camp in one trip. "Follow me," they would tell her. "But don't say I brought you." Rose would trail behind, keeping a careful distance until she came to their new campsite, and the sad cycle would start again.

There were very few people in the woods willing to help orphaned children. But one Zhetel man would welcome so many into his own family camp that he would come to be known as "the father of all children." If the virtue of his actions was any indication of the size of the man's heart, Herz Kaminsky also had the ears and nose to match. His eyes were gentle beneath a high-rising forehead and wave of rusty-brown hair. In Zhetel he had made ends meet for his family by cutting and then outfitting Zhetel's wooden houses with wooden shingles for their roofs. He also turned a penny by renting orchards from local Polish farmers. In the fall, he and the children would pick the ripe fruit and sell the harvested apples, pears, and plums in the Zhetel market square.

Kaminsky had realized early the danger the Nazi occupation posed to the Jews of Zhetel, and prepared a large *skron* underneath his house with the help of a neighboring family. Almost everyone in the two families survived the August liquidation by hiding there. When the opportunity came to flee the ghetto, Kaminsky managed to get his family to the woods.

Much like Morris Rabinowitz, Herz Kaminsky relied on his friendship with Christian farmers, in particular a very wealthy family, the Kosovskys, who helped him find food and kept him abreast of the Nazis' whereabouts. He too relied on his background in timber and the time he had spent in the local orchards to navigate his way through the forest. It was said Kaminsky had an infallible internal compass and could be counted on to find his way no matter where or how dark.

When the Nazis surrounded the woods in December 1942, the Kaminsky camp was raided and the family scattered, running from bullet spray. His wife was killed. But the terrible loss did not stop Kaminsky from taking in orphans and widows, or anyone else who was unprotected. At one point, his camp was home to more than seventy people.

As things worsened for Tuvya Weinstein—at times the verbal abuse he endured from his uncle was so bad, Rochel and Tania were frightened by the shouting—he went to see Kaminsky, the man who would take unwanted children. But Kaminsky knew that Tuvya had a home in the woods—how good or bad a home was irrelevant. There was nothing extra to spare; he could not make room for a mouth that would be fed somewhere else.

❧

There were a few happy interruptions during those months in the fall of 1943, before winter began. Nothing brought the Rabinowitz family more unexpected pleasure than Cousin Issy's visits. The sudden appearance of his dark hair and handsome eyes, that now shone with purpose and not just grief, was all it took to break the monotony. He would come to their camp in between partisan missions and raids on villages where the townspeople had turned Jews over to the Nazis. Issy always arrived with food and presents for the girls. He treated Rochel and Tania like his little sisters, and they delighted in the little toys and trinkets he found. Once he brought them a scarf, a real treasure. They had never seen anything so fine in the forest.

When it got cold, to pass the long hours in the *zemlyanka*, Luba taught Rochel how to knit. With some precious yarn and knitting needles, they sat together and measured out the stitches and designed special mittens for the partisans. These mittens required sleeves to make it easier for the partisans to shoot their guns. Rochel took to the task with heart and determination, lifted by the thought that a pair of her mittens might find their way to Issy.

The family soon learned that those mittens never reached him.

It seemed Issy had grown tired and impatient with his own weapon—the rusted old firearm was like a stodgy mule, recalcitrant and unreliable. He eyed the company's machine gun, with its bursting power, and badgered his commander to be given charge of it. Issy had done so much to prove himself and impress the partisan leaders over the months since he joined that his commander was finally persuaded and assigned the weapon to Issy.

When Ukrainian fighters from another Soviet *otriad* came

to their unit and requested the machine gun for a mission, the commander ordered Issy to give up the gun. But Issy refused. If the weapon was leaving their camp to fight, he intended to fight with it. The teenager's outsized confidence won over the commander's better judgment.

It was dangerous being an outsider and a Jew with an unfamiliar unit, but Issy felt secure as long as the gun was in his hands. The Ukrainians decided that they were going to stop in a village pub for a drink, leaving Issy to guard the door. As strangers they drew unwanted attention, and it wasn't long before a drunken brawl broke out between the locals and the Ukrainians. One of the men slipped out of the bar unnoticed and within minutes, the Nazis were firing on the pub from all sides. Issy, already out in the open, was one of the first to fight back. He managed a fierce stand, but it was never a fair fight. Issy was shot where he stood, and died.

The loss struck the family cold. The girls were heartbroken. Their beautiful cousin was never coming back.

Whenever the girls would talk about their future, and what would become of them in the forest, Rochel was the confident optimist. She had not forgotten her encounter with the old woman in the ghetto and she still took a secret kind of solace in her palm-reading fortune. "I know we will survive," she would say. But Tania, who never missed a chance to disagree, was obstinate. "No, we won't," she would tell Rochel. "We are never going to survive this, no matter what we do."

Miriam's superstitious streak—the one that drew her to the ghetto seances—had followed her into the forest, and perhaps grown even stronger in the ancient, haunting woods. Somewhere along the way she had found some figurines, tiny metal elephants so small they fit into the palm of her hand. She called them her good luck charms, and when they moved from place to place, she never left without them. When Miriam heard Tania say they were doomed with such conviction, she interpreted her youngest child's words as a distressing prophecy. From the mouths of babes, she believed, and was beside herself.

In her heart Tania didn't believe what she said to be true. In fact, she felt just like her sister—a calm kind of certainty that nothing truly bad would ever happen to them. Maybe Miriam's children could sense something the others could not.

Finally, in the last months of 1943, there was reason to be hopeful even if there was no way for them to know it.

Over the course of four days, at the end of November 1943, Franklin D. Roosevelt, Joseph Stalin, and Winston Churchill—along with their teams of delegates, emissaries, and military commanders—gathered in Tehran to game out exactly how they were going to pummel Hitler and Germany's Nazi forces with a resoundingly swift and stomping defeat. By December 1, a strategy for attack had been set and the Big Three posed for photos to mark the conference's success.

If all went according to plan, this new effort, which was gathering its forces across a host of nations, was meant to win the war and spare millions of lives in the process, including a small collection of Jews who had burrowed out a meager existence in the Belorussian forest in the middle of a war.

If only their armies could get to them in time.

CHAPTER 12

Liberation

BEFORE THE CRISP FALL AIR WHISTLED THROUGH THE forest and the ground went cold and hard, it occurred to Morris Rabinowitz that their circumstances required more than a single hiding spot; they needed a place to run to. He led a group away from the campsite, tracked a path about a mile from the edge of their clearing, and cut into the earth.

They dug a good four feet deep and six feet across, constructing a narrow underground corridor that ran some thirty feet long. Almost all the men from the campsite joined in the effort to build this bunker—even the Weinstein boys' help was accepted. Little by little, they hauled away the excess dirt, disposing of it by carrying it farther and farther away, taking care to not draw any attention to the location. At this point, Morris and the others were so well practiced at building a *skron* they had elevated it to an art form.

Unlike their other *zemlyanki,* this structure's roof was flat. The men used wood beams, branches, and logs to keep the cover flush with the ground. They padded the roof with fresh soil to encourage nearby vegetation to grow over it. By the time they had reason to flee to this, their last and final *skron*—and in due course they would—the forest floor had reclaimed the spot, hiding the bunker better than they ever could.

❦

The early months of 1944 passed with some semblance of routine for the Rabinowitz-Feldman camp. Even in the bare and more exposed winter forest, their location remained isolated. But with that safety came a new challenge: it now took longer to go back and forth to the farmers' houses for food and news. The taller the snowdrifts, the colder the temperatures, the more difficult these journeys became. In the stilling cold after a snowfall, the forest hushed into a deep quiet. There was so little noise in the woods that they could hear the voices of the family whose farm sat on the other side of the swamp. Their animals' braying calls carried over the bare trees and frozen marsh to the camp.

The Belorussian forest was frigid, but the *zemlyanki* kept them warm. Typhus made another round in the woods, and this time both Rochel and Tania contracted the disease. Fortunately, their cases were mild and they recovered from their light fevers quickly. Morris, remarkably, was never ill at all.

Before all the snow of the second winter melted, their family camp would again require the services of Dr. Miasnik. Leah Feldman was unwell. The family knew it wasn't typhus, but something else they couldn't identify was causing crippling pain in her stomach. The adults talked about it all the time. When Dr. Miasnik came, he saw at once that she needed an operation. The melting snow had left a pool of water across the *zemlyanka* floor and he stood in it, practically knee-deep, and without anesthesia did his surgeon's work with a regular kitchen knife. While the adults stood by, all their anxious attention on Leah, Tania hovered in the back of the bunker, unnoticed. It was a testament to

Dr. Miasnik's talent as a surgeon that Leah Feldman survived the operation, and recovered.

By the spring of 1944, Soviet parachutists were landing in the woods with more frequency. They shared news of the war, and finally that news was encouraging. They also left behind their large parachutes, which served no further purpose after they landed. The hiding Jews were only too happy to have them. There was a seamstress in their group, a woman who had been a dressmaker back in Zhetel, and she made clothes for the Rabinowitz girls, new dresses out of potato sacks and blouses out of the parachute fabric. Despite being undernourished, both girls had done a fair bit of growing, and they were thrilled to have new clothes made especially for them. Tania, who was still mourning the loss of that pin, was certain that her parachute blouse, with its sheen and silken feel, was the most glamorous thing she would ever own.

When it was warm enough, the girls joined their mother and Luba in the nearby fields to pick berries. On some of these outings they would see locals doing the same. Everyone was out in the open together, but the women didn't feel the need to hide. Something in the air was different.

By the start of 1944, the partisans had taken control of more than half of all the rural areas in Belorussia. And their missions had successfully debilitated central German railway lines, the main arteries used by the Nazis to send reinforcements from Berlin to the front. By the middle of March, the partisans had blown up the major supply route to the XXXVIII Army Corps in as many as three hundred places, rendering it useless for a critical period of time.

In January and April, Stalin's armies won big victories against

Germany in Leningrad and then in Odessa. The Russians were inching closer and closer to Berlin. And right in between the advancing Soviet troops and the German-occupied territories was the partisans' forest.

Just as the plan the Big Three devised in Tehran was about to spring into action, in June 1944, the partisans of the forest would play their most important role yet. On the night of June 19, a combined partisan effort halted supplies and reinforcements for four days. More than one thousand attacks were successfully launched, debilitating rail lines. The partisans held the Germans off just long enough. The Russians were on their way.

❧

During the Napoleonic Wars, Russian General Pyotr Bagration's displays of courage were so heroic that a fellow general dubbed him "the Lion of the Russian Army." It was under an operation bearing Bagration's name that Stalin's Red Army exacted their revenge on Germany, delivering a surprise attack on June 22, 1944, the anniversary of Operation Barbarossa. Three years later to the day, the Russians reversed the course that had plunged their country into a war with Hitler by launching a blitzkrieg of their own.

To guarantee their victory, the Soviets mounted an offensive far greater than was necessary, amassing a force of more than 1.5 million troops armed with no fewer than thirty thousand artillery pieces, more than three thousand tanks, and some five thousand aircraft. All across the eastern front, some 750 miles, German forces were taken swiftly and by surprise. Barely 425,000 strong, their troops were woefully ill equipped, outmanned, and outgunned.

Bagration was launched in concert with Operation Overlord, the attack the Allies landed on the beaches of Normandy just weeks earlier on June 6. The German command, completely preoccupied with the battles against the western Allies in France and the Soviets in Finland, mostly ignored the frantic cables out of the east, taking three whole days to turn its attention to the Bagration offensive.

On the morning of July 3, Russian tanks rolled into Minsk. By midday the city was under their control, the Germans overrun. Ten days later, Vilna. Within five weeks, Soviet forces pushed ahead 450 miles. By mid-August, Red Army troops would be some 300 miles from Berlin. Operation Overlord closed in on Paris on August 25, and by September 3 had liberated Brussels.

As Operation Bagration saw early victories, word of the Allies' success began making its way through the forest, landing first in the partisan camps. Sulia Rubin was at the partisans' headquarters in the woods when she heard that the "Allies had opened a second front and Hitler was definitely losing the war." She, like many others, was stunned. "One didn't dare believe it would come to an end."

By midsummer of 1944, the tide in the war against Germany had officially turned. At that point, the cost to Germany was so high—with more than four hundred thousand casualties, and the destruction of twenty-eight out of thirty-four divisions—the damage could not possibly be undone. The Red Army had the Germans on their heels.

But Moscow's successful onslaught had made the retreating Nazis more dangerous and, however unimaginably, even more murderous. Himmler issued an order to those in the path of the fast-moving Soviet troops: destroy all evidence. After so much calculated and coordinated cruelty, the Nazis were in a panic. In concentration camps, the Jews who had managed to cling to their lives for nearly five long years were being swept up and hauled onto trains where they suffocated or starved to death; or put on death marches where they were rushed to the edges of cliffs to be pushed off the edge by bullets; or herded into barns and buildings that were then set on fire. There would be no mercy.

For days and days, the sounds of artillery fire and bombs could be heard around the Rabinowitz-Feldman camp. It started off distant, but had grown louder and louder as the fighting got closer and closer. Morris had run into Russian pilots and parachutists who had told him that the Germans were losing. It was welcome news, but the fighting had trapped them.

It was now impossible for Morris and Miriam to go out of the woods to visit the Wallachs or the Belskys. It was too dangerous for anyone to leave their campsite. But on an afternoon in July, Tuvya Weinstein was nonetheless heading away from their camp on a mission to find his stolen boots.

He likely wouldn't have gone on his own accord: the boots were long gone, but his uncle, who'd been uncharacteristically generous in procuring them for his nephew, was insisting he hunt them back down.

With a remote sense of where the boots—and the person who took them—were, Tuvya followed a route he'd mapped out in his head. He passed the first farm, but when he came to the second farm, he noticed right away something that didn't belong. Tied up outside the house were two large horses, saddled for riding. All the strong horses like this had been requisitioned or stolen long ago. Just to be safe, Tuvya navigated away from the house and was working his way around to the barn when two Germans walked out the door. Tuvya stood, frozen, and then the Germans noticed him too. It took only a moment before Tuvya realized they were aiming their rifles straight at him.

In a snap, he turned and ran in the other direction, back behind the barn where there was a small creek. He could hear and feel the bullets whizzing by, and he charged even harder through the water, and kept on going. Within a few heaving paces, he reached the wooded area and the sound of gunfire stopped. The mission to find his boots was over. He shakily made his way back to the Rabinowitz-Feldman camp.

When Tuvya finally reached the *zemlyanki,* not a soul was there. He knew something must have happened to drive the entire group away from the camp. He went to hide in the swamp and waited hours for a glimpse of his uncle or cousins, or anyone from their camp to show themselves. When he finally went back to take a closer look, he saw that the potato stores had been doused with gasoline and knew the Nazis had found the camp.

For the rest of the afternoon Tuvya was lost to fear and panic while he returned to the swamp and waited alone, imagining the worst. And then he remembered the bunker.

ൾ

By late July, Jews all over the woods were once again taking refuge underground. The sounds of danger were closing in, but this time it wasn't the noises of small marauding parties but the giant booms of two warring armies clashing head to head. The Germans had failed to wrest control of the woods from the Soviet partisans. As the Russians pushed west and regained control of the area that included the forest, they sent tens of thousands of German troops running in fear for their lives.

Caught between the stalwart forest fighters they'd been fighting for years and the coming Russian army, ironically, the Nazis' route to safety was now through the woods. And many of the Germans and their collaborators, unwilling to surrender outright, were now trying to hide in the very swamps where they had labored so hard to root out their enemy. Some continued to hunt for Jews and partisans, searching the area with dogs.

Stuck right in the middle were the surrounding local farmers and villages, and the Jewish family camps. Suddenly, everything the Jews hiding in the forest wanted most, and everything they most feared, came crashing into the woods together all at once, right on top of them.

The Rabinowitz family decided to go to the bunker just in time.

❧

Everyone in the camp clambered into the space, and the last person in pulled a planter in place behind them, concealing the bunker's opening. The closure was arranged so it appeared as if it was a bush growing straight from the ground. Finally, they rubbed garlic around the edge of the small entrance so the strong odor would repel any dogs that might come sniffing. Nearly thirty people were cramped together inside. Most everyone who belonged to the Rabinowitz-Feldman camp was there, all except Tuvya Weinstein.

Other Jews hiding in the forest, just like them, took far more drastic measures to mask their odor and remain undetected. One group, who'd hidden when the partisans in their part of the woods began to retreat, dragged two dead horses to cover their cellar in the ground. With more than a dozen people hiding in a space meant to accommodate no more than five, the stench of the rotting carcasses was so foul they fainted from the lack of fresh air. The dogs wouldn't come anywhere near them. Since it was too dangerous to leave, they stayed where they were—even when the worms finished with the horses and made their way underground, they did not leave.

Soon enough Tuvya Weinstein joined the Rabinowitz-Feldman clan in the forest bunker. It was lucky he'd helped to build it, and luckier still his fast-trapping memory had locked the location in place. He was able to find his way, even in the dark. It was similarly fortunate that he did so without running into any of the hunting parties, as the Germans he'd come across at the farm were undoubtedly part of the forces infiltrating this part of the woods.

The Rabinowitz-Feldman clan hadn't been in the *skron* long before the Nazis got so close that they walked right on top of the cellar. Inside the bunker, they could hear the sound of boots on top of the leaf-laden roof, and voices speaking German. But the silence in the bunker (and its camouflage) held. As many times as the Germans tracked back and forth above, they did not notice the Jews hiding inches beneath their feet.

The relief that came when sounds of the hunting party dissipated would have only lasted so long. Without any ventilation, there was hardly any fresh air getting into the underground hideout. And, not unlike the ghetto bunker, with so many unclean bodies crowding together, the hot and humid summer temperatures soon turned the air rancid. The only time it was safe to go outside was at night, and even then they had to be extremely careful. To occupy his mind, Tuvya took a regular count of everyone in the *skron*. There were twenty-nine people inside. Rochel's hands began to itch, hot and incessant, with *kretz*. It spread, crawling like a vine all the way from her wrist to her fingers. But there was nothing Miriam could do to treat or relieve it in this space where they couldn't wash.

Like all *skrons*, this one was not built to accommodate a lengthy stay with so many people. The four-foot ceiling made it difficult for even the youngest children to stand upright. It didn't take long before the conditions wore on nerves—the stress of hiding, of hearing the Nazis walking right on top of them, was too much to take. In the ghetto they'd only hidden for two days; now they were going on more than a week. One of the men inside was losing his patience.

This man was a giant, as large as an ox, and he could hardly move inside the confined space. Finally, after seven days stretched beyond ten, he announced that he was leaving. The others in the bunker tried to stop him from going. "It's too dangerous," they warned. But nothing anyone said or did could keep the man from climbing through the hole and back into the woods.

&

After two weeks, the woods grew quiet. But no one in the bunker was ready to believe the worst was over.

In one area, an elderly Belorussian woman came out from her house and went to the field where she picked berries. She knew there were Jews from Zhetel hiding in the woods, so she called out in Russian over and over, "You can come out now! The war is over. The Germans are gone!"

But the Rabinowitzes, the Feldmans, the Weinsteins, and the rest were still waiting underground. It wasn't until there was a knock on the bunker roof, and the call of a familiar voice—a Polish man who lived nearby and traded food with them—that they dared to leave. "It's safe," he told them. "The Germans are gone." Apparently, the Nazi troops had cleared out of the woods two days earlier—two extra days that they sat in the dark waiting.

When Morris and Miriam, Luba, Beryl, and the children cautiously emerged from the bunker, they saw Russian soldiers coming through the forest, heading west, steadily widening their territory and their victory. The family made their way to the road where a Russian battalion was traveling with a Red Cross brigade. One of the Russian medics was Jewish and he came over to their group to see if they needed any medical attention. Miriam brought Rochel to show the man her hand, where the skin was raw with blisters between her fingers. The medic gently applied a cream and then bandaged her hand so it could heal.

Out there in daylight, in the company of the Russian Red Cross, the family was ready to believe that the news of their liberation was true. And then came a great rushing joy. Finally, after three long years under the cruel bootheel of Nazi occupation, there was reason to celebrate. All over this part of the woods, the Jewish partisans and people in family camps rushed to meet the Russian soldiers, crying and kissing them—just as they had when the Russians rolled into their towns and villages in 1941. Once again, it was the Soviet Red Star that symbolized their freedom.

Dr. Miasnik's nine-year-old daughter ran out with her father to watch the Russian soldiers go by, copying his gesture to offer them a salute as they passed. A soldier stopped and scooped her up in his arms, and in return she planted a kiss on his cheek. But because she had spent her time in the woods dressed as a boy—avoiding the dangers a young girl faced around the partisan men—he mistook her for one. Not that it mattered. The soldier, who was Jewish, was moved to tears just to come across a Jewish child—as he had not seen one alive in a very long time.

According to Tania, news of their liberation was delivered by a soldier riding a majestic white steed. The galloping horse flashed against the forest greens and browns, as the soldier called out to all the Jews that they were free. She wasn't sure if she dreamed it, if the horse was white or if it was a trick of the light, or if there'd been a horse at all. But that's how the seven-year-old, who'd spent the majority of her life calling a ghetto and the forest home, who'd lived almost all of her years in wartime, would remember that day.

In the last days of August and the first days of September 1944, the Jews who'd sought refuge in the forest for two years—some even longer—finally emerged as free people. The world was still at war, but their world was no longer occupied by the Nazis. Of the some eight hundred of Zhetel's Jews who managed to escape to the forest in August 1942, barely two hundred would walk out alive. It was nothing short of a miracle.

The members of the Rabinowitz-Feldman camp would find out later from the local farmers that the tall man who left their bunker had been captured by a single German with a gun.

It's likely the two men surprised each other—one separated from his unit, the other above ground for the first time in days. But one soldier with a weapon was enough. The man was brought to the Germans and they killed him. But not before they tortured and mutilated him. After surviving in the woods for two years, he was killed two days before they were liberated.

Almost two years to the day that the Rabinowitz family entered the forest, they readied themselves to leave. Morris, Miriam, Rochel, Tania, Luba, and Beryl set out in the direction of Zhetel. For the very last time, they were returning to the place they'd once called home.

At their backs stood the forest trees—the spruce, the towering oaks, the elms, and the maples—as flush and green as they'd been when the refugees had first arrived. Trees that exist in their own community. They are connected to each other by a netting between their roots underground; they share resources, nutrients, and when threatened they sacrifice the last of their nourishment and die so that younger, stronger trees can live. Perhaps the forest was more like the people who'd made a home within its hollows than any of those who survived it would ever know.

PART IV

After

CHAPTER 13

The Long Road Home

THE WAY BACK TO ZHETEL STARTED ON THE ROAD THAT for two long years Morris and Miriam Rabinowitz had taken great pains to avoid. How odd and exposed they must have felt. How difficult it would have been to trust the space of an open road, even one that had so recently been stamped with the victorious tread of Russian boots. It was too soon for it to feel anything like real freedom.

They exited the forest a great distance from where they had entered. The trip back to Zhetel took them weeks. They walked the entire way. The other Zhetelers from their camp were in tow, as were Chaim, Leah, Motie and Muley Feldman, and Nioma, Maishel, Faigel, and Tuvya Weinstein. Even in liberation, it seemed Weinstein was not ready to give up his Feldman compass. But for once, no one took issue with their company; there was no reason now to push them away.

By the time the Rabinowitzes reached Zhetel, the town didn't have much left to offer. Many of the once bustling streets with their crowded wooden buildings and little shops had been gutted or burned to the ground. Its once lively market square was sad and hollow. They scanned the houses where friends had once lived, searching the windows for signs of familiar faces, but now there was nothing but darkness.

As the Russians reclaimed the occupied territories, they wasted no time taking over what was still left standing, commandeering buildings and homes just as they had in 1939. The synagogue was being used as a warehouse, and the Rabinowitzes' former home, where Miriam ran her patent medicine shop, was filled with soldiers. Berl and Beyla's white-painted brick house sat intact, strong and sturdy on the market square. The home that had once been a mainstay of the town's Jewish life, where guests sat around tables laden with Beyla's kugels and tzimmes, was now the army headquarters.

Some neighbors were happy to see their Jewish friends alive and welcomed them back to Zhetel with warmth, doing what little they could to help. Farmers brought in food or shared clothing. One woman approached the Rozwaski family with a suit that had belonged to Dovid Rozwaski, who had been rounded up by the Germans in the summer of 1941. Of course she could not return it to him, but she insisted on giving it back to his children. It was still too big for Chaim Rozwaski, who was only nine years old, but the family kept the suit. It was these gestures that harkened back to Zhetel's onetime unique and comradely nature.

The Wallachs and the Belskys, who had been loyal friends to the Rabinowitz family throughout the war, returned to Morris and Miriam whatever remained of their left-behind possessions. It wasn't much, but Miriam and Luba's matching silk dresses—the made-to-order navy-blue frocks with white flowers from Vilna—were waiting for them in well-cared-for condition.

Not everyone was so pleased to see Jewish residents return to Zhetel. Some Christian Poles were in such disbelief that they approached their old neighbors in mesmerized caution to ask if they were ghosts. Others were worried that the Jewish homes they occupied after the massacres would be taken from them. Those who had actively supported the German occupation were fearful of Russian reprisals for their collaboration with the Nazis, and with good reason.

The Soviets had made a public show of punishing the Germans they captured as well as their enablers—Poles, Ukrainians, and Lithuanians who took active part in their occupation. Their executions were swift. For good measure, they hanged one offender in Zhetel's main square, stringing him up by the ankles. They left his body swinging outside for a week so that no one who passed through the center of town could avoid the rotting reminder of just how little mercy Russian justice would extend.

There was no official means of restitution for the returning Jews to claim what was rightfully theirs. But Marsha Senderowski was determined to get back what she knew had been pillaged from her family's home during the Zhetel ghetto liquidation. She was hiding in her family's *skron* when their neighbors came into the house. She recognized the familiar voices and listened to their conversation about how sad they were over what had happened to the Senderowskis. Not that this sympathy prevented them from rifling through the house and taking what they wanted.

The Wehrmacht soldiers who had sat at the Senderowski family table with Marsha and her sisters—the dark-haired teenage beauties with gray eyes—in the early days of the 1941 invasion had been wrong when they said all the Jews were going to die. But this thought could not have offered her solace now. While Marsha and her parents survived in the forest, her three sisters had perished in the ghetto massacres. When Marsha and her mother and father came back to Zhetel, they had nothing but the shoes on their feet and the clothes on their back.

A man who had been in the forest with Marsha volunteered to help her look for her family's possessions. He was working for the Russian police department and his presence provided authority. The officer took her from home to home, until a stitch of red thread in the corner of one tablecloth caught her eye. She recognized her sister Sonya's initials. Without a sound, she walked into the room and ripped the cloth from the table. No one made a move to stop her. Her silent fury was the only permission she needed.

❧

The Rabinowitz family took residence on Berl and Beyla's former property in a meager dwelling that registered somewhere between a small toolshed and a dilapidated shack, a space they shared with Luba and Beryl. What the place lacked in grandeur, it made up for by simply having four walls and a roof that stood above ground. Morris's hopes of unearthing the copper pots and pans he knew his parents had buried in this very yard were dashed. Multiple digs proved fruitless and the valuable kitchenware was never found.

Miriam managed to secure the girls matching outfits, just like they used to wear when they were little. They shed their potato sack dresses for wool skirts and white blouses. The clothes were mismatched and all the wrong sizes—the skirt waists rose high above their bellies while the wide-pleat hemlines fell well shy of their bare knees. Tania's short-sleeves bunched under her arms, while Rochel's blouse cuffs barely covered her wrists. In these ill-fitting clothes, the girls looked like malnourished dolls. There was no extra pudge to their upper arms or on their legs around the knees. Miriam too, looked smaller than ever, and even Morris's brawny build had gone lean. They all wore the wear of the woods on their faces.

There was little in Zhetel to provide much sustenance for body or soul. The town was in short supply of nearly everything, most critically work and food. The rations the Russians provided were hardly generous, not that they could have been. The army's supplies didn't cover rations for their own soldiers. The Jews were not long for Zhetel. Soon, the forest families began to separate. The Feldmans left. Even Nioma Weinstein decided it was finally safe enough to forge a path of his own: he took his children and his nephew Tuvya and set off for his hometown, Deretchin.

The initial flood of relief and jubilation they had experienced walking out of the woods had evaporated. The Jews who survived the forest did so by numbing themselves to the traumas that had forced them there. Now that they were no longer consumed by the all-encompassing daily fight to survive, the sting of loss began to prickle, like a sleeping limb unfolding, coming awake with full sensation.

Whatever years of happiness the Rabinowitz family had spent here in Zhetel were overshadowed by too much death. Before the winter of 1944 had a chance to test the durability of their ramshackle hut, Morris and Miriam came to the realization that it was time to leave. And they set off for the second-closest place to home, Novogrudek.

❧

The route between the two towns was familiar to everyone riding in the horse and wagon Morris had chartered. Everyone except Tania. As far as the seven-year-old was concerned, everything they encountered on this trip was new and exciting. As the wagon stumbled along, Tania spotted something on the side of the road that she thought was worth yelling about, and she called to her mother, pointing. Miriam turned to look at what was causing such a fuss, but there was nothing, just a few hens pecking at the ground. When Miriam saw Tania's face, she realized the clucking birds were the source of her daughter's fascination. It took a moment before Miriam was hit with the sad understanding that Tania, who was barely four years old when they moved into the ghetto, had been so far removed from a normal life that the child had no memory of something so commonplace as a chicken.

As they rode up to the edge of Novogrudek, they were met with what was no doubt a welcome sight: high on the hill outside the city the old castle ruins stood intact. The rest of the city, however, was a testament to defeat. The buildings and streets—which had been devastated by the bombings they were lucky to have survived—had received little if any recuperative care in the years the family had been away. The synagogue was just where they'd left it, still a crumbling mess of white stone.

Despite the disrepair, their start in Novogrudek was an improvement on the disappointments they met in Zhetel. The Dworetsky house that had belonged to Miriam's lawyer cousin, the one they'd lived in just before the German invasion, was still standing. A palace compared to their recent backyard accommodations, the house had no occupants to speak of, so the family of six was able to reclaim the property without any problems.

Miriam had not forgotten the promise she'd made to her father as the Nazis were taking over the city, before she and Luba brought the children back to Zhetel. She went to the chimney where she and Gutel had buried the Dworetsky family valuables and began to dig. One by one Miriam retrieved the items from the dirt—a silver tea set, three large silver spoons, and the stash of jewelry. Tania wouldn't know it yet, but inside that collection of family heirlooms was a jeweled pin that had belonged to Miriam's grandmother. It was much like the one she'd imagined in the woods.

That was all Miriam and Luba would uncover of their lost

family. There were no relatives waiting to welcome them back. And no further word on exactly what had happened to Gutel and Itka, or their brother, Beryl, his wife, Chana, and their child. All they knew was what they'd learned in the woods from those who had escaped the Novogrudek ghetto; just like Zhetel there had been two massacres that had left very few alive. There were multiple mass graves outside the city to prove it. Very little care if any had been taken to hide the giant mounds that sat alongside lush green fields and grazing cows. Even there the Jewish dead had not been allowed to rest in peace. Mourners who came to say Kaddish for their lost loved ones could see human bones protruding through the dirt and grass where the graves had been disturbed by scavengers.

Several hundred Jews returned to Novogrudek in the months after the forests were liberated. Mostly, it was young people who had survived the war fighting with the Bielski partisans. They arrived banded together for safety, but orphans all the same. Without family property on which to lay claim, they rented rooms together—in groups of ten, even twenty—in large houses all over the city.

Even in liberation, they were still forbidden under Soviet rule to hold religious services. But on September 26, 1944, a group of one hundred Jews gathered in a home on Zamkova Street for Kol Nidre—the evening service that marks the beginning of the holiest of Jewish holidays, Yom Kippur. An elderly man who had somehow found a prayer book led the service, chanting out the Hebrew prayers. Those in attendance were moved to tears, others wept. Red Army officers and policemen came by as the religious proceedings began. But rather than intervene, they just stood by and watched, allowing the service to continue uninterrupted.

For the first time in years, the Rabinowitz daughters were living a life like normal children. At long last, Tania Rabinowitz was going to school. Sometime in the early months of 1945, Morris and Miriam enrolled both daughters in the local public school. Nine-year-old Rochel was finally learning to read and write. But attending the Russian elementary school meant she was more than just a student, she was now a Soviet Pioneer. Every day Rochel made the pledge, and soon had it memorized.

> I, Rabinovich, Rochel, joining the ranks of the V. I. Lenin All-Union Pioneer Organization, in the presence of my comrades solemnly promise: to love and cherish my Motherland passionately, to live as the great Lenin bade us, as the Communist Party teaches us, and as required by the laws of the Young Pioneers of the Soviet Union.

With every repetition, the Russian words and their solemn promise imprinted deeper into Rochel's young mind. It would be one of the very first lessons she would remember learning, and it was one she would never forget.

While the girls settled into school, the adults looked for work. Morris managed to find a job in Novogrudek, a menial one—as were most of the jobs available at that time. But he was far more preoccupied with finding his brother, Solomon. He had mounted an exhaustive search for Solomon, who had joined the Soviet army before the German invasion and had been stationed deep in Russia. The family had lost all trail and trace of him before they entered the ghetto. Now they were hearing reports that Jews who'd escaped deep into Russia—as well as some of those who had been deported to Siberia by the NKVD before June 1941—had, in some cases, fared better than those they left behind to face the Nazis. Morris was holding out hope that his brother was on the right side of the border and still alive.

In late September 1944, the government of the Soviet Union and the interim government of Poland came to an agreement whereby any Jew who wanted to return (or repatriate) to Poland would be permitted to travel freely across those borders. However, this opportunity would only be temporary. After the allotted window of time, those borders would be all but sealed.

Most Jews decided to return to Poland. The Soviets in Novogrudek couldn't understand this. From their point of view, the Polish government and many of its citizens had treated its Jewish population with derision and discrimination, and by the numerous accounts of anti-Semitism plaguing the newly liberated Jews in Poland, they still were. But for most former residents, it was no use trying to replant roots in blood-stained ground. As one former partisan recalled, "There were too many ghosts following us."

The repatriation agreement was just the excuse Morris needed to get out from under Soviet rule. "I'm not living under the Russians anymore!" he declared.

And so, it was decided. They would go to Lublin. Though it was not a part of Poland they had ever called home, the Rabinowitz family was going back to their old country.

As the family waited together on the train platform, Morris looked over and saw that his older daughter was wearing the Pioneers' scarf, the red fabric tucked around the collar of her shirt. The sight of it infuriated him. "Rochel!" he called down to her. "Throw away the *schmatta*."

The tone of his voice shook Rochel to attention. She reached up and jerked the cloth away from her neck, stuffing it in her pocket.

A little while later, Rochel recognized a girl from her class walking through the station. A terrible thought flashed across her mind. *What if she sees me and tells the teacher?* The fear of being caught neglecting her Pioneer duties quickly supplanted any concern she felt at stoking her father's bad mood. She pulled out the neckerchief and tied it back into place. Her time in the Russian school had been brief, but its indoctrination had been profound. As soon as the scarf was back around her neck, she felt safe. Rochel Rabinovich was still a good Pioneer.

On a summer evening in 1945, Morris Rabinowitz was waiting for another train, this time at the Lublin station. The waiting area on the platform was crowded. A lot in the world had changed since the family's arrival in the Polish city. Hitler was dead. Germany surrendered to the Allies in early May. The war was all but over. Poland was swarming with some eighty thousand Jewish refugees, and Lublin, the site of Poland's interim capital and still-reforming government, was now the temporary home to more than two thousand of them. All around Europe, country borders were confused and open, and everyone was trying to get someplace else—escaping one city, or returning home to another.

If there had been more room on that platform, it's likely Morris would have preferred pacing back and forth to shake off the building anticipation. For finally, the Rabinowitz family had received some wonderful news. Not long after they had arrived in Lublin, a letter addressed to "Maeshke and Manya Rabinovich" came to their rented apartment. The handwriting belonged to Batsheva Rabinowitz, Morris's aunt, the wealthy Vilna relative who had hosted their wedding and cousin Issy's mother. She and her younger son, Simcha, were alive—they had survived the Vilna ghetto and the war, and were making a new start in Łódź.

While reviewing the community postings from Jewish families searching for relatives, an acquaintance of Batsheva's had spotted the name Morris Rabinowitz and notified her right away. When Batsheva got the news, she was overjoyed to know her nephew, his wife, and their girls were still alive. In her letter, she wrote that she was anxious to see them as soon as possible. Miriam and Morris responded immediately and invited them to visit.

Within one day of receiving their reply, Batsheva, Simcha, and Batsheva's new husband, Isaiah, and his son were packed and on their way to Lublin, pausing only to rush off a telegram to announce their imminent arrival.

Though Łódź was only a few hundred miles away, with so many passengers (most of them Jewish) making the multistop ride, the journey was neither swift nor comfortable. Batsheva and Simcha's passenger car was so full that barely half the travelers managed to get seats. Many of the men had to stand, lined up shoulder to shoulder, or they were forced to lean precariously against jumbled piles of suitcases. Even Batsheva had to perch on top of a package they'd brought with them, and Simcha, still heads shorter than most adults, was pressed in between the swaying bodies as the train chugged along.

It was well into the evening when their train finally pulled into the Lublin station. The platform was still packed full of people and Morris was still waiting. But as soon as the long-thought-lost relatives caught a glimpse of each other over the crowd, however changed they may have appeared, Morris and Batsheva knew each other straight away.

By the time Morris shepherded their guests to the apartment, it was after dark. When Miriam saw Batsheva, emotions spilled over, releasing a flood of tears that neither woman could stop.

For the children, this was really the first time they were meeting. Simcha, now eleven years old, just one year older than Rochel, looked nothing like Issy, whose masculine features had matched those of his father, Saul. Simcha, with his silken head of wavy dark hair, shared his mother's feathery eyebrows, thin dark lips, and small chin.

Batsheva had always been a comely woman, with striking owl-large eyes and high cheekbones. As a former businesswoman in the garment industry, and a wealthy one at that, Batsheva had gone to great lengths to keep up a fashionable appearance. She'd even managed to procure some makeup, and that night her cheeks were flush with rouge. Tania, who had never seen a woman wearing makeup, was transfixed. She couldn't keep her eyes from floating back to Batsheva's face to sneak another mesmerized peek at the bloom of color on her cheeks.

After they had their fill of the passionate reunion, the whole family sat down to the meal Miriam had prepared, arranging themselves around the modest apartment. Even after dinner and the long day of travel, the family was reluctant to separate. The hour was very late, but their night was only beginning. Back and forth they went, sharing their stories of all that had happened during the past few years, peeling away at the gritty details of each family's experience.

Batsheva described how her husband, Saul, had been taken almost immediately after the Nazis invaded Vilna in one of the first groups to be rounded up for an alleged work detail outside the ghetto. They never heard from him again. Left to fend for themselves, she and Simcha had endured a string of unbelievable hardships, punctuated by miraculous strokes of good luck and the intervention of generous strangers. Mother and son had escaped their ghetto and later were able to flee the notorious HKP labor camp in Vilna. When necessary, Batsheva had exhibited ferocious courage and savvy. After a truck of ghetto escapees refused them passage, she chased them down and forced her son into the back of the truck, determined he should be saved. Finally, the men relented and pulled them both inside. And in the last hours before they were liberated, when the Nazis were fighting back against the Russian onslaught, the two were caught in the middle, and for days clung to the sides of a ditch while explosions and gunfire erupted around them.

As the evening wore on, the conversation finally turned to the ghost in the room.

It would have been with great regret and sadness, perhaps even guilt, that Morris told Batsheva how they tried and failed to keep her sixteen-year-old son out of harm's way. "Issy believed you had all been killed," he explained. "He felt he had a sacred duty to avenge your deaths." He repeated the pledge Issy had made in the woods. Morris and Miriam described how hard Issy worked to join what was, by all accounts, one of the Jewish partisans' most elite battalions. Issy and his fellow fighters had fought bravely against the Nazis. There were many reasons for Batsheva and Simcha to be proud. Eventually, they got around to the details of Issy's death, or as much as they knew about it. When Morris told them that the partisans had never found Issy's body, it would've been impossible to tell if Batsheva, in all her makeup, had gone pale beneath her rouge.

While the grown-ups were talking, Rochel turned to Simcha and told him how much she and Tania had loved their handsome older cousin and how they'd always looked forward to Issy's visits. He never came to their camp empty-handed, she told him. "He brought us food and candy, even toys." When she started to describe the beautiful scarf he brought the girls shortly before he died, Rochel burst into tears. Seeing her sister cry, Tania could not help but join her.

The family sat together in the cramped room, lingering over their memories of Issy. The thought hanging over all of them: if only he had held out hope that his family was still alive, if he would have just stayed with Morris and Miriam in the woods, perhaps Issy would be in that room with them now.

❧

The next day, Morris and Miriam, Batsheva and Isaiah, and the three younger children got on the bus and rode the less than two miles to the outskirts of town to visit Majdanek, the first Nazi concentration camp to be liberated.

When the Red Army's forces arrived in Lublin in July 1944, they came upon the city so suddenly that the Nazis didn't have time to fully implement Himmler's protocol—to remove or destroy any remaining proof of their atrocities, which in this case included human evidence as well as incriminating documents. Still, there were barely five hundred prisoners alive when the Soviet soldiers entered the camp.

The following November, the Soviets opened the camp to the public as a memorial. So when the Rabinowitz family passed through the camp's main gate, located directly on the highway leading to Lublin, they saw it almost exactly as it was when the soldiers found it.

The first Soviet troops walked into the 625-acre site of former farmland without any inkling of what it was. From a distance that summer day, it appeared to be some kind of heavily guarded industrial site. They perhaps saw but didn't appreciate that the double barbed wire fence was electrified with high voltage, or was surrounded by a total of eighteen guard towers. But the lawns were manicured and the roads were tidy and paved. They noted the great chimney from afar, as well as the arrangement of squat buildings, and assumed it was a factory.

When the Russian soldiers encountered the first mountain of ash, they guessed it was industrial waste. Even more befuddling were the thousands of neatly sorted shoes, arranged into their respective pairs—men's, women's, and children's. They didn't understand what they were seeing, not even when they passed the ovens or the giant rooms with the odd showerheads protruding from the ceiling that locked behind thick steel doors. Not until a Polish officer informed them that these rooms were gas chambers did the Soviet soldiers slowly come to a dawning understanding that the debris they saw inside five giant ovens were charred bodies. They had just walked through rooms full of human remains.

Shortly after Majdanek was liberated, General Dmitrii Kudriavtsev led Lieutenant General Nikolai Bulganin on a tour of the camp. When it was over, Bulganin gave the order that every single one of his men walk through the camp before they redeployed to the front: he was adamant that his soldiers should see the scale and horror of the extermination camp so that they would be armed with a clear view of who they were fighting against, and what they were fighting for. Next, Bulganin ordered the camp be opened to journalists by invitation. A swarm of reporters—war correspondents from the Associated Press, Reuters, and newspapers from the United States, Britain, and Switzerland—came to the camp.

It was so soon after liberation that the few remaining laborers and the camp's POWs, and even the Germans who'd just been captured, were still on site. The reporters were shown the ovens with half-burned corpses, vertebrae shards, and bones. One of those first journalists on the scene was Konstantin Simonov, a reporter with the Russian outlet *Red Star*. In a warehouse he observed "shoes up to the ceilings," noting the "many children's shoes." The Nazis, he discovered, had "fertilized fields with human ashes, walking like ploughmen and sowing ashes out of bags. This fertilizer stunk and contained small bits of human bones. When it rained, the fertilizer turned red."

As Simonov worked, he was keenly aware that the horrific testimonies he was recording would not be believed, that it would take seeing evidence firsthand. After only a single day in the camp, Simonov felt he would be driven insane by what the prisoners told him, and the things he saw with his own eyes.

While the Soviets used the findings in Majdanek and encouraged the subsequent media reports on the atrocities to court public support for their continued war against the Nazis, Russia's Western allies were less eager to publish the accounts from the camp. Prompted largely by distrust of the Soviets, which had morphed into the fear of news organizations falling victim to manipulation by Russian propaganda, there was also a general paralysis and feeling of disbelief that atrocities on this massive a scale could be true. (In the immediate aftermath of the reports about Majdanek, Joseph Goebbels dismissed the news, calling it enemy propaganda.) As a result of these combined factors, news desk editors tamped down the dispatches out of Majdanek, diluting their sense of urgency, and were overall reluctant to place these stories where they would receive front-and-center attention.

When Moscow-based correspondent Paul Winterton, filed his dispatch on Majdanek to the BBC's edit desk in London, the response was unexpected. Despite the damning evidence he had to support his report, the BBC didn't broadcast it nationwide in Britain or anywhere else in the West. Instead, Winterton's report was heavily edited and its distribution limited to only overseas broadcasts a month later. Correspondent Alexander Werth reportedly faced the same incredulity. After filing his story, the home service editor balked, saying the details were "inconceivable."

Years later, memos circulated by the Foreign Office, as well as inside the BBC, surfaced, revealing why these early reports of concentration camps had not seen the light of day. One Foreign Office official warned, "Jewish sources are always doubtful." Another official stated: "The Jews tend to exaggerate German atrocities in order to stoke us up." As early as the spring of 1943, Sir Richard Maconachie, controller of the BBC's home service, wrote: "Any direct action to counter anti-Semitism would do more harm than good."

It was only when war correspondent Richard Dimbleby gave his broadcast of British troops liberating Bergen-Belsen on April 19, 1945, for the BBC that the world finally awakened to the atrocities the Nazis had been committing in these concentration camps for years.

❧

The gas chambers and piles of clothes and eyeglasses, the mountains of thousands of shoes, were all still there when the Rabinowitz family toured Majdanek. When they walked past the ovens, they could smell the charred bone and ash that was still inside.

What they saw left them in disbelief. Even Batsheva and Simcha, who'd spent so much of the war in the brutal confines of the HKP labor camp, were shocked by what they saw.

It was only afterward, when they were back in their apartment, that Rochel realized the windows in their kitchen faced the death camp. Sitting squarely in the center of that view was the large brick chimney of Majdanek's crematorium.

Many of the residents of Lublin, the Poles who lived there through the worst months of the war and through all three years that the Nazi death camp was operational, claimed they had no idea what was going on inside those electrified, barbed wire fences. But as Boris Gorbatov reported in *Pravda,* the stench billowing out of what the locals took to calling the "devil's ovens" was so unbearable and pervasive that it would have been impossible to ignore. Its wretched odor flowed into their homes through any open window.

Rochel had seen the tower many times since they'd moved to Lublin and had never given the structure a passing thought.

Now, the sight of it chilled her, and for the rest of their stay in the city, she refused to enter the kitchen without one of her parents.

Batsheva and Simcha stayed in Lublin a few more days. When it was finally time for them to leave, another kind of heartache lingered over their goodbyes. They likely would not see their Vilna cousins again for many years to come. Both families were planning to leave Poland; there was nothing left for them there.

In the wake of liberation, millions of Europeans were in upheaval, displaced and homeless, and there was a great deal of discord and disarray. Returning Jewish citizens were not only being denied their rightful homes, but, in Poland, the old animosities toward Jews were once again plaguing the country.

Fascist groups were openly threatening Jews with violence; their pamphlets, laced with inciteful language, claimed killing Jews was a signal of patriotism. Anti-Semitic attacks were on the rise. During an August riot in Kraków, a Jewish school was set on fire. Between November 1944 and October 1945, 351 Jews were murdered in Poland. On September 19, 1945, a Jewish Telegraph Agency bulletin out of London detailed reliable reports that "a pogrom atmosphere hangs over Poland," and that the Polish government was gravely concerned about "terrorist bands" who were chiefly targeting and killing Jews. Fearful for their safety, exhausted by retributive abuse, Jewish survivors wanted out of Poland and out of Europe.

"Everybody had a place to go, but the Jews," one Jewish refugee remembered. "The entire European continent, people were traveling en masse, going home, going home," she said, describing the chaos. "The trains were full. You grabbed on. People were hanging on the outside of the boxcars and in the passenger cars."

While many were looking to emigrate to Canada, the United States, South America, even South Africa, most had another, far more complicated destination in mind. It was where Miriam and Morris had set their sights as well—the one home that would embody what it meant to live a meaningful Jewish life, and one of the countries least welcoming to refugees. "We cannot go anywhere else," Morris decided. "The only place is Palestine."

❧

On the cusp of his fortieth birthday, Morris Rabinowitz was a man of few possessions, a fact that was likely made even more painfully clear as the family readied themselves to leave Lublin. The objects he had managed to keep safe through the ghetto and the years in the woods were precious and small enough to fit in his wallet: a handful of family photographs.

In one snapshot smaller than a playing card, Rochel and Tania stand on the stoop of their old house, in front of the door that opened into Miriam's shop. The girls are with a friend and all three children are bundled in winter jackets and hats. Rochel is wearing a dark coat with a fur collar and she is carrying a handsome muff. Tania is stuffed tight into a matching ensemble of white, a single dark curl escaping her woolen cap.

The pictures were worn, split and cracked all over, having been crumpled and crunched after so much rough care. It's doubtless that the effort expended to preserve them had been considerable. Now Morris faced a terrible decision—they had been told to leave these photos behind.

The Rabinowitzes, like the other tens of thousands of Jewish refugees taking leave of Poland and of Europe, were about to embark on the Jewish underground railroad with the help of a clandestine organization: the Bricha. As the war had inched its way to an end, this group worked in the shadows to help Jews get to British-controlled Palestine.

It would not be an easy journey. The Bricha routes were cut through the wilds of the mountainsides, over rivers, and across closed borders. Where the Rabinowitzes were going, the family could not be Polish, or Russian. They would all have to train themselves not to speak in Yiddish. Their forged passports and papers listed them as Greek nationals, and in preparation for their departure, they rehearsed a few Greek phrases, hoping it would help keep their cover should they be stopped along the way. They had been warned that if they were searched on trains or at border crossings, something like a family photo could give them all away.

Whether it was sentimental attachment or his inclination toward risk, Morris refused to do something he would regret. Instead he split the difference. The photographs were only a liability if they revealed that the family was Polish. All he had to do was remove the damning evidence. He gently tore away a piece of the photo that showed a Polish advertisement hanging in Miriam's shop window behind his daughters.

A short time later, Morris and Miriam took their daughters and left Poland behind in the screeching whistles of trains and the shouting sounds of the crowded Lublin station. The Rabinowitz family had joined this group of Zionist dreamers and were prepared to follow them all the way to Palestine, even if they had to brave an illegal pilgrimage to get there.

CHAPTER 14

Across the Alps and to the Sea

SOMETIME BEFORE THEY MADE IT ALL THE WAY OUT OF Poland, Miriam committed a fateful blunder. It was either a smooth-talking con man or her own fretting over the journey ahead that convinced her to exchange their gold coins for paper currency that would soon be worthless. While that crushing realization wouldn't come for months, Miriam, believing she needed to conceal their cash, sewed the bills into the girls' clothes. Not a natural seamstress, Miriam's attempt at camouflage yielded miserable results. In their smuggling outfits, Rochel and Tania took on the shape of lumpy pillows. Their torsos appeared so lopsided and irregular that one of the women traveling in their group couldn't help but comment to Miriam, "What beautiful, weirdly shaped children you have."

If Miriam didn't laugh outright at the crack, the woman at least seemed to have a sense of humor—or honesty—that she could appreciate. It was hard to know which of her mishaps to credit—the miscalculated financial investment or her limited skill with a needle and thread—but from that moment on, Miriam and Dora Kogan would be the dearest of friends.

Not long after they met, Miriam and Morris would discover that Dora and her husband, Joseph, were harboring a jittery secret. While everyone in their Bricha group was traveling with phony papers to get out of Poland, the military papers Joseph had used to get *in* were forged. The couple was desperately worried about being caught and sent back to Russia, where Joseph was very likely a wanted man.

Joseph had quite literally been in the middle of presenting his mechanical engineering thesis at the Kiev Polytechnic Institute the day the Germans bombed the Soviet-occupied territories in 1941. As a new recruit, his service in the Soviet army was short-lived as his unit was captured by the Germans within weeks, and though they killed all the Jewish men immediately, his Slavic features saved him from being discovered. He managed to break away from his captors and then handily evade the Germans for another three years by migrating through various small villages where he encountered a handful of helpful locals until liberation. Once he was back in Kiev, Joseph fully expected the Soviets to disbelieve his story about escaping the Germans as a POW and consider him at best a deserter, at worst a spy. Either way, Joseph was certain his next destination was a labor camp.

But before he fled his hometown, Joseph heard that Dora had just returned from Tashkent, Uzbekistan, where she and her sister had been evacuated during the war. The German invasion had cut short Joseph and Dora's then-burgeoning romance, but he hadn't been able to forget the woman with full lips and unmissable dark eyes. It seemed Dora had been just as smitten with Joseph, because it didn't take him long to convince her to marry him and to chance a new life with him in Palestine.

The Kogans were a welcome addition to the Rabinowitz collective. As the days turned into weeks and the weeks turned into months, their journey with the Bricha became a series of jerking starts and stops. Since leaving Lublin, they traveled to Kraków, to Bratislava in Czechoslovakia, to Hungary, and then finally into Austria. They'd gone from train to truck and from truck to train. Sometimes the Bricha guides concealed them in vehicles between destinations and safe houses; sometimes they walked out in the open. Tania, with her fair complexion, was often positioned to walk out in front of their group, where her honey brown hair could be seen. It was perhaps a feeble attempt to blend in this wayward group of Jewish refugees, but they were prepared to try anything to ward off suspicion.

It wasn't until the spring of 1946 that they started the last leg of their European journey to Italy, where they would prepare for the final trip by boat to Palestine. Just before they got on the train to Austria, they were warned that if they were asked questions of any kind, they should pretend not to understand and say nothing in reply. When the train arrived in Vienna, they were put onto trucks and dropped off a few miles away from the Italian border. The rest of the road would be traveled on foot.

Emerald green hills spiked with pine trees dipped down into valleys, only to roll back up against the great expanding mountain range of the Alps. The inclines of the mountainside were steep, jutting up like walls toward the sky where their peaks were topped with snow. At its lowest point, the Brenner Pass, one of the major border crossings between Austria and Italy, was some 4,500 feet above sea level.

Called the "great gate of Italy," this ancient route across the mountainous divide had fostered back-breaking journeys at least since the days of the Roman Empire. While there were now roads and a railway line, many of the Jewish refugees traversing this border in the aftermath of the war, between 1945 and 1947, weren't able to go through the main pass, so they had to go around it instead.

Along with a group of two dozen or so other Palestine-bound refugees, Morris and Miriam, Luba and Beryl, and the girls, and now Dora and Joseph Kogan followed their guide. They were crossing that border illegally, and their journey had to be made at night, in the dark.

This winding path they were on fatigued them all—Rochel and Tania were hiking on foot, too old now to be carried. It wasn't even a path, but a route forged through what, in many places, was the mountain's most inhospitable Alpine terrain.

The bag strapped to Morris's shoulders was getting heavier with each step. Too heavy, he was starting to believe, to haul it any further. "Manya, it's too hard to carry," he said as they trudged forward, placing one unsure foot in front of the other. "I'm throwing it away."

It's hard to imagine that there was anything Morris Rabinowitz couldn't manage on his capable shoulders. His willingness to abandon the bag and its precious cargo was a signal of just how grueling this mountain climb was.

Despite her husband's uncharacteristic cry for mercy, Miriam wouldn't hear of it. "Maeshke," she said. "It's all we have left."

Inside that satchel was everything they owned—a few pieces of jewelry, Miriam's favorite blue-silk dress, and a flatware set with three large silver spoons—generations of life reduced to the space of a single bag. They'd come too far to give them up now.

❧

In Hebrew the word *bricha* means "escape" or "flight." A fitting name for this movement, as the journey it furnished of course was both. The Bricha mission was unwaveringly singular: bring

Jewish survivors to Palestine. But the obstacles they faced were many, beginning with the White Paper, the British Mandate of 1939, which severely capped the number of Jewish refugees allowed to enter Palestine.

The Bricha was a massive, elaborate, and highly coordinated effort among multiple groups—including former Jewish resistance leaders (most notably Abba Kovner of the Vilna ghetto uprising), the men of Britain's Jewish Brigade, Zionist youth groups, and *Mossad Le'Aliyah Bet*, a branch of the underground Zionist military organization, Haganah—that operated on many, far-reaching fronts across Europe. With a network that crisscrossed the entire continent, the Bricha managed to be remarkably well organized. It helped that they were also well funded. Most of their money came from the American Jewish Committee, primarily through the American Jewish Joint Distribution Committee, or JDC, based in New York.

In its nascent form, Bricha emissaries started their work as early as 1944 and eked escape routes out of Europe from Poland to Hungary, Romania, or to American bases in Germany. Over time, the group's leaders adjusted these routes as they encountered shifting elements—harsh winter weather, river passages that proved too treacherous, and the shoring up of once-porous borders as governments banded together to stem the flow of illegal immigration. The last stop in Europe before attempting the trip to Palestine was most often Italy; its southern coastline along the Mediterranean Sea was the ideal launching point for a water crossing into Palestine.

The Bricha maintained relationships with Italian border guards, whom the British accused of abject corruption and being motivated solely by personal gain. It was true that their partnership was contingent on a system of bribes—trades of cigarettes and wine for a blind eye. But the Jewish refugees and their Bricha guides both believed that the Italian carabinieri were motivated by compassion and a desire to help a lost people.

In the summer of 1945 alone, approximately fifteen thousand Jews arrived in Italy. The British government had gotten wind that the refugees were using four Alpine passes, primarily the Brenner, to make their illegal entry, and they had put a tremendous amount of pressure on Italy to seal up these border points. With access to the main road denied, Jews and their Bricha guides often had to go up and around the pass itself, and risk a far more dangerous venture.

Group by group, these Jewish refugees—families, the elderly, women carrying babies, people with little more than the shoes and clothes on their backs—forged this difficult journey. Around the bends and curves they went, navigating the ground in front of them nearly blind in the dark. Keeping silent was an imperative. Their guides warned them to keep to a single-file line. In some places along the pass, the groups would be so close to the border crossing, they could look down and see the guards—Italian and sometimes British—manning their posts.

On the most arduous of these routes, the ground was rocky and slippery, and the inclines were impossibly steep. At times, they were told to keep one hand on the rocky wall to their side—to make sure they did not stray too close to the edge of the path. Those were the places where even stepping a handful of inches in the wrong direction would mean encountering a drop so treacherous, the fall alone would kill them. And for some who didn't listen, it did. Others drowned during river crossings, swallowed up by rushing waters.

When it was finally time to start their descent, the terrain they were traversing was so tilted it was often impossible to walk without tumbling down. Instead, they would lower their bodies against the nearly vertical incline, shimmying down the rocky mountainsides on their bottoms.

The lucky ones made it across the first time. If the Bricha

groups were caught at the border, as many were, most often they were just turned away and sent off in the direction they'd come, forced to go back over the crossing to wait until the next opportunity to try it all over again.

In the late spring of 1946, the Rabinowitz family crossed the pass on their very first try. When they made it over the border, stepping from Austria into Italy, one of the Bricha guides turned to Tania. "You're free now," he told her.

It may have felt like the end of a very long journey, and in many ways it was, but not the one they were expecting. The Rabinowitzes had just stolen their way through the back door in the dark, into a country that would be their home for far longer than they ever intended.

&

On a map, the small fishing village marked the farthest tip of Italy's craggy boot heel, where the country's jagged shoreline dipped into the great blue waters of both the Adriatic and the Ionian Seas. It was a warm, sun-drenched place, where alabaster buildings rose up like stony hills along the waterfront and the coastline curled into the water like a tail. It was a place so heavenly, it seemed that even the stars had chosen to make their home here. Instead of fading at dawn, they simply tipped out of the sky onto the water to blink their lights from the sparkling blue ocean, rising again at sunset to light up the open night sky of Santa Maria di Leuca.

A place with many namesakes, stories of Santa Maria di Leuca date back to the ancient days of Greece, when it's said that the Hellenic sailors who first navigated its open coasts were nearly blinded by its light. They christened it Leuca, a name that derives from the Greek *leukos,* meaning white. Santa Maria di Leuca had a religious lineage as well. According to legend, while on his way to Rome, Saint Peter himself came through Leuca and imparted his blessings. In his honor, a large basilica was built in homage to the Virgin Mother, for whom the town is named.

The Rabinowitz family couldn't have gotten much farther from the Lipiczany Forest's dense trees, its biting cold, or the squelching damp of its swampy grounds. The warmth of their new home with its salty, deep-blue waters suited them all. Now that they had enough to eat, Rochel and Tania began to round out, and their shapes began to soften. A healthy flush was restored to their cheeks that soon gave way to deep tans. Gone were the war-weary eyes and the jutting cheekbones, replaced by fuller faces, sun-kissed and smiling.

In other Displaced Persons (DP) camps, Jewish refugees made their homes in makeshift barracks and temporary, dome-roofed structures. In Germany, the Allied forces repurposed the Nazi concentration camps, and the Jews who had suffered internment were once again housed in the same facilities, this time as refugees.

In Santa Maria di Leuca, Jewish refugees were given accommodation in the stately villas that lined the water's edge. The United Nations Relief and Rehabilitation Administration (UNRRA) had commandeered the palatial vacation homes belonging to wealthy Italians. These manors were encircled in large stone walls with wrought-iron gates and their sweeping stone staircases that led to arching doorways and high curving balconies. So luxurious were these estates that they even had names: Daniele, D'Ambrosini, Arditi, and Meridiana.

The Rabinowitz family was provided lodging in one of the large mansions overlooking the sea. The relief organizations filled their house, and the others, to the brim, assigning dozens of families to each one. With their high ceilings and mosaic-tiled floors, the cavernous homes echoed with voices and the busy sounds of life. The wider refugee community in Santa Maria di

Leuca was broken down into kibbutzim, as they called them, and the family was suddenly surrounded by new, like-minded friends. Everything was communal: meals, chores, even sleeping arrangements were shared in too-small beds. When those were full, space was divvied up on the floor.

At night the patchworked families, united by a shared suffering and the dream of a future in Palestine, would gather for outdoor meals. They sat together around large tables in courtyards and under trellises. Balmy evenings were spent watching black-and-white films projected against the bleached villa walls. Rochel and Tania climbed onto the villas' flat rooftops with the other kids to catch a glimpse of Hollywood blockbusters like *Tarzan,* which was the first flicker of a movie they'd ever seen.

Among the families who dined on the Santa Maria sunshine and the UNRRA rations in their kibbutzim, Morris and Miriam and Luba and Ben formed close attachments with Motzke and Fruma Berger and Tina and Herz Bencianowski. Both couples had been interned in the Novogrudek ghetto. The Bergers had escaped to the woods and both husband and wife joined the Bielski partisans. Tina and Herz were able to remain hidden with the help of a Christian neighbor and survived the entire war in Novogrudek. They had come to Italy with their young daughter, Yolanda.

At six, Yolanda was a mite of a girl with sandy brown hair and a delicate face. Tania's magpie eye for shiny, out-of-place objects was quick to spot the cross hanging from Yolanda's necklace, blinking back the sun. Rochel and Tania were shocked to see a Jewish child wearing a Christian symbol. But Mrs. Bencianowski had implored the girls to ignore the necklace. "Please don't ask Yolanda anything about it," Tina had said, warning that the question would be hurtful to her daughter. Rochel and Tania promised to keep quiet. They liked Yolanda and didn't want to upset her, even if they didn't understand why. By then, all the grown-ups knew the story.

Yolanda was just a baby when the Germans invaded Novogrudek. After they barely scraped through the first massacre alive, Tina and Herz were convinced they wouldn't survive the war. When Tina saw the mothers and their young children being loaded onto a bus after the selection, sobbing and screaming to be let out, she decided they had to try and save their daughter. She appealed to a Christian woman she knew well, a wealthy landowner, and begged her to take Yolanda, who was then just eighteen months old. The woman agreed and proposed to have the child baptized as a Catholic, which would allow her to forge the necessary papers. The woman promised Tina she would see to it that Yolanda was safe.

On the morning they smuggled Yolanda out of the ghetto, Tina gave her something to make her sleep so she wouldn't cry. It was a hot summer day, but Tina wrapped Yolanda up in a bundle of heavy cloth. It had been previously arranged that a peasant woman Tina trusted would help sneak the child out of the ghetto and bring her to the wealthy woman's house.

When Tina saw her peasant friend waiting, she winked at a Jewish police officer she knew, gesturing to him that he should distract the officers guarding the ghetto entrance. Tina thrust the pile of clothes containing her daughter into her friend's arms and said in a loud voice, "Here's the laundry. Take the wash away."

Tina watched as the Polish woman put the pile of clothes into her buggy and rode out of sight, taking her sleeping baby with her. When she got back to her house in the ghetto, she broke down into tears. Tina did not cry from loss, but with a painful relief.

Much to Tina and Herz's surprise, they survived the war. As soon as she could manage the trip after liberation, Tina went to retrieve her daughter. But Yolanda, who by then was five years old, had no memory of her mother. Of course, it would have been far too dangerous for Yolanda's adoptive parents to tell such a young child that she was Jewish, and so the girl grew up knowing nothing of her real identity or her birth parents. The day Tina came for her was a wrenching experience for all of them. As far as Yolanda understood, her Christian family—who fiercely resisted giving Yolanda up—was her only family and she loved them. And Tina was the stranger who had stolen her away from them.

In the months since they made their fraught reunion and left Poland, Tina had not pushed the child to call her Mama. When Yolanda got on her knees before bed to pray to a Catholic god, Tina did not stop her. And after one attempt to unclasp the cross from Yolanda's neck while giving the child a bath, she never tried again.

Rochel and Tania didn't betray their promise to Tina, and never asked their new friend about the cross she wore. Rochel especially doted on the younger girl with the sweet shy smile and the large white bow in her hair. Luba took the children exploring with Fruma and Motzke. They wandered around the old stone steps that led straight down to the beach and waded out into the water. Rochel and Yolanda climbed on top of large rocks and posed for pictures.

All mornings in Santa Maria began with a swim. One of the women in their new and growing kibbutzim community gave Rochel and Tania swimming lessons, and each girl took to the water like happy fish. Not surprisingly the farthest waves beckoned to Tania, and she plunged into the water without fear. But Miriam, who had never learned to swim, would keep a watch over Tania's sun-bleached hair, and call to her younger daughter from the sand, "Come back! Come back!"

While the adults were assigned jobs to keep their shared households running—laundry, meal preparation, and other household upkeep—the children were enrolled in a school that functioned almost like a Zionist summer camp. They played games and lined up in rows to perform calisthenics. They wore matching high-waisted shorts and white shirts pinned with large Stars of David, reclaiming the *Juden* mark from the ghettos and wearing it now with pride. All their lessons were taught in Hebrew, and though most of the children had little to no fluency, their teachers forced it on them until slowly the new language took root. At the end of each week, the children shared special Shabbat dinners.

Ready learners, both Rochel and Tania went very quickly from being good Soviet Pioneers to Zionist pilgrims. On May 1, the residents of the DP camp marched with the Habonim Dror youth movement to show their support for socialism, workers, and Zionism. Out in front and in their best dresses, Rochel and Tania were holding banners in Hebrew and Yiddish, leading a parade of young men.

The Jewish refugees who made their temporary home in Santa Maria di Leuca from 1945 to 1946 felt touched by something freeing and paradisiacal. Just months earlier, they had been in death camps like Auschwitz, or labor camps like Dvoretz, or returning to their beaten and broken hometowns after years of hiding; now they were safe in a place full of rustic beauty and the riches of a small life. After basking in the sunshine and sea, the tension that had been coiled up in the fight for survival unwound. A new hunger for happiness blossomed in its place. These men and women got married and made babies. Here they were reborn. Here they became as close to healed and whole as life would allow.

Their jubilation was apparently contagious. The residents of Santa Maria di Leuca and the other far-flung villages in southern Italy hosting camps were, like the rest of Europe, also recovering from the war. They too were experiencing a shortage of supplies and rations. But rather than resent the infiltration of outsiders, most welcomed the Jewish refugees with open arms. For many of the local Italians, watching this bedraggled population rehabilitate on their streets and shores helped to revive their towns.

The women of Santa Maria gave away their wedding gowns so the Jewish girls could be married in white. The nuns and their Catholic assistants working at the hospital on top of the town's giant hill helped to deliver hundreds of Jewish babies and care for their new mothers. There may have been doctors, but there was no anesthesia for these women. The new life they brought came into the world screaming with pain. But even that raw labor was met with only "joy and relief," as one mother remembered. The local priest invited Jews who wanted to sing into the church's choir. And when the lucky few who were among the first to get the call that the boats arranged by the Bricha were ready to take them to Palestine, the archbishop blessed the Jewish refugees as they departed the port in Bari: "May God protect you and light your path and bring you safely to your destination."

At night bands of young Jewish men walked along the streets and beaches, singing Hebrew songs. One young Italian man, Antonio Snap from Tricase, heard them sing. He would never forget the people "with the Star of David on their chests," with the tattooed numbers on their arms. "They came grandmother and grandson, father and daughter, mother and daughter," he said, "but never an entire family." He caught the bittersweet melody of "Shalom Aleichem" rising over the sounds of the waves. And though the words meant nothing to him, he felt their meaning with his heart, and learned the verses. When he recalled the tune some fifty years later, it brought tears to his eyes.

Still, there were some Jews who couldn't move past their pain. One Italian man watched as a Jewish refugee strode into the thrashing ocean, where the waves would have easily crushed him into the rocks. He saw the man's wife step out on the balcony and call to him, but the man never even turned his head. She came running down the steps of the house and into the water after her husband, and somehow managed to pull him back to the shore, keeping him in this world even as he tried to leave it behind.

❦

In November 1946, after six blissful months in Santa Maria di Leuca, the UNRRA relocated the Rabinowitz family to another DP site, this time in Rome. The family said goodbye to their idyllic life in the seaside village and set off for the place that Lord Byron had called the "city of the soul!"

The Rabinowitz family of four moved into a stately old villa with a large garden at 41 Via Latina. They shared their new lodgings with four other families, each cordoned off into a different corner of the house. For the first time since the war began, Luba was not with them. She was no longer Luba Dworetsky, but Luba Sakier. Newly married, she and Beryl had been sent to Naples, where they began a family of their own. It was there that Luba gave birth to their first child, a happy baby girl they called Gita whose chubby face was almost perfectly round.

In Rome the Rabinowitz family quickly adapted to the more cosmopolitan trends of the city. The girls wore their long hair in two neat braids tied off in ribbons that fell past their shoulders, while their hemlines hovered high above their knees. Miriam too dabbled in new fashions, finally trading in her blue silk dress for other frocks and low kitten heels that had bow-tie leather straps around the ankles. Morris was back in a suit and tie, knotted high and tight under the neck of his collar, topped off with a cap or fedora, just as he preferred.

Their villa was near the ancient Baths of Caracalla, where families came to picnic on its wide surrounding lawns. During the war the space was used for kitchen gardens, but it was reopened to the public in 1945, and operas were once again performed in its open-air theater, as they had been for more than a hundred years. Morris and Miriam took the girls to listen to the outdoor performances under the night sky. Whether it was Giuseppe Verdi's *Aida* or another performance, Morris fell in love with Italian opera and all its pageantry.

In Rome, life for the Rabinowitz daughters was full and rich and centrally Jewish. The girls attended a Hebrew school for survivors and refugee children located in the ancient part of the city. Every morning their route to class circled around the Colosseum. They went on field trips to see Roman antiquities and celebrated Jewish holidays. They went to the shores of Ostia to swim in the ocean with their new teachers and classmates. In the summer they attended a camp in Nemi, Italy, a picturesque little town in the city's suburbs famous for its wild strawberries. Its ancient stucco-roofed townhouses were built right into the mountainside that surrounded a pristine lake as blue as the cobalt sky. Rochel flourished under the rigor of so many new academics, devouring her lessons in algebra and Latin. Both girls continued with Hebrew in preparation for their move to Palestine, but Rochel had a private tutor so she could practice her lessons after school.

Where Tania never seemed to have lost her nerve, Rochel was slowly regaining her confidence in the months since they arrived in Italy. She was given a bike, and once she mastered the balance of it, there was nothing Rochel loved more than riding along the stone-paved road of the Appian Way. She finally felt secure enough to explore, on her own, just as she had as a little girl in Zhetel.

That spring Rochel won the coveted role of Vashti in the school's Purim play, and she had a new best friend to help her celebrate. Gloria Koslowski had wild black hair and porcelain skin. Whip smart, Gloria, like Rochel, enjoyed her studies. She had also survived the war in the Białowieża Forest, living with the Bielski partisans. This shared experience was unlikely to be matched by other friendships either girl would make, even in the space of their Jewish refugee school. But Rochel and Gloria never spoke about the woods. Perhaps it was too painful, perhaps in the safety and serenity of Rome, neither girl wanted to remember the forest. Or perhaps it was just enough for each of them to know the other understood what it had been like to survive it.

On Yom Kippur, the girlfriends took a walk to no place special, ambling along the cobblestone streets. Both their bellies howled from the daylong holiday fast. Then Rochel suddenly announced, "Today, I'm so hungry, I would even eat the *pane*." And they burst into peals of laughter. Of all the delicacies and culinary delights Italy had to offer, one thing both girls found wholly unappetizing was the dry, tasteless bread. Gloria smiled. "Yes," she agreed. "I would, too."

During the summer of 1947, the last full summer they would spend in Italy, Rochel had her twelfth birthday and brushed right up against adolescence. Tania, not far behind her older sister, turned ten and edged out of the middle years of girlhood. But however quickly the girls were growing, it was in Italy that they each had their childhoods returned to them. They would always be grateful that this was the place they came to live after the war.

But happy as all the Rabinowitzes were in Italy, the dream of Palestine, and the hope for a Jewish state, was more alluring than even the great city of Rome.

ঙ

At the midnight hour on May 15, 1948, a series of long-brewing, world-changing events coincided in such close range, it was as if they'd been choreographed. In some ways, they were.

The British flag posted over the King David Hotel in Jerusalem had been replaced with the symbol of the Red Cross. At the port of Haifa, General Sir Alan Cunningham, the high commissioner of Britain's Mandate in Palestine, boarded a ship. His departure ended his nation's three-decade rule over the embattled Middle Eastern state.

In the same midnight hour, U.S. president Harry Truman issued a statement in which he confirmed to the world that the United States did indeed recognize the provisional government that had been declared by David Ben-Gurion as the "de facto authority of the new State of Israel."

At 4 P.M. on the afternoon of May 14, Ben-Gurion, now the very first prime minister of Israel, spoke at the Tel Aviv Museum during a thirty-minute ceremony. Standing before a portrait of Zionism's father, Dr. Theodor Herzl, and two large blue-and-white flags, he first asserted the right of the "Jewish people to be masters of their own fate, like all other nations, in their own sovereign state." And then Ben-Gurion, in his somber dark suit and ring of blazing-white hair, declared "the establishment of a Jewish state in Eretz-Israel, to be known as the State of Israel," and with it the end of the British Mandate. "The State of Israel," he continued, "will be open for Jewish immigration and for the Ingathering of the Exiles."

When he finished his short remarks, the audience burst into applause; some were moved to tears. It was the end of the struggle for statehood, and the beginning of the struggle to keep it. Egypt had already sent columns of marching soldiers to the border, soon to be followed by attacks from Iraq, Syria, Lebanon, and Transjordan. On May 16, the Arab-Israeli War would begin.

For Jews everywhere, however, the Zionist dream was realized, and they were celebrating even as another war was dawning.

On May 14, Jews in Rome marched together in the direction of Jerusalem and *away* from the Arch of Titus, where they believe that two thousand years before, Jewish prisoners had been led into the city. Carved into the great white stone just below the curve of the gate on the arch's inner wall is a panel showing soldiers and prisoners of war led by the victorious Emperor Titus. It's thought that in this depiction, the soldiers are parading triumphantly back into Rome, raising all the plunder they had pillaged from the temple in Jerusalem above their heads. Between two of the chiseled figures is a large menorah.

The symbolic gesture was momentous: the hundreds and hundreds of Jews in Rome—so many of them Holocaust survivors who were still refugees—walking with their backs to that arch to celebrate the new state of Israel.

Just feet away from the arch, Morris and Miriam stood in the cheering, jubilant crowd with their daughters. Morris was in a tailored overcoat and his trademark fedora, its brim riding high on his temples. Miriam, just next to him, stuck close to her husband's elbow and smiled, radiant in a dark dress. It was a happy, triumphant celebration.

For the Rabinowitz family, this day was bittersweet. Back at home, their visas were waiting; arrangements had finally been made to leave Rome. They were about to embark on the next, more permanent phase of their future. When they turned their backs on the Roman arch that day, they weren't just honoring history, they were stepping away from one life and readying to face another. Only that new life would not be in Israel.

A month later, they bade farewell to Italy and sailed to a new promised land—America.

CHAPTER 15

In America

THIS CAKE HAD LAYERS. ONE STACKED ON TOP OF THE other with a thick frosting in between. In her whole life, Tania Rabinowitz had never laid her eyes on a cake so big.

They had only been in the United States for a few days, but this cake was already just one of the many eye-widening wonders waiting for the Rabinowitz family at the large New Jersey home belonging to their cousins, the Epsteins.

From the moment their ship departed the port at Naples in June 1948, their journey was long and rocky, and without an ounce of daylight. They made the ocean crossing on the MS *Vulcania,* an Italian passenger ship with a prestigious pedigree. In its luxurious heyday in the 1920s, the *Vulcania* boasted gilded restaurants, grand ballrooms, and even an indoor pool. The rooms in the ship's top tiers featured ornate wood carvings, vaulted ceilings with dangling crystal-glass chandeliers, and elaborate mosaic-tiled floors. But the war had stripped the ship of its glitz and glamour. Drafted into service under the symbol of the Red Cross, the *Vulcania* helped repatriate Italian citizens and was later requisitioned to carry troops—first for Italy and then, after

Italy surrendered to the United States in 1943, American soldiers were shuttled to the war aboard the vessel's sturdy decks.

Traveling as third-class passengers, the Rabinowitz family didn't experience an inch of the ship's former luxuries or any of its current ones, either. Their eleven-day trip was spent entirely below deck, where hundreds of passengers shared the same large space, sleeping on cots. As the *Vulcania* made its way across the Atlantic Ocean, the ship's ceaseless pitching and rolling sent Miriam, Rochel, and Tania into the grip of seasickness. The three of them spent the duration of their voyage in green-gilled misery.

Once they docked in New York, the uneasiness of being foreigners was almost instantaneous. They felt a very long way from Europe and from the only homes they'd ever known, but it appeared that everyone else around them knew it, too. Almost from the moment they stepped off the boat, complete strangers would ask them: "How do you like America?" Rochel and Tania quickly understood that something about their outward appearance—from their Italian hemlines and long braids, to Miriam and Morris's outdated European fashions—shouted their newcomer status.

American eyes were quick to appraise, and it was clear what they saw when they looked at the Rabinowitz family: immigrants.

❧

It had taken three years in Italy before Morris and Miriam finally accepted that they were still no closer to fulfilling their dream of getting to Palestine. It was time to seek out other options. Morris placed a small notice in the *Forward,* an American Yiddish paper, identifying himself as the son of Berl and Beyla Rabinowitz from Zhetel. Years before the war, three of Berl Rabinowitz's siblings—his two sisters, Sara Rivke and Mindul, and brother Morris—had left Poland for the United States. The families had been out of touch for years, but Morris hoped it might catch the eye of one of his relatives.

Very luckily, it did.

It turned out that not only was there a large family network of Rabinowitz relatives in the United States, but they were ready and eager to help. Both of Berl's sisters were living in the Northeast: Mindul, whom everyone called Minnie, had married a man named Isaac Berman and planted roots in Elizabeth, New Jersey, where they had two children; Sara Rivke eventually settled in Connecticut with her husband, Joseph Kruchevsky, and their sizable brood of eight children. Finally, Berl's brother Morris was living with his wife, Sophie, and their four children in the Hartford area.

It was Minnie who discovered Morris's posting in the *Forward.* Thrilled to see one of her brother's children had made it through the war alive, she hurried a letter off to Italy. She wanted to know what they planned to do, and when Morris answered that they were still waiting—and hoping—to get to Palestine, Minnie was incredulous. "What are you going to do with two small children in Palestine?" she asked in a letter. By then Minnie had long been a widow, and perhaps it was a protective, familial instinct that spurred her to help Berl's only surviving child. She insisted her nephew reconsider. A new home in a country full of family was the better choice, she wrote. "Come to the United States."

The night Rochel and Tania found out they weren't going to Palestine, the girls cried themselves to sleep. The Zionist dream had been a deeply rooted expectation since they came out of the woods, and in their minds, it was the key to a happy future. But slowly, the girls came around to the prospects of the United States. All they'd ever heard about America was that it was someplace like heaven, where the streets were practically paved in gold.

The Bermans and the Kruchevskys banded together to sponsor their refugee cousins' path to the United States. They arranged for their visas and paid for their passage across the Atlantic. When the Rabinowitzes arrived, their first stop was in New Jersey, where they stayed with Minnie's daughter Sonia and her husband, Saul Epstein. Even though it had been many years since Morris had seen his cousin, he hadn't forgotten Sonia, the daring redhead who made her way to the United States when she was just sixteen years old.

Between Morris, Miriam, and the girls, the family spoke Polish, Russian, Italian, Hebrew, and, of course, Yiddish, but of their American relatives only Minnie still spoke Yiddish. Communication was mostly accomplished with a flail of hand gestures to fill in whatever gaps their combined Yiddish vocabulary couldn't manage. Despite the language barrier, Rochel and Tania warmed to their hosts Sonia and Saul in no time. A small man with a sweet and gentle nature, Saul made a special effort to see that the girls felt at home in their strange new surroundings. It was Sonia who baked the layer cake, and she treated Tania and Rochel to a very special outing—a trip to the beauty salon for their first American-style haircuts.

The family was never meant to stay in New Jersey, but still the girls were disappointed when their time with Minnie and the Epsteins came to an end. After just a few weeks, cousin Timothy Kruchevsky came in his big car and took Morris, Miriam, and the girls with him to Hartford, where the family had arranged an apartment for them.

In a stout three-story brick building at 133 Martin Street, the Rabinowitzes' new home started and ended in the span of just four small rooms—including a kitchen and a bathroom. But for a family that had shared their living space with dozens of other people for the better part of a decade—where cramped circumstances often demanded they nearly, if not literally, sleep on top of each other—having their own rooms of any kind was a dream come true. Tania marveled at their apartment and thought, *Boy, if my friends back in Italy could see the castle I'm living in.*

The Rabinowitz family's first American home was located in the city's North End, a low-income, working-class neighborhood populated largely with immigrants and African Americans—hardworking people with families. The neighbors were friendly and welcoming, and the front stoops of Martin Street were always busy with bodies and chatter. The children ran up and down the sidewalk to the corner store where a nickel was enough to score a shimmery bag of potato chips. That summer Rochel and Tania attended Jewish day camp at Camp Shalom in nearby Windsor, Connecticut. It didn't take long before both girls began to feel that maybe life in America wasn't so disappointing after all.

Family connections helped land Morris a job working in Hartford's C.J. Callaghan Paper Box Company. Miriam soon found work at the counter of Mayron's Bakery on Albany Avenue. Once the girls started school, they would join her in the afternoons and help assemble the boxes for cakes and sweets; they even got paid a handful of pennies for their labor.

Soon enough the best parts of Italy and their former lives in Europe followed them to the United States. Luba, Beryl (who would go by Ben in America), and baby Gita arrived in October 1948, and moved to upstate New York. Joseph and Dora Kogan had made arrangements to stay with family in Pennsylvania. They came to visit the Rabinowitz family and brought along their towheaded little boy, Jerry. Even Rochel's dear friend Gloria Koslowski came to America, and settled in Brooklyn to live with her older brother. The two girls weren't able to see each other often, but now they could stay in touch over the phone.

Their community of Holocaust survivors and refugees, which had served as the guardrails of the Rabinowitzes' Jewish life in Italy, was noticeably absent in Hartford. They went to synagogue for the high holiday services, and afterward they walked with the other congregants to enjoy the afternoon in nearby Keney Park. But it didn't take long for Morris and Miriam to understand that those outside Europe had experienced a very different encounter with World War II. While many Americans had loved ones fighting overseas in harm's way, the majority of the country had been an ocean away from the front lines of the war.

Even within the local Jewish community, the reaction to them as immigrants and as survivors was often complicated. Some, like their Kruchevsky cousins, viewed what the Rabinowitzes had endured with a kind of pride. It was a genuine feeling but one that perhaps strayed close to a kind of tokenism, where the Holocaust survivor was something of a cause célèbre in the American Jewish community. Oftentimes they were not embraced but pushed away from a group to which they might otherwise have believed they rightfully belonged. Rarely during those first years did the family seek out company beyond their own familiar—and now fairly far-flung—refugee community, where the gravity of their experience was fully understood and appreciated.

It had been an altogether unpleasant encounter and Morris was angry. "That's it," he told Miriam. "Never again am I going to tell them. How can they compare rationing food to what we went through?"

Most of the Rabinowitzes' extended family were proud of their Polish relatives, proud as well to have sponsored their journey to America. Morris's cousins, the Kruchevskys, regularly hosted Sunday dinners or took them to play cards. During these evening gatherings they would introduce Morris and

Miriam to their friends and encourage them to share their story with their guests. There may have been something slightly self-congratulatory in these dinner parties, but Morris and Miriam didn't seem to mind. At least not until it became clear during an encounter with Morris's uncle that not all of their American relatives understood what Morris and Miriam and their daughters had endured to survive the Nazis and the woods. Nor, it appeared, did all of them care to.

On that particular evening during dinner, Morris was relating a story about how scarce food had been while they were in the woods, when his uncle interjected. This was nothing they couldn't relate to, he said. After all, the older man continued, they too had gone without, having had to submit to food rations during the war. Furious that his uncle would compare limitations on sugar and coffee, or canned milk and fish, with near starvation and two years of hiding in the forest, Morris vowed to never discuss what they endured in their company again.

The girls had experienced crushed feelings of their own from Uncle Morris's daughters, their cousins Gloria and Shirley. When the family hosted a birthday party for Shirley, they invited Tania, as the girls were the same age. Of course, Tania didn't know anyone at the party other than her cousins. But in addition to being the new kid at the party, something else about her was different, and it was the kind of different that children hone in on, that separates them without words.

Tania overheard another girl at the party approach Shirley, and nodding to Tania, asked, "Why did you invite *her*?" Shirley replied with a burdened refrain that all children understand: "My mother made me."

A few times since they moved to Hartford, some of the other Jewish kids had called Rochel and Tania *griner,* a Yiddish word for green or naïve, but when lobbed against an immigrant it was distinctly pejorative, a way of snidely conveying that they looked "fresh off the boat." As soon as Tania realized that people could tell just by looking at her that she was an immigrant, she became determined to be as little like a refugee kid as possible. If there was a word she couldn't pronounce, she simply didn't use it. They arrived in June. By the end of the summer she was speaking English.

When Rochel and Tania started school that September, they met a similar cold shoulder. Just as with their cousins, the Jewish kids wanted nothing to do with them. Instead it was the Black kids and the Italian kids from their neighborhood who made room for them in their social circles.

Rochel never tried as hard as Tania to be accepted, and she didn't harbor the grudges against the kids who judged her. Instead, she found comfort with the kids on the margins, the ones who were a little different, the other immigrants, just like her. When Northeast Junior High hosted a talent show, she got up in front of the whole school and sang Ruggero Leoncavallo's famous "Mattinata." It reminded her of Italy, and when she sang, she was not retiring or shy, but uninhibited and proud—and she belted out the lyrics, half in Italian and half in English. The Italian kids loved her for it, and cheered her on the loudest. Watching proudly from the back of the audience was Miriam and their Kruchevsky cousins.

Though Rochel had found a group of friends, other troubles arose for the thirteen-year-old: for the first time in her young, and otherwise unstable, academic career, she flunked a test. The advancements she made in her math classes in Italy were paying off in her new school, but math is its own language, and her struggles with English tripped her up in the unlikeliest of places—her cooking class. During an exam, Rochel confused the word for yolk with egg whites, a distinction that, evidently, was a critical part of the recipe.

One invested teacher, Miss Crane, had the good sense to set up her new student Rochel Rabinowitz with an English tutor, an African American girl named Cassandra Johnson. It was a clever pairing on Miss Crane's part. Cassandra, another eighth grader, was smart and friendly, and with a few afternoon tutoring sessions at the Rabinowitz apartment, Rochel not only improved her schoolwork but she made her first true American friend.

In addition to working with Cassandra, Rochel spent some of her free time at a Jewish community center on Vine Street, where a woman named Mrs. Froth would help her with her English lessons. While she sat with Rochel, Mrs. Froth would often talk about her daughter, Ruth, an older girl who had also worked as a counselor at Camp Shalom, where the Rabinowitz girls spent part of their summers. As Rochel turned the name over in her mind, she decided that she liked the sound of it. It was not long after that Rochel announced that she wanted to be called Ruth. There was only one problem—with her still-strong accent, she had particular difficulty making the "th" sound. Understandably, there was some confusion when people asked Rochel for her name and she could only tell them "*Root*." For a short period of time, she overcame the obstacle by spelling it—"R-u-t-h."

As far as Tania could tell, no other American girls shared her name, proof that it was too foreign-sounding, and all the cause she needed to justify changing it. To find her new name, Tania sought out intrepid inspiration from the pages of her favorite reading material, narrowing her choices down to Toby, the main character in James Otis's children's novel *Toby Tyler or, Ten Weeks with a Circus*, and Terry from the popular adventure comic strip *Terry and the Pirates* (that not only appeared in the Sunday funnies but by then was also a radio show). Not surprisingly, Tania decided on Toby, the wayward scamp who ran off with the circus, and soon that was how she was known by almost everyone.

There was a short period, after his younger daughter decided to take on an American boy's name, when Morris could be overheard answering the phone only to reply, "There's no Toby here, but there is a Tania." But though Miriam would always call her daughters Rocheleh and Taibeleh, Morris and Miriam otherwise did not object to them changing their names, or in general to their campaigns to assimilate. At home the family still spoke Yiddish, and as adults, Morris and Miriam's English-language skills lagged behind their daughters'. But they recognized the pursuit to Americanize was part of their family's new life.

They may have both been working menial jobs in a foreign country without a firm grasp on the language, but something for which both Miriam and Morris had a savvy understanding was the economy of good business and the stretch of a dollar. They were hardly making lucrative wages, but they pinched and scrimped, and worked overtime, coupling business savvy with a back-breaking commitment to old-fashioned hard work. It only took them two years to put away enough savings to buy not just their own apartment, but their own building—a three-family house on Kent Street. Sometime in 1950, they said goodbye to cheery, crowded Martin Street and moved into one of the much larger apartments of the new house, and rented the other two.

For a short time, the top floor apartment was vacant. Toby didn't let the opportunity go to waste. On a couple of mornings when she and Ruth would leave for school, Toby sneaked upstairs to the third floor and hid in the empty apartment. She waited for Morris and Miriam to go to work and then came back down to run off and meet her friends. Ruth, who would never dare do anything quite so scandalous as skip school, did not join her. But Ruth never betrayed Toby's secret, still protecting her little devil of a sister.

Two years after Ruth left Northeast Junior High, Toby landed in Miss Crane's classroom. When Miriam went to see her for a parent-teacher conference, the teacher began by announcing, "Rochel and Tania are very different." Miss Crane had a reputation for being very strict, and where she had warmed to Rochel's earnest desire to be a good student, she was concerned that Toby was more interested in "socializing than minding her schoolwork."

While this observation about her daughters would hardly have struck Miriam as a revelation, in a sense, Miss Crane was right. Toby wasn't as invested in studying as her older sister. But what the no-nonsense teacher failed to see was that while twelve-year-old Toby's interests were decidedly recreational, they were not frivolous. She served on dance committees and helped with charity work for the Junior Red Cross. As a Junior Achiever (JA), she participated in the national after-school program geared at teaching teenagers about business and entrepreneurship. When Toby was a senior at Weaver High School, her work as president of Shi-Nite—a JA company that made reflector signs with the guiding sponsorship of Pratt & Whitney—won her a $150 scholarship and landed her picture in *The Hartford Courant*.

In more than one way, Toby was the ideal American teen she'd always been so determined to become. A svelte brunette with her now dark hair styled in the curled waves of a young Lauren Bacall, she was both pretty and popular. Captain of the JCC cheerleading squad, Toby had also been crowned queen at more than one big dance—she was Queen of Hillel, and then the local Jewish Community Center's Miss JCC. It just so happened that on the day the photo was taken, Toby was wearing a brand-new outfit she nabbed from Ruth's closet, a handsome navy-blue suit with white trim along the collar. Ruth always suspected Toby had taken it without asking, but Toby denied it until the newspaper story about the pageant came out. There Toby was, front and center of the accompanying photo, Miss JCC wearing Ruth's suit. But tempers never ran hot for long between the sisters, and the incident of the stolen suit was soon forgotten.

While Toby never took these competitions all that seriously, attractive and confident, she had the winning edge. When she was in college, a Hartford-area Jewish organization approached Toby. They were recruiting for the Miss Hartford contest, which was a precursor to Miss Connecticut and eventually the Miss America pageant. There wasn't a single Jewish entrant, they told Toby, and they wanted to put someone in the competition who would get noticed. As it turned out, they also wanted a young woman who had a last name that would get noticed for being Jewish, and Rabinowitz fit the bill. Toby warned her sponsors that she had no talent to perform, but they assured her that was fine. "You'll give a speech," they said. And then they helped her write it.

For Toby, competing in Miss Hartford was just a lark, a bit of fun. She did the bathing suit competition, she wore the fancy gown, and when it was time for the talent portion of the evening, Toby got up and delivered her speech: "What It Means to Be an American Citizen." She spoke about being born in Poland as Hitler was coming to the pinnacle of his power, and what it meant to be living in the United States after surviving the war. The timing was poignant: Toby had officially become a U.S. citizen just two weeks earlier. She may not have twirled batons or performed Shakespeare, but her speech was rousing, and the crowd gave her a hearty round of applause.

It didn't win her the pageant, but Toby was one of the ten finalists and the other young Miss Hartford hopefuls voted her Miss Congeniality. That year, Barbara Ann Parkhurst—a twenty-year-old aspiring actress from Farmington with blond hair and hazel eyes—was crowned Miss Hartford. Perhaps it was too much to imagine that an immigrant's story would take the competition by storm and beat out Parkhurst's performance of the song "Mon Homme," the old favorite made famous by Fanny Brice and Billie Holiday. Toby wasn't disappointed. She hadn't gone there to win. She was there to have a good time. The girl who ran through the woods without constraint was still making her own way in the world.

&

It was one year into their time in the United States that Morris and Miriam had the opportunity to pay forward the generosity that had brought them to their new home and sponsor another family member's passage out of Europe.

Unbeknownst to Miriam and Luba, one of their younger cousins, Solomon Golanski, had also survived the war. His family was from a small village just outside Novogrudek. The approximately five thousand Jews who were killed in Novogrudek after being interned in the ghetto included his parents and five siblings. In the spring of 1943, Solomon was one of the five hundred people still left in the ghetto. These men and women were highly skilled tradesmen—engineers, carpenters, electricians, and mechanics—kept alive so the Nazis could continue to benefit from their talents.

After yet another merciless culling in May 1943, the three hundred Jews who remained pursued the only conceivable option for escape—they began to dig their way out. Around the clock, day and night, these men expended the last of their waning strength to build an underground tunnel beneath the bunks in their barracks. It was a remarkable feat of construction, ingenuity, and daring. They crafted their own tools; they stole wood from the ghetto's carpentry shop and used it to keep the tunnel's walls and ceiling from collapsing; they developed a pulley system to haul the dirt out and built a false wall behind which to hide it. In between shifts the diggers traded clothes so the Germans wouldn't catch them covered in dirt. Eventually their tunnel—which measured some three feet high and two feet wide and had its own electrical lighting and ventilation system—would extend 225 yards long.

There was a blustering storm on the night of September 26, 1943. Dark and windy, the black sky provided the perfect conditions for the men to make their escape. They loosened the nails on the roof of their barracks so the howling gusts would shake the tin until it rattled, creating a cover of sound. One of the electricians in their group cut the power to the searchlights. Finally, at 9 P.M., the long line of some 250 men left the barracks one by one down into the tunnel, letting the weak and the sick go first. It took the guards in the ghetto until 4 A.M. to discover that their prisoners were getting away. In half an hour's time, SS officer Wilhelm Reuter and his men were waiting in the field at the other end of the tunnel. The escapees who were still in the tunnel climbed out into a barrage of bullets. Somehow, Solomon, running blindly toward the woods, escaped the field. He was one of only 170 who would survive that morning. Eventually Solomon found his way to the Naliboki Forest where he joined the Bielski partisans until the Russians liberated the woods in the summer of 1944.

After the war, Solomon ended up as a refugee in Rome, but there too, the cousins never crossed paths. It wasn't until Solomon was deciding where he would go to make a new life after Italy—Australia, the new state of Israel, or the United States—that he finally caught a glimpse of his relatives. While the twenty-nine-year-old debated his decision, he thumbed through the relocation center's photos of newly emigrated families in

America. He paused over a photograph of a familiar-looking family, a couple and their two daughters. Solomon was looking at his cousin Miriam Rabinowitz.

On December 3, 1949, Solomon, the only surviving member of what had once been the large Golanski family, arrived in New York. He took the train straight to Hartford, Connecticut, where Miriam and Morris were waiting for him. For a time, he lived in their apartment on Martin Street and found work as a carpenter. But the labor was hard and as the seasons turned cold, the outdoor construction sites became unbearable, so Morris got him a job at the Paper Box Company, work that came with reliably long hours and steady pay. In time, he married a Canadian woman named Etta, and they would have a baby boy and call him Alan. Shortly after, Solomon moved his family into the third-floor apartment in Morris and Miriam's building at 145 Kent Street, where rent was paid in Solomon's woodworking skills. By the time little Alan Golanski was four years old, his favorite game was playing with the boxes Solomon brought home from work. The boy arranged them all through their small apartment, creating elaborate tunnels and imagining his father, the brave carpenter, making his glorious escape to the forest.

In the early 1950s, Morris Rabinowitz had the opportunity to go in on a wholesale lumber business in Canaan, New Hampshire. He had to borrow money to put the cash together, but it was an offer with too much promise to turn down. However, Miriam—reluctant to leave the security of Hartford, where they had family and friends, for a rural town where there would be few if any Jewish prospects for her soon-to-be-of-marrying-age daughters—refused to move until her daughters were wed. Just as he didn't try to change her mind when she backed out of a civil ceremony at the Vilna courthouse, Morris must have understood this issue was also nonnegotiable. A compromise was reached: Morris would commute. Every week he would make the six-hour trip up and down Route 5.

In a way, they were reversing the guiding principle that had, for the better part of a decade, been the saving grace of their family. For so many years during the war, chances to improve their situation came at the cost of separation—whether it was Morris's job in Slonim, or a farmer friend offering to help him escape the Nazi invasion. It was only during the second ghetto selection, when Morris thought he could save his mother, sister, and nephew, that they risked making that sacrifice. Otherwise, they had remained together no matter what, even when it meant they had to go without. Now, Miriam and Morris could finally choose what was best for the family without trading it for safety or each other.

As they moved their way through the early 1950s, Morris's business grew, and their financial burdens lessened, ushering in a period of stability that the couple had not known since the early years of their marriage back in Zhetel. Now, that business-acumen potential he'd shown working for Mr. Kaplinsky's lumber mill, potential that had been cut off by the war, finally had its chance to launch. Almost twenty years later as a man nearing his fifties, Morris Rabinowitz came into his own.

But no matter how far along they got in their new American lives, they were in no hurry to disappear the ones they left behind—in Italy, in Zhetel, or even in the woods. It was unusual. For many, if not most, Holocaust survivors, any stirring of wartime memories was so painful and disturbing that they locked their experiences away, preferring to forget. Not the Rabinowitz family. It seemed like they talked about it all the time.

Every now and again, Miriam would wonder about the young boy from the ghetto selection. She would often ask her family, "What do you think happened to the boy from Bilitza?" She'd think of the boy's mother and their encounter on the street in the ghetto, and say, "The blessing of that woman saved us."

Then one day in May 1953, the telephone rang.

CHAPTER 16

A Wedding in Connecticut

THAT WHOLE MORNING, MIRIAM KEPT CHECKING THE window, looking out into the street. They'd put out some cakes and cookies, but she was too restless to sit still for long. Truth be told, this nervous excitement had been there for weeks.

When Miriam answered that ringing phone to discover the voice on the other end belonged to the boy from Bilitza, she could scarcely believe it. On that May afternoon, it was if a great cosmic question hanging over her life had finally been answered. Philip Lazowski, the boy Miriam had saved in the Zhetel Marketplace, had survived the war and, as it turned out, he'd been searching for her, too.

That night after the Brooklyn wedding and their phone call, Philip had written Miriam a letter. In scratchy cursive with still-developing English, it began:

> Dear Mama and Family,
>
> How great is my rejoicing how astonishing was I last night since I heard that you are living in the United States. . . . I didn't and couldn't forget what you did, thanks to you I am alive. I was

looking all over to find you, but as the Talmud says . . . the day will come and the day did came. No matter at what the circumstances I would be, I have promised myself even to visit you if you would be in Israel.

He said he hoped to visit her soon in Hartford. His cousin Sam owned a car, so it would not be a difficult trip. In fact, Philip wrote, he'd traveled through Hartford many times on his way to visit family in Boston and marveled that he could have been so close to Miriam without knowing it. He could not wait to see her. "Not everything is possible to write on this piece of paper, I am sure that we have lots of things to talk, or maybe more than talk, I don't want you should cry . . . what we went through it isn't easily forgotten. I have always remembered your name," he wrote. "Your name have been in my memory forever.

"Please write to me," he asked and signed the letter, "Love, Philip."

Miriam replied with a letter of her own. They corresponded back and forth, and arranged a visit.

Now, weeks after their May phone call, Miriam was waiting by the window, scanning the length of Kent Street for any sign of him.

Finally, she spotted a parking car. When Miriam saw a young man with a cap of black curls emerge from the passenger seat, she knew it was Philip and rushed out to meet him on the stoop.

As Philip started down the sidewalk toward the Rabinowitz house, he spotted a woman and knew at once it was Miriam. "Take a look, Sam," he said to his cousin. "That's the lady there."

After they kissed and embraced on the front porch, Miriam led Philip into the house and introduced him, finally, to her husband, Morris, and their two daughters. Ten years had passed, but to Philip they were all somehow familiar. Morris was still tall and broad shouldered. Miriam's daughters, who were no longer frightened little girls but now young women, still held impressions of their younger selves, Ruth with her button brown eyes and Toby with her fairer complexion. Miriam, too, was just as he had pictured, dark-haired and diminutive, with the same kind face—the one that even from a distance amid a sea of terror and tumult had appeared so welcoming to a desperate boy of eleven.

❧

In reconstructing the timeline of the Zhetel ghetto liquidation, it's highly likely that Morris Rabinowitz and Philip Lazowski escaped the *kino* within hours of each other. During those five dragging days in August 1942 that the SS and the Einsatzgruppen killing squads spent rousting Zhetel's Jews out of their hiding places, the Lazowskis' large family encountered both the best and the worst sides of fortune.

When the liquidation began, Philip—along with his mother, Chaya; his younger siblings Abraham, little Aaron, and the baby, Rachel; and his elderly grandfather—rushed into the family's hiding place under their ghetto house through a hole in the closet floor. It was such a small space, Philip's brother Rachmil and his father, Joseph, went to hide elsewhere. They managed to stay there under the floorboards in the dark for days, through the initial searches and the sweltering summer heat, coming up for fresh air only for brief moments at night.

When they heard the local Poles rummaging around the house, pillaging what little they had, they hushed themselves as best they could. But while one man was in the room above, hauling out the furniture, Philip's grandfather gave a loud rattling cough. It didn't take long before the thieves found them and alerted the Germans that they had discovered some Jews.

As they were marched out of the house, the August sun was blinding. Instinctively, the whole family raised their hands to their eyes and froze, unable to see. The SS rounded on the lot of them, beating them with rifle butts. Frightened, his grandfather, already ill and even weaker from exhaustion and dehydration, collapsed. Not willing to expend the energy to carry the elderly man to the *kino*, they continued to beat and kick him until he died right there on the ground in front of his family.

While the Germans were distracted picking through the house ruins looking for gold, Chaya whispered to Philip and Abraham to run. Both boys did as their mother instructed. Abraham, spotted almost immediately, was shot and killed. Philip didn't make it much farther before he ran into the path of a large dog and its owner, a Polish man. Seeing that Philip was Jewish, the man cursed and slapped him, then gathered him by the shirt collar and dragged him to the *kino*. The blow the man had delivered was so hard and shocking it struck Philip's most primal fear response, and he wet his pants.

Despite having been caught, Philip was happy to be with his mother again. He found her with Aaron and baby Rachel in the crowded building, and they all cried with relief.

They got word that Joseph was alive; he even sent them a package of food through his sympathetic Polish boss, and Chaya passed a message back telling her husband not to come to the *kino*. The space was jam-packed with people—all of whom had been dragged out from hiding, now scared and desolate. Some seemed to have accepted their fate.

After waiting by the window all day for word from Joseph, Philip retreated to a far corner of the *kino*'s upper floor with his mother and siblings to find room to sleep. In the morning they discovered that someone had come to the building asking in a whisper for the Lazowskis, but because the family was not native Zhetelers, no one knew who they were.

When, a little while later, Philip heard the rumbling of truck engines, he was filled with sickening dread. He'd heard that sound many times before, and the only thing that followed was death. And sure enough, the doors to the *kino* finally opened, and the Nazis began hauling out the theater's captives in large groups, pushing and pulling them onto the trucks. At the sound of the commotion—the rising cries and screams, the cruel shouting of the German officers—Philip pulled his mother and youngest siblings farther away, toward the back wall, until they were standing underneath a boarded window. There was a broken chair on the floor. Philip grabbed the pieces and thrashed them against the window until the board cracked and fell away.

He looked at Chaya, his heart thumping. "Mother, let's jump," he said. "You first." But she refused. "Not with the baby," she said. "I can't jump." Keeping hold of little Rachel and Aaron, she insisted Philip leave, and hurried him toward the now open window.

"I won't go without you," he said.

But Chaya nudged him back to the window.

"Jump," she told him. "I want you to live."

Philip climbed to the window and braced himself to launch, but his muscles seized. Seeing that her son was so reluctant to leave her, Chaya pushed him. Out the window he went, sailing down two stories to the grass below.

Unhurt, Philip glanced up and saw his mother's face in the window. Chaya was looking back down at him, and she was crying. Another moment came and went; then she turned away and was gone.

Suddenly, another boy came flying like a bird out the window after him, and landed next to Philip in the tall grass. The two stared at each other and then an SS guard, standing nearby, cast his eyes in their direction. It would have been almost impossible for him not to have seen the boys, small though they were, lying in the brush. But instead of coming after them, the guard turned back toward the spectacle of the Jews being loaded onto the trucks.

When the moment came, Philip and the other boy, who was all of nine years old, fled together, climbing over the fence just in time.

The rest of the Jews remaining in the *kino* endured another *selektion*, one that was over in a fraction of the time, conducted by Reuter. The Nazis didn't even check for *scheins*. A small number of workers were spared, the rest were taken away and shot.

For days the boys walked in the direction of Dvoretz. They were robbed of their shoes by passing Poles, harassed and even chased, but as a pair, they managed to get to the Dvoretz ghetto. It was rumored that because it was a still a functioning labor camp, the Jews there would not be massacred. Philip spent a month in that camp before word came from his father—he was sending someone to get him.

In time he would be reunited with his only surviving sibling, Rachmil, and together they eventually joined their father, Joseph. The remaining Lazowski family members would spend the next year and a half in the woods, where there was no reprieve—not from the Nazis, nor the bruising grief that trailed after them out of the ghetto.

During that spring afternoon visit on Kent Street, the Rabinowitz family learned that Philip had been in the woods closer to Bilitza, where the Lazowski family banded together in a family camp. They too had lived in *zemlyanki,* battling the same unforgiving winters, bouts of hunger and typhus, and Nazi raids. They'd survived with the help of the nearby partisans and a network of Christian farmers who had been their family's friends before the war. They too had been liberated by the Russians in the summer of 1944 and had returned to Zhetel afterward to mourn the loss of their loved ones. It's possible both families were even in the town at the same time.

Philip and his father and brother had also joined the Bricha, traveling across Europe through the American zone and finally landing in a DP camp in Bad Gastein, Austria, before also abandoning the dream of Palestine to join relatives in the United States. Philip was seventeen when he stepped off the pier in New York for the first time.

And now, five years later, he was working an assortment of odd jobs—tutoring students in Hebrew, cutting leather for car seats in a factory. He attended Brooklyn College while also pursuing the religious studies he so loved as a boy at Yeshiva University. Philip still lived with his brother and father, and his father's new wife, Feiga; they struggled together to make ends meet. Their Brooklyn apartment at 639 Rogers Avenue was just about ten city blocks away from 55 Sullivan Place, the home of Ebbets Field. He only had to lift his window to hear the sounds of the ballpark and pick up the announcers' voices shouting down the plays as the Boys of Summer embarked on what would arguably be the Dodgers' heartbreakingly best season ever.

As a more than full-time student, Philip scarcely had two pairs of shoes, let alone anything fancy enough for a wedding. But he was nonetheless eager to make friends, and so it was with a heavy chip of self-consciousness at his unfashionable hand-me-down clothes that he reluctantly attended that May wedding.

Philip was sorry to learn that the girl he'd met at that reception, Gloria Koslowski, the charming Brooklyn College student who was responsible for this very visit with the Rabinowitzes, had been killed. She had been a friend of Miriam's older daughter, he discovered, the one with the dark hair and the warm brown eyes.

It was otherwise a happy, emotional reunion. Before Philip got back into his cousin's car to leave that day, he promised he would come see them again. Miriam couldn't have been more delighted.

And see more of him they would.

❦

It was a sign of just how often Toby found herself in trouble, that when she heard all the shouting that summer morning, her first thought was, "Oh my god, what did I do now?" When the source of the uproar became clear, Toby was shocked—and then elated. For once, she wasn't the one in hot water.

It was the summer of 1952, and the Rabinowitz daughters, now aged seventeen and fifteen, had come to the Catskills to visit Luba and Ben in South Fallsburg, New York. Her aunt and uncle were the ones making all the racket and by the sounds of it, they were in a state.

The night before, Ruth had gone out on a date. At the end of the evening, she'd invited the boy back to the house. There was nothing untoward in the gesture, especially with the rest of the family at home. Ruth was just being polite. But when Luba and Ben had realized that she'd let the boy into their house, the pair of them hit the roof.

"It looks terrible!" they cried. "How could you? What will the neighbors think?"

The yelling carried on, but the idea that Ruth—who was still a certifiable goody two-shoes who had never broken a rule or a curfew—would cross the lines of propriety on a date was ludicrous.

Both sisters agreed their aunt and uncle were overreacting and that Ruth had done nothing wrong. Certainly, nothing that would've upset their own parents.

Now that Ruth and Toby were older, spending time with their aunt and uncle in South Fallsburg had revealed that there was tension in this home. The girls began to see the contrast Luba's marriage struck against their own parents' relationship, understanding a bit more the difference it would make to marry for love rather than convenience or comfort.

Marriage might have been somewhere ahead on the Rabinowitz daughters' horizons, but in the meantime, the Rabinowitz sisters were busy not just with boys, but with after-school jobs and extracurriculars. Ruth was making fifty cents an hour babysitting and both she and Toby modeled clothes for G. Fox & Co., the palatial department store in downtown Hartford that at one time was the largest privately owned department store in the United States.

By the time she was ready to graduate high school, Ruth's grades were so good that she was able to bypass the entry tests for college application and was admitted to the University of Connecticut. She was looking forward to heading off to the campus in Storrs, where she planned to pursue a business degree. In her high school senior yearbook, Ruth—or "Ruthie" as she's fondly called on the page—cut a starlet profile in a cream-colored sweater, her wavy dark hair short and stylish. The final line of her peppy write-up read: "College lies ahead if marriage doesn't get in the way first!"

Both Rabinowitz girls were a bit like their mother had been at their age. They enjoyed the attention they got from the opposite sex, but neither one had found a boy worth getting serious about. Whatever young men were in their lives, they were on the side. That is, until the summer of 1953.

❧

In the foothills of the Catskills, the Jews from greater New England, but more especially from New York City, would find sun and safe haven in the seasonal escape of a world built and run by their own kind. In the prosperous aftermath of World War II, the idea of the summer vacation expanded into widespread practice, and thousands of Jewish families began to make a mass exodus from the sweltering city heat to the cool lakesides of what would become known as the Jewish Alps.

The summer of 1953 marked the crescendo of the Borscht Belt's heyday. New Yorkers would drive their big cars to their bungalows and spend the season with their summer families. The greater American Jewish community was climbing the economic postwar boom along with everyone else and had disposable income and paid vacations to spare.

There was a place for everyone, from the super-upscale resorts to the down-home lakeside cabins. Even the ultra-Orthodox Jews had a number of kosher venues to choose from. The Pioneer Club was one of them. On the back of every postcard, the resort cast its jolly sales pitch:

> Gartenberg & Schechter's Pioneer Country Club. Modern and up-to-date hotel, superb location, beautiful lawns, all modern sports activities, large swimming pool, rooms with bath, social and athletic staff. Dietary laws strictly observed. Here truly is an adventure in luxury at modest rates. Please use Mountaindale bus and Mountaindale train.

It was at this establishment that Philip Lazowski had landed his summer job, which he was able to secure in part because he finally had his own car. One of the unforeseen advantages of this particular summer was that he was going to see Miriam Rabinowitz's older daughter, Ruth.

Before Philip had left the Rabinowitz house in Hartford that day, he had asked Ruth if it would be okay for him to write to her. Ruth hesitated, but agreed. *What harm would there be?* she thought to herself.

In the beginning they wrote back and forth about school and

there was nothing especially tender about their correspondence. But when he'd written that he would be working as a waiter at the Pioneer Club, Ruth shared that she would, in fact, be very close by, at her aunt and uncle's house in South Fallsburg, where she had a job for the summer.

It wasn't long into the season that they had their first date. Even with his summertime income, Philip was a bit skint. Instead of a restaurant dinner, he and Ruth went for a long stroll. It was a balmy summer night. The black sky was flush with stars and bright moonlight. Philip was so at ease in Ruth's company that he prattled on about his classes, letting one tangent carry into the next, perhaps to the detriment of romance. But if Ruth minded, she didn't let on. When the night came to an end, they made plans to see each other again.

As both Ruth and, especially, Philip were preoccupied with their summer jobs, neither of them had a lot of free time to spare. Ruth was working at a dress shop where she put her business classes to early practice by doing the owners' bookkeeping. Luba and Ben's house was busier that summer than it had been before. In March, Luba gave birth to their second child, a son they named Seymour. At the Pioneer Club, Philip was running all over the grounds doing a lot more than waiting tables. He was even tasked with administering insulin by needle to one very wealthy guest every morning. The woman grew fond of him. When resort management tried to send Philip home during *Bein ha-Metzarim* (the Three Weeks)—when many of the Pioneer Club's Orthodox vacationers paused their summer respites to observe the lengthy holiday and the resort suspended a good deal of their waitstaff—the lady wouldn't hear of it. As soon as she found out Philip was leaving, she called up the owner of the Pioneer Club and threatened to pack up her summer vacation right there and then. Philip was promptly reinstated.

As busy as Philip was, he and Ruth found time to spend together. They took a rowboat out onto Kiamesha Lake, just a few miles outside of South Fallsburg. Occasionally they brought along Ruth's cousin little Gita, now called Gloria, to liberate the six-year-old from a house with her new baby brother.

When the resorts packed away their lawn chairs and shuttered their pools at the end of the season, Philip and Ruth both returned to school—she to the UConn campus in Storrs and he back to Brooklyn—where their lives went on, much farther apart. Whatever spark there'd been between them during those months, it was left simmering on that summer's edge.

While Philip was overburdened with attending two universities and juggling multiple jobs and too busy for dating or having a girlfriend, Ruth had plenty of suitors—one from as far afield as Israel. A boy Ruth had met in Italy hadn't been able to forget her, and continued to send her letters. In one he included a photo of himself shaking hands with Golda Meir—well placed if not heavy-handed fodder to impress her.

It was no mystery why Ruth was attracting the attention of young men. The little girl with the round face had grown into young woman with a pinup figure, a reserved beauty in a college cardigan. She had a mind for numbers and continued to excel at her college studies. But she was as earnest as she'd been as a girl, and though she appreciated the male attention, she wasn't one to toy with anyone's affection. There was one fellow UConn student, a handsome member of her friend group, who made a special effort to monopolize her company when they all went together to watch football games. When he finally worked up the nerve to ask her for a date, Ruth, knowing that she had no future with a boy who wasn't Jewish, gently turned him down.

As the year went on, she spent more time with Philip. During winter break, Ruth traveled into the city for New Year's Eve. They huddled together in the cold at midnight and watched the great ball drop from the flagpole in Times Square. In June, Ruth returned to New York to celebrate Philip's graduation from Yeshiva University.

When the two reunited in the Catskills for another resort season in 1954, their romance began to blossom. Soon they were seeing each other as many as three or four times a week. Philip, back working at the Pioneer Club, would drive the fifteen minutes to South Fallsburg to pick her up and bring her to the resort. While he waited tables until late in the evening, Ruth danced in the ballroom. Philip didn't mind that she was having a good time without him, or even that she was being entertained by other young men. He was busy working and, having decided how much he liked her, he was just glad she was having fun. By the end of the summer, they were going steady.

For Ruth, however, getting serious about Philip Lazowski did not rest easy on her mind. While Miriam adored Philip, and was delighted Ruth was seeing him, Morris was concerned that his older daughter was getting involved with such a religiously observant young man. Yes, the Rabinowitz family kept a kosher home and attended synagogue on the high holidays, but the idea of Ruth becoming Orthodox did not sit comfortably with him.

For her part, Ruth had no desire to live a devout life or take part in all its labors of tradition. She was particularly apprehensive about the rituals that were laid at a woman's feet in Jewish Orthodoxy, like going to the *mikvah*. Finally, she sat down with a piece of paper and a pen and started to write Philip a letter, just as she'd done so many times before. As soon as she put ink to the page, all her emotions and apprehensions about what a life with him would mean came tumbling out. *Please,* she wrote, *I hope you will not expect me to go to the mikvah.* But as the letter went on, she wrote the words, *I love you.* And then she knew, her heart had already decided. This was the man she wanted to marry, *mikvah,* religion, and all. When she was finished, she tucked the letter away, knowing she would never send it, and that she would never need to.

One day in May 1955, Philip came to the Rabinowitz apartment in Hartford for one of his now regular visits to see Ruth. When they were alone for a moment in her room, he handed her something small and round. Philip didn't get down on one knee, there was no fanfare or grand speeches, just the simple offering he placed in her hand and Ruth's happy surprise. That afternoon, they met some friends in Elizabeth Park, and shining on Ruth's finger was a diamond engagement ring.

Seven months later, at noon on December 11, 1955, Ruth Rabinowitz and Philip Lazowski were married. It was a crisp winter afternoon, but the social hall at Beth David Synagogue in West Hartford, Connecticut, was full and warm. An arrangement of palms, white chrysanthemums, and pink pompons stood next to the chuppah.

The Society and Clubs section of the *Hartford Courant,* the city's premier newspaper, devoted an entire column to the affair. Their reporter gave full breadth to the event's details, from the bridesmaids' crystalette gowns with their "waltz-length skirts" to their "old-fashioned bouquets of coral flowers."

Naturally, Ruth, the bride, won the most attention on the page. "The bride chose a gown of Chantilly lace over white satin, fashioned with a scoop neckline, fitted bodice and a full skirt in a front with pleated net and ending in a cathedral train. Her fingertip veil of French illusion fell from a lace cap trimmed with sequins and pearls, and she carried a Bible adorned with stephanotis and an orchid." Missing from the clipping is how

Ruth's dark complexion struck a becoming contrast against the white of her dress, how her brown hair curled under her veil, and that her expression was at once serene and happy.

Toby, the maid of honor, carried carnations in the same shade of blue as her Chantilly lace dress. Six-year-old Gloria Sakier was the flower girl and her little brother, Seymour, who was just two years old, was the ring bearer. Morris and Miriam walked ahead of their daughter down the aisle to their seats.

Waiting for Ruth at the chuppah with his groomsmen, Philip looked smart in a black tuxedo and skinny black bow tie, a white carnation pinned to his satin lapel. Standing by his side was his brother Rachmil (now called Robert). His father, Joseph, and his wife, Feiga, were sitting nearby.

In a small sea of folding chairs, a crowd of family and friends sat watching. There were Luba and Ben, the Rabinowitzes and the Kruchevskys, but also Joseph and Dora Kogan and a host of familiar faces from the woods, including Tuvya Weinstein. Months earlier, when Philip had handed Ruth his list of wedding guests, she was startled to come across a familiar name. "I know him," she said. "That's the boy with the frozen feet!" When Philip was in a DP camp in Bad Gastein after the war, he made two very special friends: Willie Molczadski and Tuvya Weinstein. Although Tuvya hadn't come at the Rabinowitzes' invitation, they were certainly glad to see him.

For all the chairs occupied with familiar smiling faces, there was still perhaps a palpable loss in that room. On such a joyful occasion, how could the family not feel Chaya's absence, and that of the lost Lazowski children? How could they not wonder how many seats might have been filled? Or, had it all been different, would Gutel and Berl and Beyla have been there to watch their granddaughter marry?

When the afternoon of dining and dancing was finally over, Ruth and Philip changed into their traveling clothes and left Beth David Synagogue for their honeymoon in Florida. When the newlyweds returned to Hartford, school would be waiting for the twenty-year-old third-year UConn student and the twenty-five-year-old attending Trinity University's graduate program. But their adventure as a young married couple had just begun. Ahead of them was a whole lifetime they were eager to meet together, smiling and ready.

Epilogue

THREE YEARS LATER, ON THE EVENING OF APRIL 20, 1958, in a candlelit ceremony, Toby Rabinowitz took her turn down the aisle at Beth David Synagogue. She married her summer sweetheart, Richard Langerman, or as she called him, Dickie, a boy she met when they were both counselors at Camp Shalom. That fall, the twenty-one-year-old college junior transferred from UConn and moved to Chicago, where her new husband was starting law school.

Both Rabinowitz daughters were now married to Jewish men and beginning families of their own. A woman of her word, Miriam made good on her promise to Morris to move to New Hampshire, where, just like her daughters, she embarked on a new phase of her own life.

This was a peaceful period in the lives of Morris and Miriam Rabinowitz. They found new friends in Canaan and kept close the ones they already had. The lumber business that Morris worked to build—where his employees never called him Mr. Rabinowitz, but always Mr. Morris—thrived. Miriam discovered a passion for refinishing antique furniture and spent her time making old things beautiful. She took classes and learned how to cane a chair. They finally traveled to Israel.

They became grandparents. Ruth and Philip had three sons: Barry, Alan, and David. Toby and Dickie had a boy and a girl: Scott and Toni. At last, Morris got the boys he'd always wanted. When Barry was born, Morris arrived at the hospital to meet his first grandchild with a teddy bear in hand.

Eventually, Morris and Miriam bought a plot of land with a house alongside a lake, where they brought their grandchildren up from Connecticut and Massachusetts to spend the summers. Morris took the grandchildren fishing, Miriam peeled them apples. They picked blueberries. They bickered. Morris teased Miriam about her cooking. "*Epes iz felndik*. There's something missing," he'd say at dinner after taking a bite of her latest effort, infuriating her, and then he'd wink at the assembled company. While Morris worked in the yard, Miriam scolded him through open windows, yelling that he shouldn't be wearing his good shoes.

They were happy.

When her young grandsons would beg, "Grandma, tell me about the woods," Miriam would entertain them with details of their time in the forest. These bedtime stories thrilled the children. To them it was a fantastical, faraway place where their parents and grandparents loomed as large as the trees—heroes in their family's very own fairy tale.

The Rabinowitzes' New Hampshire home was an oasis for many of their friends and relatives. Every summer Solomon Golanski's family would make their annual pilgrimage to visit their cousins in New Hampshire. Young Alan Golanski, especially, loved these visits to Maeshke and Manya's house in Canaan. Morris would bring him along to the lumberyard, where the boy would sit on top of the woodpiles and help Morris tally the different kinds of timber.

By then, it was the mid-1960s, and Morris owned a huge stretch of property, including many rolling acres of woods. One summer afternoon Morris took ten-year-old Alan along with him on an expedition. Morris delighted the boy by pointing out the different kinds of trees and helping him hunt for salamanders. They followed the trail of brilliant-colored markers tied to the tree branches that signaled they were on Morris's property. After a while, they lost track of time. Soon it became clear they'd lost track of where they were as well. There were no more markers in sight.

The afternoon began to fade, and so did the light in the woods. Even though he understood they were lost, Alan wasn't worried—he was with Maeshke. Finally, they heard the sawing rumble of a lawnmower and they followed the sound until they came to a man riding the machine across a yard. He was neighborly, and directed them to the road. Morris and Alan walked all the way back to the car.

It was dark by the time they returned to the house, where Miriam and Etta Golanski, Alan's mother, were in a fit of worry. "Where have you been?" they demanded.

After all those years, perhaps it was the ultimate triumph over his past that Morris Rabinowitz, the man who navigated his way around one of the earth's last primeval woodlands, should get safely lost in a forest of his very own.

❧

For nearly twenty years, Morris and Miriam lived a good life in Canaan—content with their past and their present. Then, in 1980, Miriam was diagnosed with ovarian cancer.

By the time the doctors discovered it, the disease had already spread throughout her body. Despite the bleak prognosis, Morris insisted that Miriam have surgery, a new procedure he'd read about in the newspaper. It had saved the life of another woman with the same kind of cancer, he reasoned, so why not his wife, too? Miriam agreed to have the operation. Morris arranged a private room for her at St. Francis hospital in Hartford. For the entire month of her difficult recovery, he was by her side day and night. Afterward, Morris insisted they move to Miami Beach, where the sun was bright and warm, convinced it would restore her, as he believed it had once before.

"I saved her in the woods," he told his daughters. "I can save her now, too."

For a time, Miriam's health improved. But in the end, there was no earthly way to replicate the healing Morris had brought to his wife in the forest. Miriam died on January 19, 1981, at the age of seventy-three.

The following year, Morris became terribly ill. Ruth and Toby rushed to be with him. While Ruth sat by her father's bed in the hospital, Morris handed her a crumpled piece of paper. In Yiddish he had scrawled, *Ikh vil shtarbn. I want to die.* A few hours later, on December 13, 1982, he did. He was seventy-six years old.

Morris Rabinowitz and Miriam Dworetsky—Maeshke and Manya to all their friends and family—were married for forty-eight years, just shy of half a century. But if anyone was really keeping score, it might be more accurate to say that from the time the small spitfire laid eyes on her daring gambler, the two packed many lifetimes into the single one they shared.

That this couple, who suffered what they suffered—the war, the Nazis, and the forest—should come out the other side wanting more life, wanting more joy, defies logic. It is a testament to what extraordinary individuals Morris and Miriam were. More than that, it is a testament to the idea that life's true saving grace is just what we imagine it to be: love.

Author's Note

When I was six years old and my sister, Gail, was three, we took home first place in our synagogue's annual Purim costume contest. Many of the other girls came as Queens Esther or Vashti (costumes that entailed glittering gowns and headband tiaras), but my mother dressed us up as hamentashen cookies—the signature pastry of this holiday.

I remember wearing soft, shapeless brown fabric that vaguely resembled, or actually might have been, pillowcases. Which is all to say, I don't believe my sister and I won that contest because we had the most creative ensembles. Instead, it was likely that the person awarding the prizes that night felt a special affinity for us, the two curly-haired little girls dressed up like brown blobs. The judge of that competition was Ruth Lazowski.

My father likes to say that when he and my mother began searching for a Jewish community of their own sometime around 1984, their decision was cemented in a single moment. While touring Beth Hillel Synagogue in Bloomfield, Connecticut, a boisterous group of kids charged past my parents, bursting with anticipation to get to the end of the hallway. Waiting to greet them with his famous smile and pockets full of candy was Rabbi Philip Lazowski. "The kids just loved him," my father says. "That's when we knew we found our rabbi."

⸙

In 1962, just a few years after he and Ruth were married, Philip Lazowski was ordained. In 1969, he became the rabbi of the Beth Hillel Synagogue congregation. Ruth, who made a career in accounting work, also taught in the synagogue's Hebrew school. Together they became the much-adored stewards of this community for forty-five years.

Since I was five years old, the Lazowskis have been steady and beloved figures in my family's life. They have been to my parents' home for holidays and parties. They were with us to celebrate my thirtieth birthday. When they've taken trips to Los Angeles, they've visited my sister. On their travels to Washington, D.C., they've visited me. I call them Ruth and Rabbi.

Rabbi Lazowski presided over my bat mitzvah, and then my sister's three years later. He officiated my Grandpa Isadore's funeral, and then my Grandma Pauline's. He married my cousin, Michael, and his wife, Laura, but only after he guided Laura through her conversion to Judaism, while Ruth taught Laura about keeping a kosher house. Rabbi has visited my relatives who were sick in the hospital or grieving in their homes. He calls me Beckelah; Ruth calls me Becky.

In 1975, Rabbi Lazowski published *Faith and Destiny*, a memoir of his experience during the Holocaust. It is a powerful retelling of his childhood and his story of survival. Inside that story is his lifesaving encounter with Miriam Rabinowitz and how they were reunited after the war, which, of course, led him to Ruth.

Where I grew up in the suburbs outside Hartford, Philip

and Ruth Lazowski's Holocaust love story is the stuff of local legend.

It wasn't long after finishing my first book that I started to turn over the idea that there might be room to put the Lazowskis' love story into its own book. It was only after I first reached out to Ruth in October 2015 about the possibility of writing such a book that I realized how much of the story hadn't been told. There was an almost wholly unknown side of their combined history—Ruth's side, the Rabinowitz side.

In the months and years that followed I would discover the other love story at the center of this book: the one between Miriam and Morris Rabinowitz. I was introduced to two generations of women and brave sisters—Miriam and Luba Dworetsky, and Ruth (Rochel) and Toby (Tania) Rabinowitz.

On display in Ruth and Rabbi's house are the photographs Morris was able to hide away in the ghetto and carry with him to the woods, across the Alps, and into postwar life. Ruth showed them to me one at a time, holding each up as she told its tale. One shows Miriam as a girl with the ribbon-set curls, her face serious, almost pinched. Another stands out—it's the photo from which Morris had to tear away pieces of Polish while they were traveling illegally through Europe after the war. The third is the photo of Ruth and Toby in the family's Zhetel yard, just before the Germans invaded. The sisters are wearing their matching buckle shoes and wool coats with the same wide collars; they're holding hands and smiling.

Finally, Ruth pulls the fourth photo from the shelf. This one is of her kindergarten class. There are thirty children, boys and girls arranged in rows against a wooden fence at their Jewish school. Their teachers, two young women, are pictured too, each with her arms stretched around the students standing next to her. It is easy to see that it's a warm day—the girls are in capped-sleeved dresses and the boys are wearing shorts. The sun is bright and some of the kids squint their eyes toward the camera. Ruth remembers a few of her classmates, how she envied this little girl's embroidered blouse, how that little boy was always crying.

In a lineup of photographs of joyous family occasions—Philip and Ruth on their wedding day, glamorous and glowing, chubby-cheeked babies, grandchildren's bar mitzvahs—this one is haunting. "All of them were killed," Ruth told me as she set down the frame. "I am the only one in this photo who lived."

Also in the Lazowskis' living room is a painting rich with earthy warm colors. It's a scene of clustered wooden houses with drooping tin roofs and stout chimneys. There's a slanting fence next to a flower garden and a pumpkin patch. It's a cheery painting. Ruth purchased it from a hotel in Poland when she, Philip, and Toby went back for the first time in July 1993. It reminds her of Zhetel, the way she remembers it—or, at least, the way she chooses to remember it.

During that visit, twenty-eight years ago, Ruth, Philip, and Toby traveled not only to Poland but also to Lithuania and Belarus to pay their respects to their lost loved ones and to face their past. Their last stops were to visit their childhood homes in Bilitza and Zhetel. It was not like she remembered. The *kino* was gone. Berl and Beyla's house was still standing, as it had been after the war, but it had been remodeled and painted, stripped of its columns and its former grandeur. On the plane ride back, Ruth, overcome by emotion, put her feelings down on paper.

"I have longed to see my grandfather's house again," she wrote, "but it is no more. Gone are the Jews of Zhetel, all that is left are graves."

While they were there, Philip, Ruth, and Toby had visited

the mass graves on the opposite sides of town. In one was Berl, and in the other Beyla, Cherna, and little Simcha, as well as Philip's mother, Chaya, and his brothers, Abraham and Aaron, and his baby sister, Rachel.

On Yom HaShoah, Ruth would always gather her Hebrew school students together and talk to them about the Holocaust. She would say that it's "something that we should never forget. We should learn from it, and we should speak up when we see things wrong, not only just for Jews but for any people. We can't just stand back and watch it happen."

I can only imagine the impression this made on students who were the same age as Rochel Rabinowitz was during the Holocaust. (My mother still considers it one of the great misfortunes of my formative years that I did not have Ruth as a Hebrew school teacher. The year I was meant to be in her class, one of the upper grades was without a teacher, and Ruth stepped in to fill the vacancy.) In 1996, after one of her young students heard Ruth describe the doll that was snatched away from her in the ghetto, the girl returned to her class a few days later with a gift. It was a doll.

It's hard to know now, at the end of writing this book, how much these past five years have changed my impression of Ruth and Rabbi—they are still the life-loving people I've always known. It would be more accurate to say I understand better how remarkable it is that they are the people they are. People who have traveled the world over many times, always ready—even now—to take in all that life has to offer.

During my many visits to their house, I took whatever chance I could to admire that painting in their living room. I can understand what drew Ruth to it, now that I know what her home meant to her, and all the happiness she is still able to draw from those memories. The driving force in Ruth's heart is a true hunger for life. It has been there ever since she was Rochel Rabinowitz, hiding in the woods, knowing deep down that no matter what happened, somehow, they would survive.

Working on this book, I've spent countless hours in the Lazowski home, in a kitchen chair I have come to think of as my own. As Ruth opened her photo albums, her diaries, and her memories, there was more joy in them than I would have thought possible for such a dark and devastating time.

The afternoon when Ruth told me about her junior high talent show, where she performed the Italian song "Mattinata," we found the music online together—a rendition by Andrea Bocelli. She serenaded me right there in the kitchen. Ruth remembered every word and every note. She still loves to sing.

Acknowledgments

It's a delicate business, rooting around other people's pasts. Memories are personal and they are emotional. They are imperfect.

And this is a book built on memory.

In order to tell the story of the Rabinowitz family, decades of history had to be excavated, untangled, and deciphered, and then rearranged into order. Many of the details that color these pages were long thought lost, and many of them were mired deep in trauma.

The majority of that work fell to a small handful of people who provided the wellspring of information that enabled me to tell the Rabinowitz family's story and the stories that surrounded them—from Zhetel and Novogrudek, from the ghetto and the woods, from the war and all that followed. Chief among them, of course, were Ruth Lazowski and Toby Langerman.

Both Ruth and Toby gave me unconditional access and placed two lifetimes' worth of their personal experiences into my hands. There were times over the past five years when my communication with Ruth and Toby was almost constant. They took literally hundreds of my phone calls; they met my endless questions with endless patience. There were dozens of visits to West Hartford to talk with Ruth. When I left Toby's Brookline apartment after meeting her in person for the first time in August 2019, she sent me off with a bag of cherries for the ride back to Hartford. I've been on the receiving end of her generosity ever since. Toby's commitment to surfacing old—and sometimes painful—memories as she helped me piece together this story line was nothing short of heroic. (Many thanks to her grandson Zachary Krausman for his help collecting family photos.)

I am grateful for the trust Ruth and Toby put in me, and the faith they placed in this project. My affinity and admiration for these incredible women only continues to grow.

Rabbi Philip Lazowski was just as open with his time and his memories, as well as with his wealth of written material. Our many conversations added indispensable perspective and rich detail to the people at the center of this book. His contribution to this work means a great deal.

Special thanks as well to Colleen Braham, who has been a part of organizing the Lazowski household for years and who was always kind and helpful during my visits to their home.

All the Lazowski and Langerman children—Alan, Barry, David, Toni, and Scott—showed nothing but warm support and enthusiasm for this project. The memories they shared of their grandparents were essential to my understanding of Morris and Miriam's years in New Hampshire, and the last years of their life together. In considering the spirit of this family's legacy, it feels right and good to remember Jack Langerman, for though his life was cut much too short, the time he had was so well lived.

I'm especially thankful to have met Ted Winestone—or Tuvya Weinstein, the boy with the frozen feet—and his wife, Jocelyn, and daughter Rebecca Gerber, who graciously welcomed me into their corner of Memphis, Tennessee. Ted's remarkable capacity for names, dates, and chronology was essential for constructing a timeline of the Rabinowitz-Feldman camp's movements in the forest. At the end of my visit, when I marveled at his amazing memory, Ted was less enthusiastic about it. "It's not good," he told me. "The last week in anticipation of you being here, I haven't slept yet." But not once during our hours-long conversations did he refuse to answer a single one of my questions, no matter how unpleasant the memory. Ted was willing to talk as long as I needed.

Chaim Weinstein, another surviving resident of the Rabinowitz-Feldman camp, was kind enough to speak with me from Israel and send me *Zhetel, Our Town*, a book to which he contributed. "You're doing a mitzvah," he told me. I'm so pleased he thinks so. I owe thanks to his daughter Tsafrit Grinberg for helping coordinate our correspondence.

❧

There are two people whose steadfast support made the dream of this book a reality. Their enthusiasm for the Rabinowitzes' story and all its potential never wavered. When there was some early discouragement that a book about the Holocaust might be a difficult if not impossible sell, my agent Esmond Harmsworth brushed away the doubts. His certainty in our endeavors is always fortifying, his support is always reassuring, and his advice is never short of brilliant.

I will forever consider myself lucky that my editor at St. Martin's Press, Elisabeth Dyssegaard, waited patiently while I labored for months getting the proposal for this book to her. It is not lost on me what a gift it is to have the confidence of someone with Elisabeth's talents. This book is seeing the light of day in its best version because of her editing attention and care.

I'm grateful for the team at St. Martin's Press, whose time and expertise have been spent not only putting this book together, but putting it out into the world. Thank you to Jennifer Fernandez, Alex Brown, and Carla Benton for overseeing its production, and to Katy Robitzski, Michelle Cashman, Sara LaCotti, Katie Bassel, and Jessica Zimmerman for all the rest—from the publicity outreach to the beautiful packaging.

The facts in this book—which span all manner of wide-ranging World War II history, from obscure Nazi minutiae to Harry Truman's signature on a press release—have been safeguarded by the dauntless fact-checking abilities of Colleen Connolly and Hilary McClellen. Handing the book's passages over to them provided nothing short of sweet relief.

The same can be said for this book's copy editor, Bill Warhop. A formidable keeper of all things style and grammar, these pages benefited greatly from his corrections and attention to . . . everything. Many thanks as well to Rima Weinberg and Laura Michelle Davis for their page-proofing work on this text. Together, their comments and suggestions have ensured this book not only reads smarter, but *is* smarter.

The list of resources I engaged to educate myself on not only the Rabinowitz family but also the vast and complex Holocaust history that surrounded their experiences, is very long. And there were a great many people I enlisted to help me make sense of that material.

Thanks to Alexandra MacDougle and June Rain for their work transcribing testimonies and putting them into order. And special thanks to Ron Pricop for his Hebrew translation, and to Jerrold Landau, who helped me research and navigate the yet-to-be translated portions of the Zhetel Memorial book. It was with his assistance that I was able to find the accounts detailing Issy Rabinowitz's partisan activity and the circumstances of Meirim Dworetsky's death. Thanks also to Binny Lewis at the JewishGen Yizkor Book Project for his assistance in navigating this resource. And special thanks to Sam Menefee-Libey for lending a helping hand.

I owe a tremendous debt to Elise Bath at the Wiener Holocaust Library in London. Her dedication to tracking down multiple leads in the museum's International Tracing Service Archive produced absolutely essential documents and information that helped guide me to a far more complete understanding of the family's refugee experience.

When I traveled to New York in January 2020 to meet Tamara Vershitskaya of Novogrudek's Museum of Jewish Resistance, I didn't expect to find myself at what was essentially a Bielski family reunion. When it comes to partisan history, Tamara is an educational army of one. I'm also grateful to have made contact with Leonid Smilovitsky of Tel Aviv University's Goldstein-Goren Diaspora Research Center, whose depth of research on the Holocaust experience in Belarus is truly unprecedented. And thanks to Peter Duffy, author of *The Bielski Brothers*, and Jeffrey Cuyubamba, whose work charting the Novogrudek-Lida region enabled the very talented illustrator Kevin Tong and me to put together the map in this book.

I'm especially indebted to Allan Levine, whose book *Fugitives of the Forest* was by far the most comprehensive account of the broader partisan history I encountered. It became a compass I returned to multiple times as I worked to reconstruct the Rabinowitz family's experience in the woods. The comments and feedback he offered on my own manuscript were invaluable.

❧

After five years of research, I can honestly say that I know more about the Rabinowitz family history than I do my own. But reporting and researching this book brought me home in a way I would never have anticipated. The middle of this work happened to coincide with the onset of the pandemic, and I found myself in the entirely unusual situation of quarantining with my parents, Meyer and Sheila Frankel, at my childhood home in West Hartford, Connecticut. The experience brought our family—including my sister, Gail, and her partner, Nick Dominguez—closer together. It was an unexpected and special gift of time no other collision of circumstances could've provided. Those months reinforced what I already knew: They are wonderful people and I'm blessed to call them my family.

In the marathon of book writing, it was Jennie Rothenberg-Gritz who coached me across the finish line. I'm grateful to have had her thoughtful, compassionate feedback on multiple drafts of this book. I'm equally lucky to have had Karin Tanabe's support—every one of her book-writing pep talks was a straight shot of gumption. I'm very fortunate, too, that after nearly a decade, the incomparable David Rothkopf is still in my corner.

It's a wonderful thing to have friends who believe, without condition, that what feels impossibly out of reach is already within your grasp. The following people are those kinds of friends: Rachel Wozniak and Chris Wozniak, Michal Mizrahi, Claire Bohnengel, Brandon Van Grack, Erica Sandler, Sarah Longwell, Tenaya Britton, Jessica Pavone, Jeremy Berlin, Jackie Leventhal, Nick Vilelle, Hanna Berman, and Ty McCormick.

I owe a special kind of gratitude to Pete Kiehart. It was all grit and no glamour, but the care and support he provided during the final months of completing this book were nothing short of saintly. There was more happiness than should have been allowed, and for that I'll always be grateful.

❧

I knew early on that it would be impossible for me to rest the entirety of this book on the shoulders of two women who experienced the majority of these events (many of them horrific) as young children. A child's perspective is illuminating, but it is also limited.

This is how I encountered the people I have come to think of as the chorus characters of this book. These individuals may never have crossed paths with the Rabinowitz (or Dworetsky) family members, but they were there. They were in Zhetel and Novogrudek before the war, or in the ghetto. They were in the Lipiczany Forest in a family camp or fighting with the partisans. They were in Poland after the war or trying to find their way to Palestine. They crossed the Alps into Italy and were on the beaches of Santa Maria di Leuca or exploring the streets of Rome. Learning their stories gave me critical information and insight that not only helped verify the Rabinowitz family history, but contextualized it, and brought it to richer life on the page.

The full list of these individual accounts that helped to inform and shape the details in this book is far too long to include here, but I cannot close the pages of this book without acknowledging the following people, almost all of whom I will never be able to thank directly.

Brothers Morris Abrams and Irving Abramowich, and their lifelong friend Arel Laro, who throughout my research I fondly referred to as "The Three Men from Zhetel." Morris Rosnow and his partisan-fighter sisters, Sara Rosnow (previously Raznow) and Mira Shelub; Chaim Rozwaski and his sister Miriam Beigun; the surviving children of Herz Kaminsky: Samuel, Zelick, and Genia Krolewiecki. As well as: Gertrude Bayorski, Tina Nussbaum Benson, Ann Benjamin-Goldberg, Sonia Berenshtein, Miriam Miasnik Brysk, Rose Feigenbaum, Mina Fried, Jack Kagan, Isak Kleber, Gdalia Krolewiecki, Ruth Lapidus, Kalman Minuskin, Sonia Minuskin, Harold Minuskin, Sulia Rubin, Irving Shiloff, Marsha Taplin, Herby Troyetsky, Michael Zamkov, Sonia Zissman, and Harold Zissman.

These people left behind pieces of themselves—by giving interviews and recording their testimonies, by sharing their family photos and memorabilia, by writing memoirs—so that their stories would live on beyond their own lifetimes. These are the institutions that made it possible: the Shoah Foundation's Visual History Archive, the United States Holocaust Memorial Museum, the Fortunoff Archive for Holocaust Testimonies at Yale University, Yad Vashem, and the Jewish Partisans Educational Foundation. There's no limit to the gratitude I feel for the community of people who did the long, hard work of collecting these testimonies and preserving them, and then made them available to the world so that we will never forget these men and women and what they survived. Their efforts will also ensure that we remember those who did not live to tell their own stories.

❧

While doing some research on memory, I came across this line from Mary Karr's memoir *The Liar's Club*: "When the truth would be unbearable the mind often just blanks it out. But some ghost of an event may stay in your head."

I encountered a lot of ghosts while writing this book.

I don't remember the first time I heard Miriam Rabinowitz's voice, but I remember the second. When Ruth gave me the interview she recorded shortly before Miriam died, it was at the very beginning of this process; I listened to parts of it and then put it away. By the time I played it again, I'd been writing and researching for three years, by which point I'd conjured up a fully dimensional portrait of Miriam. I felt I knew her. Then, suddenly, there she was, a voice in my ear.

I think about Miriam a lot.

I think about that moment on April 30, 1942, when she chose to rescue eleven-year-old Philip, even though helping him meant risking her life and the lives of her daughters. I also think about Luba who, after days of hiding in their cramped ghetto bunker while a massacre was happening around them, volunteered to be the first one up out of the trapdoor to see if it was safe to leave.

From time to time, I find myself thinking of a woman the Rabinowitz family likely never knew. A woman who, understanding she was in the final moments of her life, stood up straight and fierce, to face the policeman who had just kicked her while she was on the ground and "gave him two such ringing slaps, that his snout was torn open and he was splattered from head to foot with blood."

The witness who recounted this moment only refers to this woman as Sastonovich, but he was there to see what happened next: "They shot her right away." I can't imagine the man she struck ever forgot her.

Neither will I.

Notes

Prologue

xiii the New York City Clerk's archive: "NYC Marriage Index, Brooklyn 1953," Reclaim the Record, https://archive.org/details/nycmarriageindex.

xiii Morning after morning: Philip Lazowski, author phone interview, June 12, 2018.

xiv spring wedding: Philip Lazowski, author phone interview, June 12, 2018.

xv The operator's voice: Philip Lazowski, author phone interview, June 12, 2018; Philip and Ruth Lazowski, author interview, March 3, 2019, West Hartford, CT.

xv *Jewish population of Europe in 1945*: United States Holocaust Memorial Museum Encyclopedia, https://encyclopedia.ushmm.org/content/en/article/remaining-jewish-population-of-europe-in-1945.

xvi *Gloria Koslowski's death*: "New York, New York, U.S., Death Index, 1949–1965," Philip and Ruth Lazowski, author interview, March 3, 2019; Ruth Lazowski, author interview, February 26, 2019, West Hartford, CT.

Chapter 1: A Wedding in Vilna

3 at the Vilna courthouse: Miriam Rabinowitz, interview by Ruth Lazowski, 1980.

4 *Vilna home of Saul and Batsheva Rabinowitz*: Simcha Ben-Shaul, *Childhood in the Holocaust* (Tel Aviv: Unpublished autobiography, 1997), 8–9.

4 *Morris and Miriam Rabinowitz's wedding*: Miriam Rabinowitz, interview by Ruth Lazowski, 1980.

5 *Gutel the widower*: Miriam Rabinowitz, interview by Ruth Lazowski, 1980.

6 *Rochel Dworetsky's funeral*: Miriam Rabinowitz, interview by Ruth Lazowski, 1980.

6 *Miriam's teenage years*: Miriam Rabinowitz, interview by Ruth Lazowski, 1980.

8 *Miriam opens a pharmacy*: Miriam Rabinowitz, interview by Ruth Lazowski, 1980.

8 "How much did you pay?": Miriam Rabinowitz, interview by Ruth Lazowski, 1980.

9 *Miriam refuses a matchmaker*: Miriam Rabinowitz, interview by Ruth Lazowski, 1980.

9 "I'm not going to marry": Miriam Rabinowitz, interview by Ruth Lazowski, 1980.

9 *Miriam in Hashomer Hatzair*: Ruth Lazowski, diary entry/personal papers, November 14, 2010.
10 *Morris's hands and hats*: family photos between 1945 and 1948.
10 "love at first sight": Miriam Rabinowitz, interview by Ruth Lazowski, 1980.
11 two years of unhurried courtship: Miriam Rabinowitz, interview by Ruth Lazowski, 1980.
11 "What are you waiting for?": Miriam Rabinowitz, interview by Ruth Lazowski, 1980.
12 lebensraum: Philip W. Blood, *Hitler's Bandit Hunters: The SS and Nazi Occupation of Europe* (Washington, DC: Potomac Books, 2008), 30–31, 42; "Lebensraum," *The Holocaust Encyclopedia*, United States Holocaust Memorial Museum, https://encyclopedia.ushmm.org/content/en/article/lebensraum.
12 *Blut und Boden*: Blood, *Hitler's Bandit Hunters*, 31.

Chapter 2: The Town Named After a Bird

14 *History of Zhetel*: Irene Newhouse, "Dzyatlava," *Today in Belarus and Lithuania*, https://kehilalinks.jewishgen.org/Lida-District/dzyat.htm; "Dzyatlava guidebook," *Shtetl Routes*, http://shtetlroutes.eu/en/dzyatlava-guidebook/.
14 *Grand Duchy through Second Polish Republic*: Ina Sorkina, "Dzyatlava guidebook," *Shtetl Routes*, n.d., http://shtetlroutes.eu/en/dzyatlava-guidebook/.
14 *Growth of Zhetel*: Newhouse, "Dzyatlava."
16 to see Lazerowich the shoemaker: Morris Abrams, Irving Abramowitz, Arel Laro, interview, Tape 3, 8:20–9:25. United States Holocaust Memorial Museum Collection, Gift of Charles Abrams, 1991, 1993.
16 *Vilna's Yiddish theater troupe*: Morris Abrams, Irving Abramowitz, Arel Laro, interview, Tape 3, 6:43. United States Holocaust Memorial Museum Collection, Gift of Charles Abrams, 1991, 1993; Mayhill Fowler, "Review of *Yiddish Empire: The Vilna Troupe, Jewish Theater, and the Art of Itinerancy* by Debra Caplan," *In geveb* (February 2019), https://ingeveb.org/articles/review-of-yiddish-empire-the-vilna-troupe-jewish-theater-and-the-art-of-itinerancy-by-debra-caplan.
16 *Boys singing in Zhetel streets*: Edward Hait, interview 7561, Tape 1, 7:30, Northbrook, IL, Visual History Archive, USC Shoah Foundation (hereafter, "VHA"), 1995.
16 "It was a very happy little Jewish town": Edward Hait, interview 7561, Tape 1, 9:30.
16 "All the towns near Zhetel": "The Way of Life in Zhetel," in *Zhetel Our Town: Commemorating the Sixtiety* [sic] *Anniversary of the Destruction of the Community of Zhetel 1942–2002*, ed. Chaya Lipsky, Rivka Lipsky-Kaufman, and Yitzchak Ganoz (Israeli Zhetler Association, 2002), xi.
17 *Muslim population in Novogrudek region*: Yehuda Bauer, "Nowogrudek—The Story of a Shtetl," *Yad Vashem Studies* 35 (2007): 5–40.
17 "Lefties, Righties": Morris Abrams, Irving Abramowitz, Arel Laro, interview, Tape 3, 3:30–3:50. United States Holocaust Memorial Museum Collection, Gift of Charles Abrams, 1991, 1993.
18 "An unusual city": Sonia Heidocovsky Zissman, interview, transcript, and recording, Jeff and Toby Herr Oral History Archive, United States Holocaust Memorial Museum, 1995, RG-50.030.0332.
18 *Rabinowitz home in Zhetel*: Ruth Lazowski, interview 25646, Bloomfield, CT, VHA, 1997, Tape 1, 5:50–6:20; 13:38–14:11.
19 "Oh, Maeshke, you had another girl": Ruth Lazowski, author interview, March 3, 2019, West Hartford, CT.

19 "I have to hang my own head": Toby Langerman, author phone interview, March 19, 2020.

20 Taibeleh: Toby Langerman, author phone interview, February 2021.

20 "little devil": Ruth Lazowski, author interview, April 30, 2017, West Hartford, CT.

21 *Berl and Beyla's house*: Ruth Lazowski, author interview, April 27, 2017, West Hartford, CT.

21 amply constructed: photo of Beyla: Jacob Weiner, *9 Generations: 200 Years of Our Family* (Tel Aviv: 1970), 48–49. Note: This book was not published for commercial distribution.

21 long line of rabbis: photo of Berl: Weiner, *9 Generations*, 48–49.

22 Cherna was full-figured: Photo, circa 1935, Rabinowitz family collection.

23 "I was Dworetska until the war": Miriam Rabinowitz, interview by Ruth Lazowski, 1980.

23 leadership of Marshal Józef Piłsudski: Stefan Korbonski, *The Jews and the Poles in World War II* (New York: Hippocrene Books, 1989), 7–10; Allan Levine, *Fugitives of the Forest* (Toronto: Stoddart, 1998) xxviii; Michał Leśniewski, "Piłsudski, Józef," *International Encyclopedia of the First World War*, October 8, 2014, https://encyclopedia.1914-1918-online.net/article/pisudski_jozef.

24 *Polish government anti-Jewish policies*: Yisrael Gutman and Shmuel Krakowski, *Unequal Victims: Poles and Jews During World War Two* (New York: Holocaust Library, 1986), 21. **Author's Note:** In their assessment of the Polish government's treatment of its Jewish community leading up to the German invasion of 1939 (after the death of Piłsudski), authors Gutman and Krakowski are careful to demonstrate that at no point did it actively condone or incite violence. But they do make a case that its clear lack of a robust and resolute response condemning "the increasing acts of violence and spreading atmosphere of violence, [while giving] its blessing to the economic boycott, i.e., the economic war against the Jews" was "interpreted as the government's acquiescence." On page 20, they quote sociologist Jacob Lestchinsky, who said that "it is impossible to accuse the Polish government of organizing savageries against the Jews. But it is possible, and necessary, to accuse it of laying the foundations of the pogroms."

24 "On the Principles of Catholic Morality": Allan Levine, *Fugitives of the Forest*, 2nd ed. (Guilford, CT: Lyons Press, 2008), xxix–xiviii; James Carroll, "Pope Francis and the Problematic Sainthood Cause of Cardinal August Hlond," *New Yorker*, July 11, 2018, https://www.newyorker.com/news/daily-comment/pope-francis-and-the-problematic-sainthood-cause-of-cardinal-august-hlond. **Author Note:** As James Carroll writes in his article, Hlond was "the Primate of Poland during the Second World War, and a famous opponent of the Nazis. Indeed, he was the only cardinal to be arrested by the Gestapo, which occurred in 1944, when he was in exile in France."

24 "the whip of God": Gutman and Krakowski, *Unequal Victims*, 20.

24 Radical nationalist groups escalated their protests: Celia S. Heller, *On the Edge of Destruction: Jews of Poland Between the Two World Wars* (New York: Columbia University Press, 1977), 115–19.

25 *Polish government fails to curb anti-Jewish riots*: Gutman and Krakowski, *Unequal Victims*, 19–22.

25 "Go to Palestine": Gdalia Krolewiecki, interview 44016, Tape 1, 18:30–20:09, Caulfield South, Melbourne, Victoria, Australia, VHA, 1998.

25 *Anti-Semitic signs on Zhetel's Catholic church*: Morris Abrams, interview 54994, Tape 1, 15:20–16:20, Houston, TX, VHA, 1994.

25 "The Church will not allow this to happen": Morris Abrams, interview 54994, Tape 1, 15:20–16:20.

25 *Priest cautions against bigotry*: Mira Shelub and Fred Rosenbaum, *Never the Last Road: A Partisan's Life* (Berkeley, CA: Lehrhaus Judaica, 2015), 12.

25 *Priest apologizes*: Morris Abrams, interview 54994, Tape 1, 15:20–16:20.

26 *Field trip to Warsaw and Gdynia*: Ann Benjamin-Goldberg, interview 11455, Tape 1, 6:55–8:00, Huntington, NY, VHA, 1995.

26 "In a way, Zhetel was a cocoon": Shelub and Rosenbaum, *Never the Last Road*, 13.

26 *News of pogroms reaches Zhetel*: Morris Abrams, interview 54994, Tape 1, 14:25–15:40.

27 "dictatorial powers unequaled": Frederick T. Birchall, *New York Times*, August 20, 1934.

Chapter 3: The Russians Invade

31 Wieluń: Alan Taylor, "World War II: The Invasion of Poland and the Winter War," *The Atlantic*, June 26, 2011, www.theatlantic.com/photo/2011/06/world-war-ii-the-invasion-of-poland-and-the-winter-war/100094/.

31 Białystok and Grodno, Łódź, and Kraków: Lionel Marson, "The Invasion of Poland," BBC News, September 1, 1939, www.youtube.com/watch?v=ktn_P5z5MK4.

31 *Warsaw is hit*: No author attributed, "1939: Germany Invades Poland," *On This Day*, BBC, http://news.bbc.co.uk/onthisday/hi/dates/stories/september/1/newsid_3506000/3506335.stm.

31 *Polish defenses destroyed*: Stefan Korbonski, *The Jews and the Poles in World War II* (New York: Hippocrene Books, 1989), 21–22.

32 *Morris leaves to fight for Polish army*: Ruth Lazowski, diary entry/personal papers, November 14, 2010.

32 *Jews of Zhetel decide to follow Polish troops*: Morris Abrams, interview 54994, Tape 1, 19:00–22:41, Houston, TX, VHA, 1994.

32 *Red Army invades Poland*: Jeremy Hobson and Jackson Cote, "80 Years After Germany's Invasion of Poland, a Look at World War II's Toll on the Country," *Here and Now*, WBUR, September 6, 2019, www.wbur.org/hereandnow/2019/09/06/poland-world-war-two.

32 *Poland surrenders*: Otto D. Tolischus, "Modlin Surrenders and Nazis Achieve War Aims in East—Distrust of Soviet Seen," *New York Times*, September 29, 1939; No author cited, "The Second World War," *The Holocaust Explained*, Wiener Holocaust Library, www.theholocaustexplained.org/life-in-nazi-occupied-europe/the-second-world-war/invasion-of-poland/.

33 fifty miles short of Zhetel: Morris Abrams, interview 54994, Tape 1, 19:00–22:41.

33 *Zhetel's Jewish residents welcome Russians*: Morris Rosnow, interview 40913, Walnut Creek, CA, VHA, 1998.

33 *Kissed the tanks*: Arel Laro, interview by Anthony Young, February 5, 1992, interview, transcript, and recording, United States Holocaust Memorial Museum, Permanent Collection, accession number 1992, RG-50.233.0065.

33 last fighting men of the Polish army: No author cited, "Last 8000 Polish Troops Surrender," AP dispatch, Berlin, October 6, 1939.

34 "The theory behind it sounded very good": Ann Benjamin-Goldberg, interview 11455, Tape 1, 19:00–19:52, VHA, 1995.

34 rounded up members of the Polish elite: Allan Levine, *Fugitives of the Forest* (Toronto: Stoddart, 1998), 13–14. **Author's Note:** Levine details the ruthless side of Soviet

rule and its brutality against the Polish population. He writes: "During the twenty-one months of Russian occupation, approximately 500,000 people, mostly men, were incarcerated. Torture and beatings were common, and at least 1.5 million Poles were deported to Siberia in unheated cattle cars. Half of them died en route."

34 "Nothing was private anymore": Sulia Wolozhinski Rubin, *Against the Tide: The Story of an Unknown Partisan* (Jerusalem: Posner & Sons, 1980), 49.

35 *Three Jewish families to Siberia*: Morris Abrams, interview 54994, Tape 1, 19:30–21:30.

35 *NKVD interrogations*: Chaim Rozwaski, interview 23619, Tape 1, 22:00–23:17, East Meadow, NY, VHA, 1996.

36 *The Belsky farm*: Ruth Lazowski, author interview, 2018, West Hartford, CT.

36 "Oh, you finished this time": Miriam Rabinowitz, interview by Ruth Lazowski, 1980.

37 *Soviet jobs went to Jews who spoke Russian*: Irving Shiloff, interview 3467, Tape 2, 5:00–5:45, Brooklyn, NY, VHA, 1995.

37 *Morris finally finds a job*: Miriam Rabinowitz, interview by Ruth Lazowski, 1980.

37 *Russians hunt for counterrevolutionaries*: Morris Abrams, interview 54994, Tape 1, 19:26–21:30.

38 *Novogrudek's Jewish population*: Yehuda Bauer, "Nowogrudek—The Story of a Shtetl," *Yad Vashem Studies* 35 (2007): 5–40.

38 keeping the light from entering Gutel's bedroom: Ruth Lazowski, author interview, February 2018, West Hartford, CT.

38 *Chestnuts delight children of Racelo Street*: Dov Cohen and Jack Kagan, *Surviving the Holocaust with the Russian Jewish Partisans* (Portland, OR: Vallentine Mitchell, 1998), 25.

39 "When your family left Zhetel": Ruth Lazowski, diary entry/personal papers, November 14, 2010.

Chapter 4: The Germans Invade

42 "Today at 4 o'clock A.M.": Vyacheslav Molotov, "Reaction to German Invasion of 1941," Fordham University, Modern History Sourcebook. Translation: https://sourcebooks.fordham.edu/mod/1941molotov.asp.

42 "German troops attacked our country": Radio address of the USSR's Chairman of the Council of People's Commissars and the People's Commissar for Foreign Affairs, V. M. Molotov, June 22, 1941, United States Holocaust Memorial Museum, courtesy of Imperial War Museum, https://collections.ushmm.org/search/catalog/irn1000646.

42 *Communique from Ribbentrop*: Raymond James Sontag and James Stuart Beddie, *Nazi-Soviet Relations, 1939–1941: Documents from the Archives of the German Foreign Office as Released by the Department of State* (New York, DIDIER, 1948).

43 "The Führer has therefore ordered": Sontag and Beddie, *Nazi-Soviet Relations.*

43 "Why did you sign the non-aggression pact": *World War Two: Behind Closed Doors,* PBS documentary series (2008), episode 1: 55:00–56:24.

43 "obvious absurdity": The German Ambassador in the Soviet Union (Schulenburg) to the German Foreign Office/Telegram/Moscow, June 14, 1941, https://www.ibiblio.org/pha/nsr/nsr-09.html#23.

43 Hitler had lied: Gustav Hilger and Alfred G. Meyer, *The Incompatible Allies: A Memoir-History of German-Soviet Relations 1918–1941* (New York: Macmillan, 1953).

43 late-April meeting in Berlin: Oleg Yegorov, "How One German Tried to Stop WWII," *Russia Beyond,* September 13, 2019.

43 "You can't stand in the way of destiny": *World War Two: Behind Closed Doors,* episode 1, 55:00–56:24.

43 the exact date and timing: Professor Richard Overy, "The Soviet-German War 1941–1945," BBC, February 17, 2011, www.bbc.co.uk/history/worldwars/wwtwo/soviet_german_war_01.shtml.

44 wiretapped phone calls: Jessie Greenspan, "When Stalin Was Caught Napping," History Channel, updated: March 11, 2019; original: June 22, 2016.

44 seventy-one border violations: Sontag and Beddie, eds., *Nazi-Soviet Relations*, 341–342.

44 "Soviets, Soviets, the war is coming!": Patrick Jackson, "Barbarossa Hitler Stalin: War Warnings Stalin Ignored," BBC News, June 21, 2011.

44 At 3:15 a.m.: Erik Sass, "Operation Barbarossa: The Biggest Military Adventure in History," *Mental Floss*, June 21, 2011, www.mentalfloss.com/article/28033/operation-barbarossa-biggest-military-adventure-history.

44 demolished nearly a quarter of the Russian air force: "World War II: Operation Barbarossa," Jewish Virtual Library, https://www.jewishvirtuallibrary.org/operation-barbarossa; Mitchell G. Bard, *The Complete Idiot's Guide to World War II*, 2nd ed. (New York: Alpha Books, 2004).

44 before Schulenburg had reached Molotov's office: Geoffrey Roberts, *Molotov: Stalin's Cold Warrior* (Washington, DC: Potomac Books, 2012), chapter 2.

44 "Victory will be ours!": Molotov, "Reaction to German Invasion of 1941," Fordham University, Modern History Sourcebook.

45 *German planes fly over Novogrudek*: Lyuba Rudnicki, trans. from Yiddish by O. Delatycki, "Under the German Yoke," in *Navaredok Memorial Book, Translation of Pinkas Navaredok*, ed. E. Yerushalmi and Alexander Harkavy, Navaredker Relief Committee (Tel Aviv and United States: 1963), 241.

45 *The Russians evacuate Novogrudek*: Dov Cohen and Jack Kagan, *Surviving the Holocaust with the Russian Jewish Partisans* (Portland, OR: Vallentine Mitchell, 1998), 36–37.

45 *Radio broadcasts from Moscow and Minsk*: Yaakov Kivelevich, trans. from Hebrew by Aviva Kamil, "On the Threshold of the Shoah," in Yerushalmi and Harkavy, *Navaredok Memorial Book*, 230.

45 *Russian occupiers don't show up to work*: Rudnicki, "Under the German Yoke," 241.

45 "See you soon!": Jack Kagan, interview 7715, Tel Aviv, Israel, VHA, 1995.

46 *Russians in retreat*: Kivelevich, "On the Threshold of the Shoah," 230.

46 *Distance from rivers and bridges*: Sulia Wolozhinski Rubin, *Against the Tide: The Story of an Unknown Partisan* (Jerusalem: Posner & Sons, 1980), 63–65.

47 *Families debate evacuating male members*: Rudnicki, "Under the German Yoke," 241.

47 *Rabinowitz family moves in with Dworetsky cousin*: Miriam Rabinowitz, interview by Ruth Lazowski, 1980.

48 *German advance, tanks and planes*: John Graham Royde-Smith, "Operation Barbarossa," *Encyclopedia Britannica*, www.britannica.com/event/Operation-Barbarossa; Sass, "Operation Barbarossa."

48 one hundred military divisions: *Time to Remember*, season 2, episode 11, "1941: Operation Barbarossa," produced by Peter Baylis, narrated by Anthony Quayle, aired December 31, 1963, British Pathé TV's History Collection.

48 fifty miles: Royde-Smith, "Operation Barbarossa."

48 under a mandate: Felix Römer, "The Wehrmacht in the War of Ideologies: The Army and Hitler's Criminal Orders on the Eastern Front," in *Nazi Policy on the Eastern Front, 1941: Total War, Genocide, and Radicalization*, ed. Alex J. Kay, Jeff Rutherford, and David Stahel (Rochester, NY: University of Rochester Press, 2012), 73–85.

48 "total war": Romer, "Wehrmacht in the War of Ideologies," 83.

48 stamp out Communism: Leonid Rein, "The Radicalization of Anti-Jewish Policies in Nazi-Occupied Belarus," in Kay, Rutherford, and Stahel, *Nazi Policy on the Eastern Front,* 220.

49 nine planes: Rudnicki, "Under the German Yoke," 237.

49 *Others ran to the castle ruins*: Rubin, *Against the Tide,* 63–65.

49 his own dismembered leg: Rubin, *Against the Tide,* 63–65.

49 *Wouldn't risk burial*: Kivelevich, "On the Threshold of the Shoah," 230.

49 thirty people were killed: Rudnicki, "Under the German Yoke," 237.

49 fires from the attack: Rubin, *Against the Tide,* 63–65.

49 She brought her hands hard: Ruth Lazowski, author interview, July 24, 2019, West Hartford, CT.

50 *Novogrudek loses government authorities*: Cohen and Kagan, *Surviving the Holocaust,* 38–39.

50 *Russian POWs*: Photographer unknown, "[German motorcycle troops and infantry pass a long column of Russian prisoners during the advance into the Soviet Union, 1941]," photograph from Imperial War Museum, https://www.iwm.org.uk/collections/item/object/205260127.

50 *Defeated Russian soldiers*: Shmuel Openheim, trans. from Yiddish by O. Delatycki, "The Days of Annihilation in the Nazi Hell," in Yerushalmi and Harkavy, *Navaredok Memorial Book,* 251.

51 *Returning home for Shabbat*: Rudnicki, "Under the German Yoke," 237.

51 abandoned property: Rudnicki, "Under the German Yoke," 237.

51 wails of the Stuka dive-bombers: Footage of German propaganda film with Luftwaffe Junkers Ju 87 Stuka, original source unknown, www.youtube.com/watch?v=5uvqhA4_2tU; Original source unknown, Luftwaffe Aerial Combat Footage of Ju 88, Me 109, Me 110, Stuka, www.youtube.com/watch?v=gJooYDwvWwo.

51 *Houses catch fire*: Cohen and Kagan, *Surviving the Holocaust,* 38–39.

52 bombing went on for hours: Yehoshua Yaffe, trans. from Yiddish by O. Delatycki, "They Burned the Town," in Yerushalmi and Harkavy, *Navaredok Memorial Book,* 74.

52 tidal waves, one after the other: Openheim, " Days of Annihilation in the Nazi Hell," in Yerushalmi and Harkavy, *Navaredok Memorial Book,* 251.

52 *In the bunker during the bombing*: Ruth Lazowski, interview 25646, Bloomfield, CT, VHA, 1997.

52 the city wouldn't go dark: Rubin, *Against the Tide,* 63–65.

52 choking cloud of smoke: Yaffe, "They Burned the Town," 274.

52 *Family surveys damage after bombing*: Miriam Rabinowitz, interview by Ruth Lazowski, 1980.

53 The man who ran a hardware store: Yaffe, "They Burned the Town," 274.

53 *Racelo Street destroyed*: Cohen and Kagan, *Surviving the Holocaust,* 138.

53 *Soldiers at the Alter family's house*: Rubin, *Against the Tide,* 63–65.

53 "Thank God, we got rid of Communists": Michael Zamkov, interview 23383, Tape 1, 18:48, New Haven, CT, Visual History Archive, USC Shoah Foundation, 1996.

54 *Cherna's fair skin and blue eyes*: Photographer unknown, Photograph of Cherna Rabinowitz, family collection, date circa 1935.

54 Cherna, holding Simcha: Ruth Lazowski, interview 25646, Tape 1, 24:49–25:17.

54 "Their house was bombed": Ruth Lazowski, interview 25646, Tape 1, 25:47–26:05.

54 burning in Lida: Morris Abrams, interview 54994, Tape 1, 22:27–23:12, Houston, TX, VHA, 1994.

55 *Thousands lose homes*: Yaffe, "They Burned the Town," 274.
55 *"Reisepass! Paszport!"*: Morris Abrams, Irving Abramowitz, Arel Laro, interview, Tape 4, 3:00–10:00, United States Holocaust Memorial Museum Collection, Gift of Charles Abrams, 1991, 1993.
55 *Morris's altercation with German soldiers*: Miriam Rabinowitz, interview by Ruth Lazowski, 1980.
56 *Spot on Morris's eye*: Toby Langerman, phone interview, March 19, 2020.
56 "Manya, remember where it is": Miriam Rabinowitz, interview by Ruth Lazowski, 1980.
56 "If somebody survives this": Miriam Rabinowitz, interview by Ruth Lazowski, 1980.

Chapter 5: Back to Zhetel

58 *Carnage on the road to Zhetel*: Chaim Rozwaski, interview 23619, Tape 2, 5:50–7:05, East Meadow, NY, VHA, 1996.
58 *German graves by the side of the road*: Chaim Rozwaski, interview 23619, Tape 2, 6:55–7:05.
59 *Soldier gestures with thumb*: Morris Abrams, Irving Abramowitz, Arel Laro, interview, Tape 4, 10:04, United States Holocaust Memorial Museum Collection, Gift of Charles Abrams, 1991, 1993.
59 *German soldiers hand out candy*: Mira Shelub and Fred Rosenbaum, *Never the Last Road: A Partisan's Life* (Berkeley, CA: Lehrhaus Judaica, 2015), 75.
59 gray eyes: Marsha Senderowski Taplin, interview 12746, Las Vegas, NV, VHA, 1996 (Family image).
59 "*Shada, shada*": Marsha Senderowski Taplin, interview 12746, Tape 1, 9:10–9:50.
60 "when the SS come": Arel Laro, interview by Anthony Young, February 5, 1992, interview, transcript, and recording, United States Holocaust Memorial Museum, Permanent Collection, accession number 1992, RG-50.233.0065.
60 Their trip by horse and buggy: Miriam Rabinowitz, interview by Ruth Lazowski, 1980.
60 Myetchansky Street: Miriam Rabinowitz, interview by Ruth Lazowski, 1980.
61 Issy tagged along: Simcha Ben-Shaul, *Childhood in the Holocaust* (Tel Aviv: unpublished autobiography, 1997), 64–68.
61 dig their own graves with spoons: Abrams, Abramowitz, and Laro, interview, Tape 4, 3:00–10:00.
61 *Bilitza rabbi tied to horse*: Philip Lazowski, *Faith and Destiny* (Barkhamsted, CT: Goulet Printery, 2006), 27.
61 "We came back": Miriam Rabinowitz, interview by Ruth Lazowski, 1980.
62 *Jurisdiction of* Gebietskommissar *Wilhelm Traub*: Yehuda Bauer, "Nowogrudek—The Story of a Shtetl," *Yad Vashem Studies* 35 (2007): 5–40.
62 posted their first decree: Yitzak Arad, Shmuel Krakowski, and Shmuel Spector, eds., *The Einsatzgruppen Reports: Selections from the Dispatches of the Nazi Death Squads' Campaign Against the Jews, July 1941–January 1943*, Holocaust Library (New York: Yad Vashem Martyr's Remembrance Authority, 1989), 43.
62 not allowed to walk on sidewalks: Sonia Minuskin, *My Children, My Heroes: Memoirs of a Holocaust Mother* (Prescott, AZ: Allegra Printing and Imaging, 2009), 1–2.
63 ages of sixteen and seventy: Morris Abrams, interview 54994, Tape 1, 28:45, Houston, TX, VHA, 1994.
63 report to the market square: Morris Rosnow, interview 40913, Walnut Creek, CA, VHA, 1998.
63 Shifra Dunyetz: Shelub and Rosenbaum, *Never the Last Road*, 75–76.

63 *Zhetel's most influential Jewish citizens*: Abrams, Abramowitz, and Laro, interview, Tape 4, 11:00–12:15.

63 "You stay. I'll go": Morris Abrams, interview 54994, Tape 1, 28:45, and Tape 2, 2:40–3:23, Houston, TX, VHA, 1994.

63 "There were no nice Germans": Morris Abrams, interview 54994, Tape 2, 2:40–3:23.

64 darted into the crowd: Chaim Rozwaski, interview 23619, Tape 2, 9:15–11:50, East Meadow, NY, VHA, 1996.

64 *Build a new road in Smolensk, SS lies*: Abrams, Abramowitz, and Laro, interview, Tape 4, 16:30.

66 "If you speak of this to anyone": Morris Abrams, interview 54994, Tape 3, 1:15–3:59; Abrams, Abramowitz, and Laro, interview, Tape 4, 17:20–1925.

67 first day of October 1941: "Zdzieciol (Zhetel)," *Holocaust Encyclopedia*, United States Holocaust Memorial Museum, https://encyclopedia.ushmm.org/content/en/article/zdzieciol-zhetel.

67 end of November: "Zdzieciol (Zhetel)," *Holocaust Encyclopedia.*

68 they shot her dead: Abrams, Abramowitz, and Laro, interview, Tape 4, 21:00–22:00.

68 rip the fur off coat collars: Abrams, Abramowitz, and Laro, interview, Tape 5, 00:30–2:00.

68 the coldest winter in the twentieth century: Harald Lejenäs, "The Severe Winter in Europe 1941–42: The Large-Scale Circulation, Cut-Off Lows, and Blocking," *Bulletin of the American Meteorological Society* 70, no. 3 (March 1989): 271–353.

68 averaged −4 degrees: Lejenäs, "Severe Winter in Europe 1941–42," 271–353.

69 taking axes to the beams of their homes: Morris Abrams, interview 54994, Tape 2, 6:10.

69 General Winter, General Frost, and General Snow: Boris Egorov, "'General Frost': How the Russian Winter Terrified the Country's Enemies History," *Russia Beyond*, December 13, 2018.

69 *German soldiers battle Russian winter*: Bruce C. Paton, "Cold, Casualties, and Conquests: The Effects of Cold on Warfare," *Medical Aspects of Harsh Environments*, vol. 1 (Washington, DC: Office of the Surgeon General, Department of the Army, 2001), ch. 10, 313–49.

69 "The Führer wants to know when Moscow will be captured": Paton, "Cold, Casualties, and Conquests," 313–49.

70 Kremlin's windowpanes: "Operation Barbarossa and Germany's Failure in the Soviet Union," Imperial War Museum, www.iwm.org.uk/history/operation-barbarossa-and-germanys-failure-in-the-soviet-union.

70 near unanimous vote—save one: "Tally Sheet for Declaration of War Against Japan," December 8, 1941, https://history.house.gov/Records-and-Research/Featured-Content/Tally-Sheet/.

70 Hitler declared war: Adolf Hitler, "Speech Declaring War Against the United States," December 11, 1941, Speech to the Reichstag, as recorded by the Monitoring Service of the British Broadcasting Corporation. Translation, Source: Jewish Virtual Library: https://www.jewishvirtuallibrary.org/hitler-s-speech-declaring-war-against-the-united-states.

70 4,500 men, women, and children: Dov Cohen and Jack Kagan, *Surviving the Holocaust with the Russian Jewish Partisans* (Portland, OR: Vallentine Mitchell, 1998), 45–49; 140–50.

70 temperatures that dipped to four below: the rabbi's testimony is dated March 20, 1942; see Cohen and Kagan, *Surviving the Holocaust*, page 150.

70 downy flakes of snow: Sulia Wolozhinski Rubin, *Against the Tide: The Story of an Unknown Partisan* (Jerusalem: Posner & Sons, 1980), 71.

71 While sipping cognac: Peter Balakian, "Wannsee: Place and Deed," *The Chronicle*, January 20, 2014.

71 debated, in horrific detail: "The Minutes from the Wannsee Conference, January 20, 1942," United States National Archives, Holocaust Education & Archive Research Team, www.holocaustresearchproject.org/holoprelude/Wannsee/wanseeminutes.html.

71 five hundred thousand Jews: Jurgen Matthaus, Jochen Bohler, and Klaus-Michael Mallmann, *War, Pacification, and Mass Murder 1939: The Einsatzgruppen in Poland* (Lanham, MD: Rowman and Littlefield, 2014), 154.

Chapter 6: The Ghetto

72 *Belsky brings bad news*: Ruth Lazowski, interview 25646, Tape 2, 1:23–1:43, Bloomfield, CT, VHA, 1997.

72 "Jews who leave their designated districts": Stefan Korbonski, *The Jews and the Poles in World War II* (New York: Hippocrene Books, 1989), 43.

72 shot on sight: Sonia Minuskin, *My Children, My Heroes: Memoirs of a Holocaust Mother* (Prescott, AZ: Allegra Printing and Imaging, 2009), 101.

73 "We'll want it back": Miriam Rabinowitz, interview by Ruth Lazowski, 1980.

73 *Zhetel ghetto description*: Arel Laro, interview by Anthony Young, February 5, 1992, interview, transcript, and recording, United States Holocaust Memorial Museum, Permanent Collection, accession number 1992, RG-50.233.0065; Pessya Mayevsky, trans. David Goldman, "This Is How We Lived in the Zhetel Ghetto," in *Navaredok Memorial Book, Translation of Pinkas Navaredok*, ed. E. Yerushalmi and Alexander Harkavy, Navaredker Relief Committee (Tel Aviv and United States: 1963), 373.

73 *Ghetto fence*: Arel Laro, interview by Anthony Young, February 5, 1992, interview, transcript, and recording, United States Holocaust Memorial Museum, Permanent Collection, accession number 1992, RG-50.233.0065.

74 pulling a heavy log: Chaim Rozwaski, interview 23619, Tape 2, 22:30–24:26, East Meadow, NY, VHA, 1996.

74 *Rabinowitzes move into a home that had belonged to a Christian family*: Ruth Lazowski, diary entry/personal papers, November 14, 2010.

75 *Zhetel ghetto rations*: Philip Lazowski, *Faith and Destiny* (Barkhamsted, CT: Goulet Printery, 2006), 35.

75 well after dark: Chaim Rozwaski, interview 23619, Tape 2, 25:25–27:04.

75 Meager rations: Minuskin, *My Children, My Heroes*, 3.

75 *Smuggling food into ghetto*: Miriam Rozwaski Biegun, interview, Voice/Vision Holocaust Survivor Oral History Archive, University of Michigan-Dearborn, 1983.

76 the novel as a call to action: Stefan Ihrig, *Justifying Genocide: Germany and the Armenians from Bismarck to Hitler* (Cambridge, MA: Harvard University Press, 2016), 2. Excerpt in *Tablet*, April 2016, www.tabletmag.com/sections/arts-letters/articles/from-musa-dagh-to-masada.

76 *Miriam Rabinowitz attends a séance*: Ruth Lazowski, interview 25646, Tape 2, 6:13–7:21.

77 "*Habe sich, tischele!*": Mira Shelub and Fred Rosenbaum, *Never the Last Road: A Partisan's Life* (Berkeley, CA: Lehrhaus Judaica, 2015), 81–82.

77 "Kitty-cat, you can't do that!": Pessya Mayevsky, trans. David Goldman, "This Is How We Lived in the Zhetel Ghetto," in *Navaredok Memorial Book, Translation of Pinkas Navaredok*, ed. E. Yerushalmi and Alexander Harkavy, Navaredker Relief Committee (Tel Aviv and United States 1963), 373; Shelub and Rosenbaum, *Never the Last Road*, 81–82.

77 swarms of crowing blackbirds: Marsha Senderowski Taplin, interview 12746, Las Vegas, NV, VHA, 1996.

78 *Matzah in ghetto*: Miriam Rabinowitz, interview by Ruth Lazowski, 1980.

79 *Death of Yoseph Rozwaski*: Chaim Rozwaski, interview 23619, East Meadow, NY, VHA, 1996.

79 "Can I look at your hand?": Ruth Lazowski, author interview, 2017, West Hartford, CT.

Chapter 7: The Resistance

81 Miriam and Luba started packing knapsacks: Ruth Lazowski, diary entry/personal papers, November 14, 2010.

82 *six hundred thousand Jews interned in ghettos*: Allan Levine, *Fugitives of the Forest* (Toronto: Stoddart, 1998), 52.

82 "We were like someone who is about to drown": Levine, *Fugitives of the Forest,* 52.

82 "*Fang den Juden!*": Ruth Lapidus, interview 20801, Tape 3, 7:17–8:21, Brooklyn, NY, VHA, 1996; Werner's Dog, Donner: An account of the Lida ghetto, Chaim Basist, "The Story of the House of Plotnik-Monco-Basist," Museum of Family History, 2008, www.museumoffamilyhistory.com/ce/ghetto/lida.htm.

82 "God, why can't I turn into a bird?": Ruth Lapidus, interview 20801, Tape 3, 8:33–8:40, Brooklyn, NY, VHA, 1996.

83 "That was my dream": Ruth Lapidus, interview 20801, Tape 3, 8:47–11:03.

83 *Gebietskommissar* Traub's headquarters: Dov Cohen and Jack Kagan, *Surviving the Holocaust with the Russian Jewish Partisans* (Portland, OR: Vallentine Mitchell, 1998), 51.

83 "In areas occupied by the enemy": Joseph Stalin, "Radio Broadcast July 3, 1941," Translation, www.marxists.org/reference/archive/stalin/works/1941/07/03.htm.

84 "partisan units and sabotage groups": Yitzhak Arad, *The Holocaust in the Soviet Union* (Lincoln: University of Nebraska Press, 2009), 505–509.

84 the most noticeable thing about Dvoretsky was his spectacles: photo, *Zhetel Memorial Book, Translation of Pinkus Zhetel,* ed. Baruch Kaplinski (Tel Aviv: Zhetel Association in Israel, 1957).

84 *Alter Dvoretsky education and family*: "Alter Dvoretsky as the Head of the Judenrat Until Forced to Transfer into the Ghetto," in *Zhetel Our Town: Commemorating the Sixtiety* [sic] *Anniversary of the Destruction of the Community of Zhetel 1942–2002*, ed. Chaya Lipsky, Rivka Lipsky-Kaufman, and Yitzchak Ganoz (Israeli Zhetler Association, 2002), xv.

85 "The Germans couldn't understand": Morris Rosnow, interview 40913, Walnut Creek, CA, VHA, 1998.

85 *Dvoretsky never under illusions*: Zeev Barmatz, *Heroism in the Forest: The Jewish Partisans of Belarus* (Tel Aviv: Kotarim International Publishing, 2013), 53 (Translated from the Hebrew by Anna Mowszowski).

85 "The Germans didn't come here to employ us": Barmatz, *Heroism in the Forest,* 53.

85 *Forging relationships with Christian Poles*: Mira Shelub and Fred Rosenbaum, *Never the Last Road: A Partisan's Life* (Berkeley, CA: Lehrhaus Judaica, 2015), 79.

86 preparing for a massacre: Barmatz, *Heroism in the Forest,* 53–63.

86 *Built trust with Soviets*: "Alter Dvoretsky as the Head of the Judenrat," xviii.

86 small dark eyes: "A Gathering of Zhetel Survivors, 1945," Minuskin Family Archive, Museum of Family History, photo, www.museumoffamilyhistory.com/pfh.dzyatlava-minuskin.htm.

86 "I am not trying to save my life": Arel Laro, interview by Anthony Young, February

5, 1992, interview, transcript, and recording, United States Holocaust Memorial Museum, Permanent Collection, accession number 1992, RG-50.233.0065.

86 The underground's first meeting: Arel Laro, interview by Anthony Young.

86 Dvoretsky was on edge: Morris Abrams, Irving Abramowitz, Arel Laro, interview, Tape 5, 4:55, United States Holocaust Memorial Museum Collection, Gift of Charles Abrams, 1991, 1993.

86 an oath of silence: Abrams, Abramowitz, and Laro, interview, Tape 5, 06:36, 12:10.

88 weapons hidden in the ark: Sonia Berenshtein, interview by Nathan Beyrak, June 18, 1993, Language: Hebrew, United States Holocaust Memorial Museum, Permanent Collection, accession number 1995.A.1272.10, RG-50.120.0010.

88 a three-act diversion: Leib Sholem Gerling, "The Underground in the Zhetel Ghetto," in *Zhetel Memorial Book, Translation of Pinkus Zhetel*, ed. Baruch Kaplinski (Tel Aviv: Zhetel Association in Israel, 1957), 372.

89 Vanya: Arel Laro and Irene Laro, interview by Anthony Young, February 5, 1992, interview, transcript, and recording, United States Holocaust Memorial Museum, Permanent Collection, accession number 1992, RG-50.233.0065.

89 "I want one of you to go with me": Arel Laro, interview by Anthony Young; Abrams, Abramowitz, and Laro, interview, Tape 6, 8:08–9:23.

89 face like a sparrow: photo of Shalom Fiolon, in Lipsky, Lipsky-Kaufman, and Ganoz, *Zhetel Our Town*, 59.

90 *Irene recognized Vanya*: Arel and Irene Laro, interview by Anthony Young.

90 the gun jammed: Gerling, "Underground in the Zhetel Ghetto," 372.

90 Razinsky, the blacksmith: Barmatz, *Heroism in the Forest*, 53.

90 "I will not betray you": Abrams, Abramowitz, and Laro, interview, Tape 6, 11:30–12:00; Gerling, "Underground in the Zhetel Ghetto," 372.

91 "How can you leave us in this moment?": Abrams, Abramowitz, and Laro, interview, Tape 6, 14:34–15:15.

91 Nothing Dvoretsky could say: Gerling, "Underground in the Zhetel Ghetto," 372.

91 Dvoretsky's wife and mother: Tamara Vershitskaya and Avinoam Patt, "Zdzieciol" (Zhetel); *Encyclopedia of Camps and Ghettos, 1933–1945*.

91 a bounty of 25,000: "Catching Shalom Fyulon," in *Zhetel Our Town: Commemorating the Sixtiety* [sic] *Anniversary of the Destruction of the Community of Zhetel 1942–2002*, ed. Chaya Lipsky, Rivka Lipsky-Kaufman, and Yitzchak Ganoz (Israeli Zhetler Association, 2002), VII.

Chapter 8: The First Selection and the Boy from Bilitza

92 Philip Lazowski was wide awake: Philip Lazowski, *Faith and Destiny* (Barkhamsted, CT: Goulet Printery, 2006), 39; Philip Lazowski, interview 25650, Tape 1 and 2, Bloomfield, CT, VHA, 1997.

93 They lived in a comfortable white house: Lazowski, *Faith and Destiny*, 8–9.

94 single tooth extraction: Lazowski, *Faith and Destiny*, 12.

95 Gestapo and the Lithuanian officers: Lazowski, *Faith and Destiny*, 39; Tape 1 and 2, Bloomfield, CT. VHA, 1997.

95 "*Raus! Raus! Raus!*": Morris Rosnow, interview 40913, Tape 4, 2:17, Walnut Creek, CA, VHA, 1998.

96 "I came back for my coat": M. A. C. Lynch, "Ruth and Rabbi Philip Lazowski: Holocaust Survivors Reunited in Hartford," *Hartford Courant*, July 10, 2011.

96 The Jews called these militia men crows: Chaim Leibovitz, trans. O. Delatycki, "The Great Destruction, A. 'How 300 Jews saved themselves,'" in *Navaredok Me-*

morial Book, Translation of Pinkas Navaredok, ed. E. Yerushalmi and Alexander Harkavy, Navaredker Relief Committee (Tel Aviv and United States: 1963), 498–507.

96 "A Reminder to the Belorussian Policeman": Leonid Smilovitsky, *Holocaust in Belorussia, 1941–1944*, trans. Judith Springer (Tel Aviv, 2000), 349. **Author Note:** The pamphlet advised these forces to "remember that alcohol is no less an enemy of yours than the Bolsheviks. By being drunk, you poison your body and soul and disgrace the name 'policeman' before the people. Only sober people can conscientiously perform the honorable duties of policemen in the struggle against Bolshevism."

97 *Traub's boots*: Morris Rosnow, interview 40913, Tape 4, 2:30.

97 dancing to music only they could hear: Philip Lazowski, interview 25650, Tape 1, 20:26–20:44.

97 beautiful spring day: "Chaim Weinstein Who Was 12 at This Time—A Story of a Survivor," in *Zhetel Our Town: Commemorating the Sixtiety* [sic] *Anniversary of the Destruction of the Community of Zhetel 1942–2002*, ed. Chaya Lipsky, Rivka Lipsky-Kaufman, and Yitzchak Ganoz (Israeli Zhetler Association, 2002), xviii. **Author Note:** A high-ranking SS officer spotted Lazerowich, the shoemaker in line, and approached him with a register of surprise on his face. "What are you doing here?" he demanded. The question was absurd, but this man—Jew or not—was the one who made the officer's boots, and so he told the elder Lazerowich to collect his family and they were sent back home to the ghetto.

98 "Don't stand next to us": Philip Lazowski, interview 25650, Tape 1, 21:15–21:23.

98 gathering to check papers: Miriam Rabinowitz, interview by Ruth Lazowski, 1980. **Author Note:** Miriam explained in 1980: "When the first selection came, we thought they said controller of documents. And since we had documents, we thought we are safe. So, we went to the Marketplace. We went there and they made a selection, and that is when Philip came to us."

98 black leather trench coat, a giant dog: Sara Rosnow, interview 41158, Tape 2, 22:00, Walnut Creek, CA, VHA, 1998.

99 "If the Nazis let me live with two children": Ruth Lazowski, author interview, April 2017, West Hartford, CT.

99 Her young face: "Sara Rosnow: A Young Woman in the Forest: A Jewish Partisan Story of Survival," Jewish Partisan Educational Foundation, Jewish Partisan Community, www.jewishpartisancommunity.org/partisans/sara-rosnow/.

100 held on to her grandchildren: Sara Rosnow, interview 41158, Tape 2, 23:54–24:38.

100 "I'm only a grandmother!": Morris Rosnow, interview 40913, Tape 4, 5:25–6:27; Sara Rosnow, interview 41158, Tape 2, 23:54–24:38.

100 safety pin: Ruth Lazowski, author interview, April 2017, West Hartford, CT.

100 "*Das ist mein Mann!*" Ruth Lazowski, interview, April 2017, West Hartford, CT.

101 Bashe Rozwaski and her children were in this unfortunate group: Chaim Rozwaski, interview 23619, Tape 3, 8:29–11:30, East Meadow, NY, VHA, 1996.

102 *Gebietskommissar* Traub: "Chaim Weinstein Who Was 12 at This Time," xviii; Chaim Rozwaski, interview 23619, Tape 3, 11:35–12:20.

103 Bashe Rozwaski was still holding her infant son: Miriam Rozwaski Biegun, interview, Voice/Vision Holocaust Survivor Oral History Archive, University of Michigan-Dearborn, 1983.

103 he noticed one old woman crying silently: Chaim Rozwaski, interview 23619, Tape 3, 14:12.

103 someone brought the Rozwaski family a shawl: Miriam Rozwaski Biegun, interview, 1983.
103 *Last-minute reprieve by pits*: "Chaim Weinstein Who Was 12 at This Time," xviii.
103 *Nazis run out of ammunition*: Philip Lazowski, interview 25650, Tape 1, 25:00.
104 *Judith Moszkowski climbs out of mass grave*: Sara Rosnow, interview 41158, Tape 2, 24:30.

Chapter 9: The Escape

106 piles of sand: Toby Langerman, author phone interview, 2018; Ruth Lazowski, author interview, February 2018, West Hartford, CT; Toby Langerman, author interview, August 2019, Brookline, MA.
106 *Cooperman house residents*: Miriam Rabinowitz, interview by Ruth Lazowski, 1980.
107 Skron *in Coopermans' garage*: Ruth Lazowski, author interviews, July 2016, April 2017, February 2018, West Hartford, CT.
108 professed envy: Sonia Minuskin, *My Children, My Heroes: Memoirs of a Holocaust Mother* (Prescott, AZ: Allegra Printing and Imaging, 2009), 8.
108 *deliberated suicide by poison*: Minuskin, *My Children, My Heroes*, 3.
108 *mothers dress children in grown-up wardrobe*: Pessya Mayevsky, trans. David Goldman, "This Is How We Lived in the Zhetel Ghetto," in *Navaredok Memorial Book, Translation of Pinkas Navaredok*, ed. E. Yerushalmi and Alexander Harkavy, Navaredker Relief Committee (Tel Aviv and United States: 1963), 373.
108 "*Mein Herr*, let me live": Mayevsky, "This Is How We Lived in the Zhetel Ghetto," 373.
109 "You shed more tears for that doll": Toby Langerman, author phone interview, April 25, 2020.
110 "I see the woman who saved my life!": Philip Lazowski, *Faith and Destiny* (Barkhamsted, CT: Goulet Printery, 2006), 46.
111 *Nazi troops storm the ghetto*: Lazowski, *Faith and Destiny*, 55.
111 He had to try: Ruth Lazowski, interview 25646, Tape 3, 1:50–2:40, Bloomfield, CT, VHA, 1997.
112 "Find the forester": Ruth Lazowski, author interview, July 31, 2016, West Hartford, CT.
112 *Loudspeaker in the ghetto*: Mira Shelub and Fred Rosenbaum, *Never the Last Road: A Partisan's Life* (Berkeley, CA: Lehrhaus Judaica, 2015), 86.
112 impenetrable ring: Arel Laro, interview by Anthony Young, February 5, 1992, interview, transcript, and recording, United States Holocaust Memorial Museum, Permanent Collection, accession number 1992, RG-50.233.0065.
113 *Schneider!* (Tailor!) *Schuster!*: Morris Abrams, Irving Abramowitz, Arel Laro, interview, Tape 6, 27:38–29:00, United States Holocaust Memorial Museum Collection, Gift of Charles Abrams, 1991, 1993.
113 "Go": Ruth Lazowski, interview 25646, Tape 3, 16:15–17:25.
113 *Lazerowich the shoemaker*: Abrams, Abramowitz, and Laro, interview, Tape 6, 4:00.
113 locked eyes: Abrams, Abramowitz, and Laro, interview, Tape 6, 29:30.
113 two hundred tradesmen: Arel Laro, interview by Anthony Young.
114 put on trucks: Morris Abrams, interview 54994, Tape 3, end, Tape 4, beginning, Houston, TX, VHA, 1994.
114 *Conditions inside the* kino: Abrams, Abramowitz, and Laro, interview, Tape 6, end, Tape 7, beginning; Lazowski, *Faith and Destiny*, 61.
114 *Judenrein*: Leonid Smilovitsky, "Ghettos in the Gomel Region: Commonalities and Unique Features, 1941–42," Tel Aviv University, https://www.jewishgen.org/Belarus/newsletters/gomel/GomelGhettos/index.html.

114 "It's over!": Abrams, Abramowitz, and Laro, interview, Tape 6, 35:10.

115 "Who has relatives hiding?": Morris Abrams, interview 54994, Tape 3, 3:59.

115 "My family was killed already": author Ruth Lazowski, interviews, April 2017, February 2018, West Hartford, CT.

115 As the hours passed: Ruth Lazowski, interview 25646, Tape 3, 2:00–4:11.

116 gunshots and cries: Morris Rosnow, interview 40913, Tape 4, 15:40–16:40, Walnut Creek, CA, VHA, 1998.

116 "Jews were here": Ruth Lazowski, interview 25646, Tape 3, 3:04–3:30; Tania Langerman, interview 16470, Tape 1, 11:32–11:55, Brookline, MA, VHA, 1996.

117 *Coopermans' daughter-in-law hysterical*: Toby Langerman, author interview, August 7, 2019, Brookline, MA; Tania Langerman, interview 16470, Tape 1, 12:50–13:00.

117 "We better be quiet": Ruth Lazowski, author interviews, July 2016, 2018, West Hartford, CT; Ruth Lazowski, interview 25646, Tape 3, 3:29–3:54; Toby Langerman, author interview, August 7, 2019, Brookline, MA; Tania Langerman, interview 16470, Tape 1, 12:00–12:40.

117 could hear the moans: Marsha Senderowski Taplin, interview 12746, Las Vegas, NV, VHA, 1996.

117 One mother watched: Minuskin, *My Children, My Heroes,* 10.

117 Another dabbed urine: Minuskin, *My Children, My Heroes,* 10.

118 second day of hiding: Sonia Berenshtein, interview by Nathan Beyrak, June 18, 1993, Language: Hebrew, United States Holocaust Memorial Museum, Permanent Collection, accession number 1995.A.1272.10, RG-50.120.0010.

118 saw that a woman with a baby: Shelub and Rosenbaum, *Never the Last Road,* 87.

118 One moment he was crying: Morris Rosnow, interview 40913, Tape 4, 14:30–15:30.

118 When they left, they took the child: Miriam Rozwaski Biegun, interview, Voice/Vision Holocaust Survivor Oral History Archive, University of Michigan-Dearborn, 1983.

119 *two mothers in tunnel*: Anonymous, Bilitza, Zhetel, Dvoretz Survivor. The interview is in Hebrew, RG-50.120.0144, Jeff and Toby Herr Oral History Archive, United States Holocaust Memorial Museum, May 6, 1993.

119 "We knew. We knew": Samuel Kaminsky, interview 38977, Tape 3, 12:15, Melbourne, Victoria, Australia, VHA, 1997.

119 *Conditions in the* kino: Morris Abrams, interview 54994, Tape 3, 3:59.

120 "I'll have you in hell": Ruth Lazowski, author interview, 2016, West Hartford, CT; Ruth Lazowski, author interview, April 30, 2017, West Hartford, CT.

120 "Maeshke, I have a way to get into the attic": Ruth Lazowski, author interview, April 2017, West Hartford, CT; Ruth Lazowski, interview 25646, Tape 3, 18:48–19:36.

121 *Final workers put on trucks*: Abrams, Abramowitz, and Laro, interview, Tape 6, end, Tape 7, beginning.

121 *Inside the* skron: Ruth Lazowski, interview, July 2016, West Hartford, CT.

122 *Luba volunteers to leave the bunker*: Toby Langerman, author interview, August 2019, Brookline, MA; Tania Langerman, interview 16470, Tape 1, 13:30.

122 "Manya, lift up the kids": Ruth Lazowski, interview, July 31, 2016, West Hartford, CT.

123 "I'm not going with her": Toby Langerman, author interview, August 2019, Brookline, MA.

123 no lights in the ghetto: Marsha Senderowski Taplin, interview 12746, Tape 1, 24:28–25:50.

123 "Where is *Rocheleh*?": Ruth Lazowski, author interviews, July 2016, April 2017, February 2019, West Hartford, CT.

124 air was bitterly cold: Samuel Kaminsky, interview 38977, Tape 3, 13:47.

124 black coat: Ruth Lazowski, interview, February 2019, West Hartford, CT.
124 "Your mother left you": Ruth Lazowski, author interview, July 2016, West Hartford, CT.
124 "*Rocheleh*, where are you?": Ruth Lazowski, author interview, July 2016, West Hartford, CT.
125 "I could hear the weak and feeble": Minuskin, *My Children, My Heroes*, 15.
128 "Manya, are you crazy?": Ruth Lazowski, author interview, July 2016, West Hartford, CT.
128 "My God, she's lost her mind": Tania Langerman, interview 16470, Tape 1, 15:00–15:23.
128 "If I had known what was waiting": Toby Langerman, author interview, August 7, 2019, Brookline, MA.

Chapter 10: The First Winter

131 last remaining primeval woodlands: World Heritage Data Sheet, page 6, http://www.yichuans.me/datasheet/output/site/bialowieza-forest/.
131 580 square miles: Bogdan Jaroszewicz, Olga Cholewińska, Jerzy M. Gutowski, Tomasz Samojlik, Marcelina Zimny, and Małgorzata Latałowa, "Białowieża Forest—A Relic of the High Naturalness of European Forests," *Forests* 10 (10) (September 29, 2019): 849, https://www.mdpi.com/1999-4907/10/10/849.
131 180 feet above the forest floor: Jaroszewicz et al., "Białowieża Forest."
131 six feet in diameter: Jaroszewicz et al., "Białowieża Forest."
132 Russian czars: Erik Hoffner, "Forest Medieval: Poland's Bialowieza Is One of the Only Old Growth Forests in Europe. Despite Being a World Heritage Site, It's Threatened by Logging," *Earth Island Journal* (Winter 2010), www.earthisland.org/journal/index.php/magazine/entry/forest_medieval/.
133 running from towns: Yitzhak Arad, *The Holocaust in the Soviet Union* (Lincoln: University of Nebraska Press, 2009), 508.
134 torn the yellow *Juden* stars: Mira Shelub and Fred Rosenbaum, *Never the Last Road: A Partisan's Life* (Berkeley, CA: Lehrhaus Judaica, 2015), 94.
134 devout Christian woman: Sonia Minuskin, *My Children, My Heroes: Memoirs of a Holocaust Mother* (Prescott, AZ: Allegra Printing and Imaging, 2009), 17–19.
135 kissed the dirt in thanks: Morris Rosnow, interview 40913, Tape 5, 14:00, Walnut Creek, CA, VHA, 1998.
135 *Familiar faces around the campfire*: Morris Abrams, Irving Abramowitz, Arel Laro, interview, Tape 8, 00:32, United States Holocaust Memorial Museum Collection, Gift of Charles Abrams, 1991, 1993.
135 eight hundred Jews from Zhetel: Abrams, Abramowitz, and Laro, interview, Tape 8, 4:00.
136 *Morris and Miriam set off for supplies*: Ruth Lazowski, interview 25646, Tape 3, 20:35–21:40, Bloomfield, CT, VHA, 1997.
137 *Peeling birch bark*: Ruth Lazowski, interview 25646, Tape 3, 21:54–22:22.
137 "He had maps in his head": Ted Winestone, interview 15385, Tape 6, 8:46, Memphis, TN, VHA, 1996.
138 "You don't belong to anybody": Sulia Wolozhinski Rubin, *Against the Tide: The Story of an Unknown Partisan* (Jerusalem: Posner & Sons, 1980), 115.
140 singing songs: Herby Troyetsky, interview 22740, Tape 4, 8:27–9:17, Long Island, NY, VHA, 1996.

141 "the worst give away in the woods": Ted Winestone, interview 15385, Tape 5, 22:00, and Tape 7, 26:00.

141 "Rabinovich was the man to follow": Ted Winestone, author interview, February 2020, Memphis, TN.

141 advertised reward: "Eyewitness Testimony 55: Children in the Forest, Y.L. Born in Bielcia in 1933," recorded by A. Yerushalmi in Tel Aviv, Israel, 1947, in *Jewish Responses to Nazi Persecution,* ed. Isaiah Trunk (New York: Stein and Day, 1979), 302–4.

141 single cup of sugar: "Eyewitness Testimony 23. Life in the Lublin Forest," in *Jewish Responses to Nazi Persecution,* ed. Isaiah Trunk (New York: Stein and Day, 1979), 169.

141 active or just passive humanitarians: Leon Smilovitsky, "Jewish Family Camps and Groups in Belarus, 1941–1944," Diaspora Research Center of Tel Aviv University, trans. Anya Karasik, www.jewishgen.org/yizkor/belarus/bel119.html#6.

142 "Here, everything is ours": Gertrude Salutski Boyarski, interview 2633, Tape 2, 7:04–9:30, West Palm Beach, FL, VHA, 1995.

143 belt of grenades around his waist: Minuskin, *My Children, My Heroes,* 113. **Author's Note:** This section of the book is attributed to material from a relative's book: Kalman Minuskin, *The Ghetto in the Forest* (Kfar Saba: self-published in Hebrew, 1990).

144 *Kitchens and a bakery*: Herby Troyetsky, interview 22740, Tape 4, 6:14.

144 Kolya: Shelub and Rosenbaum, *Never the Last Road,* 96.

144 *Kaplinsky and Atlas brigades*: Arad, *Holocaust in the Soviet Union,* 508–9.

144 *Partisan missions*: Arad, *Holocaust in the Soviet Union,* 508–9.

144 *Partisan operations in the fall of 1942*: Moshe Kahanowitz, "Organizers and Commanders," in *The Ghetto Fighters: The True Story of the Jews Who Fought a Gallant but Hopeless War Against the Nazi Hordes sent to Destroy Them,* trans. and ed. Meyer Barkai (New York: Belmont Tower Books, 1962), 137.

144 *Battle in Ruda Yavorska*: Minuskin, *My Children, My Heroes,* 113. Note: This section of the book is attributed to material from a relative's book: Kalman Minuskin, *The Ghetto in the Forest* (Kfar Saba: self-published in Hebrew, 1990); "The Zhetler Battalion Attacks German Strongholds in Towns and Villages," in *Zhetel Our Town: Commemorating the Sixtiety* [sic] *Anniversary of the Destruction of the Community of Zhetel 1942–2002,* ed. Chaya Lipsky, Rivka Lipsky-Kaufman, and Yitzchak Ganoz (Israeli Zhetler Association, 2002), xxi.

144 "These men were absolutely fearless": "Eyewitness Testimony 39," in *Jewish Responses to Nazi Persecution,* ed. Isaiah Trunk (New York: Stein and Day, 1979), 228–29.

145 "Comrades, forward!": A group of partisans, "People of Zhetel in the Lipiczanski Partisans," in *Zhetel Memorial Book,* ed. Baruch Kaplinski (Tel Aviv: Zhetel Association in Israel, 1957), 379.

146 "Issy, stay with us": Ruth Lazowski, interview 25646, Tape 4, 00:55–1:37.

146 "The Germans killed my entire family": Simcha Ben-Shaul, *Childhood in the Holocaust* (Tel Aviv: Unpublished autobiography, 1997), 66; Ruth Lazowski, interview 25646, Tape 4, 00:55–1:37.

146 "What do you want?": Yuri Suhl, ed., *They Fought Back: The Story of the Jewish Resistance in Nazi Europe* (New York: Schocken Books, 1967; second paperback printing 1975).

147 upward of 150,000 partisans: Allan Levine, *Fugitives of the Forest* (Toronto: Stoddart, 1998), 161 and 237.

147 "the soulmate of *lebensraum*": Philip W. Blood, *Hitler's Bandit Hunters: The SS and Nazi Occupation of Europe* (Washington, DC: Potomac Books, 2008), 303.

147 "This partisan war again has some advantage": Waitman W. Beorn, "A Calculus of Complicity: The Wehrmacht, the Anti-Partisan War, and the Final Solution in White Russia, 1941–42," *Central European History* no. 44 (2011): 308–37.
148 Luftwaffe planes: Levine, *Fugitives of the Forest*, 145.
148 *Partisans ordered not to let the Nazis in the woods*: Herby Troyetsky, interview 22740, Tape 3, 4:17.
148 *Kaplinsky shot in the back*: Herby Troyetsky, interview 22740, Tape 3, 4:51.
150 "Many of the camps fell into the hands of the murderers": Arad, *Holocaust in the Soviet Union*, 512.
151 *Nazi cable to Himmler, December 20, 1942*: Philip W. Blood, *Hitler's Bandit Hunters: The SS and Nazi Occupation of Europe* (Washington, DC: Potomac Books, 2008), 199. **Author Note:** The cited material is footnoted as UN Charges Against German War Criminals, July 1947, evidence against Georg Henning Graf von Bassewitz-Behr (pages 87–88).
151 "Why did we want to live": Abrams, Abramowitz, and Laro, interview, Tape 8, 8:18–8:45.
151 just in time for Christmas: Abrams, Abramowitz, and Laro, interview, Tape 8, 8:45–9:03.
153 *Symptoms of typhus*: Arthur Allen, "How Scientists Created a Typhus Vaccine in a 'Fantastic Laboratory,'" *Fresh Air*, NPR, July 22, 2014.
153 *No strength to bury them*: Morris Abrams, interview 54994, Tape 3, 30:00–30:25, Houston, TX, VHA, 1994.
154 *Succumb to cold*: Ted Winestone, interview 15385.
154 *Morris and Rochel run from* oblava: Ruth Lazowski, author interview, West Hartford, CT.
155 *The pin*: Toby Langerman, author interview, August 2019, Brookline, MA; Toni Langerman, author phone interview, January 2020; Tania Langerman, interview 16470, Tape 1, 13:30, Brookline, MA, VHA, 1996.
157 *Dr. Miasnik the surgeon in the woods*: Miriam Brysk, *Amidst the Shadows of Trees: A Holocaust Child's Survival in the Partisans* (East Stroudsburg, PA: Gihon River Press, 2013), 45; Miriam Brysk, interview 55093, Farmington Hills, MI, VHA, 1991; Miriam Brysk, interview 55650, Farmington Hills, MI, VHA, 2012.
158 "She is going to die": Ruth Lazowski, interview 25646, Tape 3, 25:46–26:30.
159 *Meirim Dworetsky's last mission*: Chana Majewski-Klar, "The Years in the Forest," in in *Zhetel Memorial Book, Translation of Pinkus Zhetel*, edited by Baruch Kaplinski, Zhetel Association in Israel, (Tel Aviv, 1957), 397; Group of partisans, "Brief biographies of heroic partisans," in *Zhetel Memorial Book, Translation of Pinkus Zhetel*, edited by Baruch Kaplinski, Zhetel Association in Israel, (Tel Aviv, 1957), 420.
159 *Sara Alpert*: Group of partisans, "Brief biographies of heroic partisans," in *Zhetel Memorial Book*, 420.

Chapter 11: The Second Summer and the Boy with the Frozen Feet

162 *Description of the camp and its residents*: Ted Winestone (formerly Tuvya Weinstein), author interview, February 2020, Memphis, TN; Ted Winestone, interview 15385, Tape 7, 22:06–22:50, Memphis, Tennessee, VHA, 1996.
165 "the boy with the frozen feet": Ruth Lazowski, author interview, April 27, 2017, West Hartford, CT; Ruth Lazowski, author interview, February 26, 2019, West Hartford, CT.
165 Tuvya Weinstein had a gentle face: Ted Winestone, family photos.

166 *Weinstein vacations*: Ted Winestone, author interview, February 17, 2020, Memphis, TN.

166 *Tuvya's fiddle and medals*: Ted Winestone, author interview, February 17, 2020; Ted Winestone, interview 15385, Tape 3, 12:26–13:20.

167 a wall of people: Ted Winestone, interview 15385, Tape 5, 00:20–4:00; Ted Winestone statement, 2010: family website: https://tuvyastory.com/about-ted.

167 *Dvoretz camp liquidated*: "Commemoration of Jewish Victims: Dworzec," from *The Untold Stories: The Murder Sites of the Jews in the Occupied Territories of the Former USSR,* Yad Vashem, www.yadvashem.org/untoldstories/database/commemoration.asp?cid=1185.

168 "You're already hallucinating": Ted Winestone, interview 15385, Tape 5, 00:20–4:00.

171 "She gave it a *kinehora*": Toby Langerman, author interview, August 2019, Brookline, MA.

171 entertained male guests: Ruth Lazowski, author interview, February 2019, West Hartford, CT.

172 *Abortions in the woods*: Miriam Miasnik Brysk, interview, Oral History Department at the Holocaust Memorial Center Library Archive, Farmington Hills, MI, Ann Arbor, MI, 2004, www.holocaustcenter.org/visit/library-archive/oral-history-department/index-summaries/brysk-miriam-miasnik/; Sulia Wolozhinski Rubin, *Against the Tide: The Story of an Unknown Partisan* (Jerusalem: Posner & Sons, 1980), 109.

173 *Russian leaflets*: Rubin, *Against the Tide*, 63–65.

173 this increased morale: Sonia Minuskin, *My Children, My Heroes: Memoirs of a Holocaust Mother* (Prescott, AZ: Allegra Printing and Imaging, 2009), 113. (Kalman Minuskin selected excerpt.)

173 "Moscow was far away": Rubin, *Against the Tide*, 63–65.

173 *Join family camps with Bielskis*: Herby Troyetsky, interview 22740, Tape 4, 9:20, Long Island, NY, VHA, 1996.

174 "I would rather save one old Jewish woman": No author attributed, "Tuvia Bielski: Rescue Is Resistance," Jewish Partisan Educational Foundation, https://www.jewishpartisans.org/content/resist-curriculum.

174 *Bielski brothers' camp*: Allan Levine, *Fugitives of the Forest* (Toronto: Stoddart, 1998), 237.

174 *City of marshlands*: Nechama Tec, *Defiance* (Oxford: Oxford University Press, 1993), 146–47.

174 *Evacuate the woods*: Rubin, *Against the Tide*, 239.

174 pending attack: Tec, *Defiance*, 159.

174 massive assault: Peter Duffy, *The Bielski Brothers: The True Story of Three Men Who Defied the Nazis, Built a Village in the Forest, and Saved 1,200 Jews* (New York: Harper Perennial, 2003), 173.

175 to clear the stinging from their eyes: Rubin, *Against the Tide*, 138.

175 having sex with a minor: Duffy, *Bielski Brothers*, 172; Richard Rhodes, *Masters of Death: The SS-Einsatzgruppen and the Invention of the Holocaust* (New York: Vintage Books, 2003), 248. **Author Note:** As Rhodes points out, in 1934, the age of consent in Germany was fourteen.

176 "the butcher": Włodzimierz Nowak and Angelika Kuźniak, "My Warsaw Madness. The Other Side of the Warsaw Uprising," *Gazeta Wyborcza*, August 27, 2004.

176 "the most evil man in the SS": Chris Bishop and Michael Williams, *SS: Hell on the Western Front* (London: Amber Books, 2003), 92.

176 "whipping scene at Minsk": Trials of War Criminals Before the Nuremberg Military Tribunals Under Control Council Law No. 10, Nuremberg, October 1946–April 1949: Case 11: U.S. v. von Weizsaecker (Ministries case), 533. **Author Note:** The memo referenced was dated May 4, 1944, and references another earlier letter. This letter was presented in evidence at the Nuremberg trials.

176 Even Himmler called Dirlewanger an "oddity": French L. MacLean, *Thank God That Sow's Gone to the Butcher . . . : 2000 Quotes from Hitler's 1000-Year Reich* (Atglen, PA: Schiffer, 2007), 128.

176 Dirlewanger was an effective, even excellent leader: Peter Longerich, *Heinrich Himmler: A Life* (Oxford: University Press, 2011), 831.

176 more than ten thousand lives: Duffy, *Bielski Brothers,* 173.

176 July 13 to August 11, 1943: Philip W. Blood, *Hitler's Bandit Hunters: The SS and Nazi Occupation of Europe* (Washington, DC: Potomac Books, 2008), 199.

176 tally of "bandits" slaughtered: Blood, *Hitler's Bandit Hunters,* 199–201.

177 ham fat: Miriam Rozwaski Biegun, interview, Voice/Vision Holocaust Survivor Oral History Archive, University of Michigan-Dearborn, 1983.

177 kerosene: Rubin, *Against the Tide,* 114.

177 "Get away!": Ted Winestone, interview 15385, Tape 6, 14:57–18:12.

178 "I just couldn't risk it": Ruth Lazowski, author interview, April 27, 2017, West Hartford, CT.

178 tobacco substitute: Ruth Lazowski, author interview, February 2018, West Hartford, CT.

179 playing cards: Sonia Minuskin, *My Children, My Heroes: Memoirs of a Holocaust Mother* (Prescott, AZ: Allegra Printing and Imaging, 2009), 113.

179 he took a sharpened blade: Miriam Brysk, *Amidst the Shadows of Trees: A Holocaust Child's Survival in the Partisans* (East Stroudsburg, PA: Gihon River Press, 2013), 55.

181 *Rose Salman escapes to the woods*: Rose Feigenbaum, interview 3014, Tape 2, 18:40, Riverdale, NY, VHA, 1995.

182 "I'd rather die from you": Rose Feigenbaum, interview 3014, Tape 2, 18:40.

182 "take me away": Rose Feigenbaum, interview 3014, Tape 2, 18:40.

182 "the father of all children": Genia Krolewiecki (daughter of Herz Kaminsky), interview 44031, Tape 4, 18:00, Melbourne, Victoria, Australia, VHA, 1998.

183 *Kaminsky camp is raided*: Genia Krolewiecki, interview 44031, Tape 1, 9:00–12:00.

183 *Running from bullets*: Zelick Kaminsky, interview 33785, Melbourne, Victoria, Australia, VHA, 1997.

183 *Kaminsky's wife is killed*: Genia Krolewiecki, interview 44031, Tape 1, 9:00–12:00.

183 more than seventy people: Genia Krolewiecki, interview 44031, Tape 4, 18:00.

183 Rochel and Tania were frightened at the shouting: Ruth Lazowski, author interview, April 27, 2017, West Hartford, CT.

185 *Issy Rabinowitz's death*: Simcha Ben-Shaul, *Childhood in the Holocaust* (Tel Aviv: Unpublished autobiography, 1997), 13, 67.

185 "I know we will survive": Ruth Lazowski, author interview, February 26, 2019, West Hartford, CT; Toby Langerman, author interview, August 7, 2019, Brookline, MA.

186 Big Three posed for photos: "American staff car enters through a gate of a Russian Embassy building in Tehran, Iran," clip 65675053418, *CriticalPast*, December 1, 1943, www.youtube.com/watch?v=g477uMMEaac.

Chapter 12: Liberation

187 *Building the bunker*: Ted Winestone, author interview, February 17, 2020, Memphis, TN; Ted Winestone, interview 15385, Tape 7, 27:50–28:25, Memphis, TN, VHA, 1996.

188 *Typhus, mild cases*: Toby Langerman, author interview, August 2019, Brookline, MA.

188 *Mrs. Feldman's operation*: Toby Langerman, author interview, August 7, 2019, Brookline, MA.

189 parachute blouse: Toby Langerman, author phone interview, March 19, 2020; Tania Langerman, interview 16470, Tape 1, 13:30, Brookline, MA, VHA, 1996.

189 more than half of all the rural areas: Leonid Smilovitsky, "Jewish Family Camps and Groups in Belarus, 1941–1944," trans. Anya Karasik, Diaspora Research Center of Tel Aviv University, www.jewishgen.org/yizkor/belarus/bel119.html#6.

189 three hundred places: Pat Mctaggart, "Soviet Partisans: The Rag-Tag Scourge Along WWII's Eastern Front," https://warfarehistorynetwork.com/2016/12/16/soviet-partisans-the-rag-tag-scourge-along-wwiis-eastern-front/.

190 *Between Soviet troops and German troops*: Allan Levine, *Fugitives of the Forest* (Toronto: Stoddart, 1998), 291.

190 On the night of June 19: Mctaggart, "Soviet Partisans."

190 More than one thousand attacks: Robert Beckhusen, "Everything Went Wrong for the Axis During Operation Bagration," *War Is Boring*, December 22, 2017, https://warisboring.com/everything-went-wrong-for-the-axis-during-operation-bagration/; Mctaggart, "Soviet Partisans."

190 some 750 miles: Anjan Basu, "Operation Bagration: A June 22 Hitler Had Not Bargained For," *The Wire*, June 22, 2020, https://thewire.in/history/a-june-22-hitler-had-not-bargained-for.

190 Barely 425,000 strong: Beckhusen, "Everything Went Wrong."

191 Russian tanks rolled into Minsk: Mike Bennighof, "Red Victory: Operation Bagration, Part One," online series, May 2018, www.avalanchepress.com/Bagration1.php.

191 Soviet forces pushed ahead 450 miles: David Reynolds, "The Other D-day—and the Onset of Cold War," *The Guardian*, June 21, 2014, www.theguardian.com/books/2014/jun/21/we-must-not-forget-the-other-d-day.

191 "Allies had opened a second front": Sulia Wolozhinski Rubin, *Against the Tide: The Story of an Unknown Partisan* (Jerusalem: Posner & Sons, 1980), 140.

191 twenty-eight out of thirty-four divisions: Peter R. Mansoor, "Operation Bagration and the Destruction of the Army Group Center," *Military History in the News*, Hoover Institution, June 24, 2019, www.hoover.org/research/operation-bagration-and-destruction-army-group-center.

192 Russian pilots and parachutists: Ruth Lazowski, author interview, February 2018, West Hartford, CT.

192 *The mission for Tuvya's boots*: Ted Winestone, interview 15385, Tape 7, 27:50–28:25.

193 *Germans still hunting Jews in the woods*: Minuskin, *My Children, My Heroes*, 113; Avraham Leibovich, written testimony, 15 pages, handwritten, in Yiddish, Israel Kaplan collection, Ghetto Fighters House Archives, June 28, 1941, www.infocenters.co.il/gfh/notebook_ext.asp?book=110715&lang=eng.

194 *Bunker planter and garlic*: Ted Winestone, interview 15385, Tape 7, 11:24.

194 two dead horses: "Eyewitness Testimony 55," 302–4. **Author Note:** After reading this testimony and recognizing the similarities to Philip Lazowski's experience, I realized

this was testimony of Philip's brother Rachmil Lazowski, who changed his name to Robert Lesser after the war.

195 *Rochel has* kretz: Ruth Lazowski, author interview, February 22, 2018, West Hartford, CT; Ruth Lazowski, interview 25646, Tape 4, 11:15–12:04, Bloomfield, CT, VHA, 1997.

196 "It's too dangerous": Ted Winestone, author interview, February 17, 2020, Memphis, TN.

196 "You can come out now": Minuskin, *My Children, My Heroes,* 75.

196 Russian medics: Ruth Lazowski, author interview, February 2018, West Hartford, CT; Ruth Lazowski, interview 25646, Tape 4, 11:15–12:04.

197 *A salute and a kiss*: Miriam Brysk, *Amidst the Shadows of Trees: A Holocaust Child's Survival in the Partisans* (East Stroudsburg, PA: Gihon River Press, 2013), 63; Miriam Brysk, interview 55650, Tape 1, 1:48:00–1:49:00, Farmington Hills, MI, VHA, 2012.

197 *Man on a white horse*: Toby Langerman, author interview, August 2019, Brookline, MA.

198 one soldier with a weapon was enough: Ted Winestone, interview 15385, Tape 7, 27:30–28:25.

198 *Forest trees are connected*: Suzanne Simard, interview with Jad Abumrad and Robert Krulwich, "From Tree to Shining Tree," *Radiolab,* podcast audio, July 30, 2016, www.wnycstudios.org/podcasts/radiolab/articles/from-tree-to-shining-tree.

Chapter 13: The Long Road Home

202 *Zhetel houses are dark*: Zelick Kaminsky, interview 33785, Tape 3, 8:00, Melbourne, Victoria, Australia, VHA, 1997.

202 *Synagogue warehouse*: Sonia Heidocovsky Zissman, interview, transcript, and recording, Jeff and Toby Herr Oral History Archive, United States Holocaust Memorial Museum, 1995, RG-50.030.0332.

202 *Berl and Beyla's house*: Tania Langerman, interview 16470, Tape 2. 8:40–9:00, Brookline, MA, VHA, 1996.

202 *Dovid Rozwaski's suit*: Miriam Rozwaski Biegun, interview, Voice/Vision Holocaust Survivor Oral History Archive, University of Michigan-Dearborn, 1983.

203 *Russians hanged one offender*: Miriam Rozwaski Biegun, interview, 1983.

203 *Wehrmacht soldiers at Senderowski table*: Marsha Senderowski Taplin, interview 12746, Las Vegas, NV, VHA, 1996.

204 copper pots: Ruth Lazowski, diary entry/personal papers, undated, titled "Crossing the Alps."

204 *Rochel and Tania's mismatched clothes*: Family photo, marked "Poland, 1945."

206 *Novogrudek after liberation*: Sulia Wolozhinski Rubin, *Against the Tide: The Story of an Unknown Partisan* (Jerusalem: Posner & Sons, 1980), 65–66.

206 a crumbling mess: Yehoshua Yaffe, "People of Novogrudok After Liberation," in *Navaredok Memorial Book, Translation of Pinkas Navaredok,* ed. E. Yerushalmi and Alexander Harkavy, Navaredker Relief Committee (Tel Aviv and United States: 1963), 357.

206 *Family possessions*: Lazowski diary, "Crossing the Alps."

207 grazing cows: Rubin, *Against the Tide,* 169.

207 bones protruding: Dov Cohen and Jack Kagan, *Surviving the Holocaust with the Russian Jewish Partisans* (Portland, OR: Vallentine Mitchell, 1998), 96.

207 *Yom Kippur service*: Cohen and Kagan, *Surviving the Holocaust,* 97.

208 *Russian school*: Cohen and Kagan, *Surviving the Holocaust,* 96.

209 The Soviets in Novogrudek couldn't understand: Cohen and Kagan, *Surviving the Holocaust,* 98.

209 anti-Semitism plaguing the newly liberated Jews in Poland: Yisrael Gutman and Shmuel Krakowski, *Unequal Victims: Poles and Jews During World War Two* (New York: Holocaust Library, 1986), 365–374.

209 "There were too many ghosts following us.": Rubin *Against the Tide*, 186.

209 "I'm not living under the Russians anymore!": Ruth Lazowski, interview 25646, Tape 4, 13:00, Bloomfield, CT, VHA, 1997.

209 "Throw away the *schmatta*": Ruth Lazowski, author interview, 2018, West Hartford, CT; Ruth Lazowski, interview 25646, Tape 4, 14:20–14:59.

210 *Rochel Rabinovich is a good Pioneer*: Ruth Lazowski, author interview, February 21, 2018, West Hartford, CT.

210 eighty thousand Jewish refugees: Yehuda Bauer, *Flight and Rescue: Brichah* (New York: Random House, 1970), 113.

210 Poland's interim capital: Gutman and Krakowski, *Unequal Victims*, 354.

211 Within one day of receiving their reply: Simcha Ben-Shaul, *Childhood in the Holocaust* (Tel Aviv: Unpublished autobiography, 1997), 64–68.

212 *Batsheva's makeup*: Toby Langerman, author phone interview, March 19, 2020.

213 "He brought us food and candy, even toys": Ben-Shaul, *Childhood in the Holocaust*, 64–68.

214 Red Army's forces arrived in Lublin: "Lublin/Majdanek: Key Dates," *Holocaust Encyclopedia*, United States Holocaust Memorial Museum, https://encyclopedia.ushmm.org/content/en/article/lublin-majdanek-key-dates?series=20374.

214 opened the camp to the public: Museum of Majdanek, www.majdanek.eu/en/mission.

214 located directly on the highway: Majdanek Concentration Camp, archival footage, untitled documentary, part 1 of 5, www.youtube.com/watch?v=hk-TAq8CiIw&t=263s.

214 625-acre site of former farmland: Majdanek Concentration Camp, untitled documentary, part 1 of 5.

215 five giant ovens: Majdanek Concentration Camp, untitled documentary, part 1 of 5.

215 rooms full of human remains: Bernhard Storch, interview 19921, South Nyack, NY, VHA, 1996.

215 General Dmitrii Kudriavtsev: Anita Kondoyanidi, "The Liberating Experience: War Correspondents, Red Army Soldiers, and the Nazi Extermination Camps," *Russian Review* 69 (July 2010): 438–62.

215 Bulganin gave the order: Majdanek Concentration Camp, untitled documentary, Youtube, part 1 of 5, https://www.youtube.com/watch?v=hk-TAq8CiIw&t=263s.

215 "fertilized fields with human ashes": Kondoyanidi, "Liberating Experience," 438–62. **Author Note:** As discussed in this article, Simonov wrote a serialized article on Majdanek titled "The Extermination Camp," published by *Red Star* on August 10, 11, and 12, 1944.

216 enemy propaganda: Majdanek Concentration Camp, untitled documentary, Youtube, part 3 of 5, https://www.youtube.com/watch?v=lqFFYagEwYg&t=133s.

216 *Winterton and Werth*: Untitled documentary, production date unknown, A Chronos U.K. production, www.youtube.com/watch?v=hk-TAq8CiIw&t=263s.

216 "Jewish sources are always doubtful": Marion Milne, "The Holocaust: Why Auntie Stayed Mum: The BBC Knew About the Nazi Death Camps Two Years Before the First Reports from Belsen, Says Marion Milne," *The Independent*, May 9, 1995, www.independent.co.uk/news/media/the-holocaust-why-auntie-stayed-mum-1618801.html; *What Did You Do in the War, Auntie?*, BBC Documentary, 1995, https://www.youtube.com/watch?v=5bL8FsORE20&t=8s. **Author Note:** In his onscreen

interview for this documentary, former BBC editor Leonard Miall commented on the news organization's editorial decision-making at the time. "We were being very careful to try and avoid giving currency to rumors which might not be true, and which would then jeopardize our general credibility. In the process, undoubtedly, we did play down the extent of the Holocaust horrors."

217 It was only when war correspondent Richard Dimbleby: "Broadcast at Bergen-Belsen, narrated by Richard Dimbleby," BBC, April 19, 1945, https://www.bbc.co.uk/archive/richard-dimbleby-describes-belsen/zvw7cqt. **Author Note:** As the BBC archives state: "The BBC initially refused to play the report, as they could not believe the scenes he had described, and it was only broadcast after Dimbleby threatened to resign."

217 shocked by what they saw: Ruth Lazowski, author interview, February 2018, West Hartford, CT; Ben-Shaul, *Childhood in the Holocaust*, 63–68.

217 the "devil's ovens": Kondoyanidi, "Liberating Experience," 438–62. (This is from Boris Gorbatov's detailed article in *Pravda*, August 11, 1944.)

218 Anti-Semitic attacks were on the rise: Laura Jockusch and Tamar Lewinsky, "Paradise Lost? Postwar Memory of Polish Jewish Survival in the Soviet Union," *Holocaust and Genocide Studies*, December 2010; Gutman and Krakowski, *Unequal Victims*, 365–374; Bauer, *Flight and Rescue*, 115; David Engel, "Patterns of Anti-Jewish Violence in Poland, 1944–1946," *Yad Vashem Studies* (1998): 43–85; Jan T. Gross, *Fear: Anti-Semitism in Poland After Auschwitz* (New York: Random House, 2006), 35; "Anti-Jewish Violence in Poland After Liberation," Yad Vashem, https://www.yadvashem.org/articles/general/anti-jewish-violence-in-poland-after-liberation.html.

218 351 Jews were murdered in Poland: Bauer, *Flight and Rescue*, 115.

218 "a pogrom atmosphere hangs over Poland": *JTA Daily News Bulletin*, September 20, 1945.

218 "Everybody had a place to go, but the Jews": Lisa Nussbaum Derman, interview, transcript, and recording, Jeff and Toby Herr Oral History Archive, United States Holocaust Memorial Museum, 1994, RG-50.030*0300.

219 "We cannot go anywhere else": Ruth Lazowski, interview 25646, Tape 4, 15:22–15:50.

Chapter 14: Across the Alps and to the Sea

221 "What beautiful, weirdly shaped children you have": Toby Langerman, interview, August 7, 2019, Brookline, MA.

222 *Story of Joseph and Dora Kogan*: Jerry Kogan, author phone interview, February 2021; "Joseph Kogan, Obituary," *Missoulian*, August 9, 2006, https://missoulian.com/news/local/obituaries/04wed/joseph-kogan/article_d309b8f5-f7c0-5599-b7fe-8fab174fb88b.html; "Dora Kogan, Obituary," *Missoulian*, February 7, 2012, https://missoulian.com/news/local/obituaries/dora-kogan/article_03ab24fe-519a-11e1-ac9a-001871e3ce6c.html.

223 *months-long Bricha journey journey*: "Dora Kogan, Obituary," *Missoulian*, February 7, 2012.

223 *Route from Lublin to Austria*: Lisa Nussbaum Derman, interview, transcript, and recording, Jeff and Toby Herr Oral History Archive, United States Holocaust Memorial Museum, 1994, RG-50.030*0300.

223 pretend not to understand: Ruth Lazowski, interview 25646, Tape 4, 16:05–17:15, Bloomfield, CT, VHA, 1997.

223 the "great gate of Italy": *Encyclopaedia Britannica: Aus to Cal* (Cambridge, 1910), 495–96.

224 "Manya, it's too hard to carry": Ruth Lazowski, diary entry/personal papers, undated, titled, "Crossing the Alps."

225 Bricha emissaries started their work as early as 1944: Yehuda Bauer, *Flight and Rescue: Brichah* (New York: Random House, 1970), 4–23.

225 *Italian carabinieri turn a blind eye*: Susanna Kokkonen, "Jewish Displaced Persons in Postwar Italy, 1945–1951," *Jewish Political Studies Review*, April 25, 2008, Jerusalem Center for Public Affairs, Israeli Security, Regional Diplomacy, and International Law, https://jcpa.org/article/jewish-displaced-persons-in-postwar-italy-1945-1951/.

226 *Number of Jews entering Italy 1945*: Kokkonen, "Jewish Displaced Persons."

226 *Crossing with the Bricha, see the guards*: Isak Kleber, interview 25066, Tape 3, 19:00–30:00, Montréal, Quebec, Canada, VHA, 1997.

226 too close to the edge: Mina Fried, interview 531, Tape 3, 6:00, Cedarhurst, NY, VHA, 1995.

228 forces repurposed the Nazi concentration camps: "Survivors and the Displaced Persons Era, Wiener Holocaust Library, https://www.theholocaustexplained.org/survival-and-legacy/survivors-and-dp-era/dp-camps/.

228 *Vacation homes had names*: *Shores of Light: Salento 1945–1947*, directed by Yael Katzir (2015; Israel: Katzir Productions), 08:30, https://vimeo.com/119858386.

229 *Kids on roof to watch* Tarzan: Toby Langerman, author interview, August 7, 2019, Brookline, MA.

229 *Tania notices Yolanda's cross*: Toby Langerman, author phone interviews, May 2020.

229 "Please don't ask Yolanda anything about it": Toby Langerman, author phone interview, March 6, 2021.

230 *Tina Bencianowski gives up her child*: Tina Nussbaum Benson, interview 9291, Tape 5, 16:00–23:22, Freehold, NJ, VHA, 1995.

231 *Yolanda prays*: Tina Nussbaum Benson, interview 9291, Tape 8, 23:50–24:26.

231 "Come back!": Toby Langerman, author interview, August 7, 2019, Brookline, MA.

232 special Shabbat dinners: Chaim Bank Collection, Ghetto Fighters House, photo.

232 Rochel and Tania were holding banners: Ghetto Fighters House, photo archive: Donated by Drori (formerly Schwartz) Yaakov & Shulamit, May 1, 1946.

233 "May God protect you": *Shores of Light*, directed by Yael Katzir, 26:00.

233 "with the Star of David on their chests": *Shores of Light*, directed by Yael Katzir, 9:57.

233 tears to his eyes: *Shores of Light*, directed by Yael Katzir, 9:57.

234 never even turned his head: *Shores of Light*, directed by Yael Katzir, 44:00.

234 "city of the soul!": Lord Byron, Bartleby.com, 2013, www.bartleby.com/205/.

234 41 Via Latina: Ruth Lazowski, interview, February 22, 2018, West Hartford, CT.

234 chubby face: Photo, Luba and baby, Italy, 1947, family collection.

234 two neat braids: Family photo, Rabinowitz and Kogan family, Santa Maria di Leuca, 1946.

234 *Miriam in new heels*: Family photo, Santa Maria di Leuca, courtesy of Toby Langerman.

234 *Baths of Caracalla in World War II*: "Caracalla," Teatro Dell'Opera di Roma, www.operaroma.it/en/locations/caracalla-2/.

235 outdoor performances: "An Evening at Caracalla in 1939 to Watch 'Aida,'" *Rome in the Footsteps of an XVIIIth Century Traveller*, blog credited to Roberto Piperno, www.romeartlover.it/Caracall.html. Features original playbills.

235 celebrating Jewish holidays: "Youngsters from a School for Refugee Children, Visiting Titus' Gate in Rome on an Outing for the Holiday of Lag B'Omer," Catalog No. 18039, 1947, Chaim Bank Collection, Ghetto Fighters House Archives.

235 shores of Ostia: "Students and Teachers of a School for Holocaust Survivors in Postwar Rome, at the Seashore in Ostia," Catalog No. 21595, August 5, 1947, Chaim Bank Collection.

235 summer they attended a camp: "A Summer Camp for Refugee Children from Rome and Its Environs, Held in Nemi, Near Rome," Catalog No. 18040, 1947, Chaim Bank Collection.

235 *Rochel at school in Italy*: Ruth Lazowski, author interviews, 2017 and 2018, West Hartford, CT.

235 *Rochel as Queen Vashti*: Family photo, Italy, of Ruth, Gloria Koslowski, and Toby.

236 "Today, I'm so hungry": Ruth Lazowski, author interview, April 27, 2017, West Hartford, CT.

237 Sir Alan Cunningham: Obituary, "Sir Alan Cunningham; Palestine Commander," Reuters, February 1, 1983.

237 three-decade rule: *Newsweek* Staff, "Declaring the State of Israel on May 14, 1948," *Newsweek*, May 14, 2015.

237 *President Truman press release*: "U.S. Recognition of the State of Israel," National Archives, May 14, 1948, https://www.archives.gov/education/lessons/us-israel.

237 Zionism's father: "Ceremony of the Declaration of the State of Israel: David Ben-Gurion Reading the Proclamation of Israel's Statehood, Tel Aviv Museum, May 14, 1948," photograph by Robert Capa, Alfred and Ingrid Lenz Harrison Fund, Minneapolis Institute of Art, online.

237 blue-and-white flags: "Natural and Historic Right," *The Manchester Guardian*, May 15, 1948.

237 "Jewish people to be masters of their own fate": David Ben-Gurion, "The Declaration of the Establishment of the State of Israel," Provisional Government of Israel *Official Gazette*: Number 1; Tel Aviv, May 14, 1948, www.knesset.gov.il/docs/eng/megilat_eng.htm.

237 burst into applause: No author attributed, "Natural and Historic Right," *The Manchester Guardian*, May 15, 1948.

237 Egypt had already sent: "The Jewish State Born/Proclamation of 'Israel' /US Recognition/Martial Law in Arab States," *The Guardian* (Manchester), May 15, 1948.

238 a panel showing soldiers: Arch of Titus: Video: *The Spoils of Jerusalem Being Brought into Rome*, Arch of Titus, Rome, Khan Academy, www.khanacademy.org/humanities/ancient-art-civilizations/roman/early-empire/v/arch-of-titus-relief.

238 cheering, jubilant crowd: "Jewish Displaced Persons Celebrate Israeli Independence by Gathering by the Arch of Titus in Rome," May 14, 1948. No photographer credit, family collection.

Chapter 15: In America

239 *MS* Vulcania*'s luxurious 1920s*: Photograph album of MS *Vulcania*, accession number XB2010.09.1, University of Florida, George A. Smathers Libraries.

239 *MS* Vulcania *during World War II*: "Saturnia," Italian Liners Historical Society, www.italianliners.com/saturnia-en.

240 *MS* Vulcania *in 1943*: "Maritime Monday for March 5, 2012—Mare Nostrum, Part Uno," *Gcaptain* (a maritime blog), March 5, 2012, https://gcaptain.com/maritime-monday-march-five-twentytwelve-mare-nostrum-part-uno/#.

240 "How do you like America?": Toby Langerman, author interview, August 7, 2019, Brookline, MA.

240 *Rabinowitz family history*: Jacob Weiner, *9 Generations: 200 Years of Our Family* (Tel Aviv: 1970), 48–49. Note: This book was not published for commercial distribution.

241 "two small children in Palestine?": Ruth Lazowski, interview 25646, Tape 4, 19:43–20:39, Bloomfield, CT, VHA, 1997.

241 paved in gold: Toby Langerman, author interview, August 7, 2019, Brookline, MA.

242 *Morris remembers Sonia*: Toby Langerman, author interview, August 7, 2019, Brookline, MA.

242 *Layer cake and beauty salon*: Toby Langerman, author interview, August 7, 2019, Brookline, MA.

242 133 Martin Street: Photo labeled "Hartford: May 29, 1950," family archive.

243 *Front stoops and potato chips*: Toby Langerman, author interview, August 7, 2019, Brookline, MA.

244 "Never again": Ruth Lazowski, author interview, February 26, 2019, West Hartford, CT.

245 limitations on sugar and coffee: No author attributed, "Rationing," National WWII Museum, New Orleans, no publication date listed, https://www.nationalww2museum.org/war/articles/rationing.

245 "Why did you invite *her*?": Ruth Lazowski, author interview, April 8, 2018, West Hartford, CT; Toby Langerman, author interview, August 7, 2019, Brookline, MA.

245 *griner*: Ruth Lazowski, author interview, April 8, 2018, West Hartford, CT; "Evolution of the Greenhorns," *The Forward*, June 6, 2003, https://forward.com/news/8973/evolution-of-the-greenhorns/.

246 *Rochel sings "Mattinata" in the school talent show*: Ruth Lazowski, author interview April 30, 2017, West Hartford, CT; Ruth Lazowski, author interview, April 8, 2018, West Hartford, CT.

247 *Rochel changes her name to Ruth*: Ruth Lazowski, author interview, July 31, 2016, West Hartford, CT.

247 *Rochel pronouncing Ruth*: Toby Langerman, author phone interview, February 9, 2021.

247 *Toby the circus boy or Terry the pilot*: Toby Langerman, author phone interview, February 9, 2021.

249 "Rochel and Tania are very different": Ruth Lazowski, author interview, April 8, 2018, West Hartford, CT.

249 *Toby borrows Ruth's suit*: Ruth Lazowski, author interview, February 2018, West Hartford, CT.

250 "You'll give a speech": Toby Langerman, author phone interview, January 4, 2021.

250 Barbara Ann Parkhurst: "Farmington Secretary Crowned Miss Hartford," *Hartford Courant*, April 27, 1957.

251 three hundred Jews who remained: Solomon Golanski, testimony, December 1983, 829583, Tapes 1 and 2, Fortunoff Video Archive for Holocaust Testimonies, Yale University Library; Dov Cohen and Jack Kagan, *Surviving the Holocaust with the Russian Jewish Partisans*, OR (Portland, OR: Vallentine Mitchell, 1998), 78.

252 *9 P.M. to 4 A.M.*: Cohen and Kagan, *Surviving the Holocaust*, 179–80.

252 *Tunnel and escape*: Solomon Golanski, testimony, December 1983, 829583, Tapes 1 and 2; Cohen and Kagan, *Surviving the Holocaust*, 83.

253 *Solomon comes to the United States*: Solomon Golanski, interview 25649, Tape 4, 28:20–29:30, West Hartford, CT, VHA, February 9, 1997.

253 *Tunnels made out of paper boxes*: Alani Golanksi, author phone interview, February 9, 2021.

253 *Morris borrows money*: Alani Golanksi, author phone interview, February 9, 2021.

254 *Hartford to New Hampshire*: Ruth Lazowski, author interview, July 31, 2016, and April 30, 2017, West Hartford, CT.

255 "The blessing of that woman saved us": Ruth Lazowski, author interview, 2017, West Hartford, CT.

Chapter 16: A Wedding in Connecticut

256 *Philip's letter to Miriam*: Philip Lazowski, family archive, May 1953.

258 *Lazowski family discovered*: Philip Lazowski, *Faith and Destiny* (Barkhamsted, CT: Goulet Printer, 2006), 58–60; Philip Lazowski, interview 25650, Tape 3, 3:40–5:11, Bloomfield, CT, VHA, February 9, 1997.

259 *Abraham killed*: Philip Lazowski, interview 25650, Tape 3, 5:49.

259 Chaya passed a message: Lazowski, *Faith and Destiny*, 61.

260 "Jump": Lazowski, *Faith and Destiny*, 62–63; Philip Lazowski, interview 25650, Tape 3, 11:04–12:20.

261 conducted by Reuter: Morris Abrams, interview 54994, Tape 3, 4:37–7:30, Houston, TX, VHA, October 27, 1994.

262 stepped off the pier: Lazowski, *Faith and Destiny*, 143.

262 *Rogers Avenue to Ebbets Field*: Philip Lazowski, author interview, March 3, 2019, West Hartford, CT.

264 "Ruthie": Weaver High School Yearbook, 1953. Family papers.

265 the Jewish Alps: David Levine, "History of Borscht Belt Hotels and Bungalow Colonies in the Catskills," *Hudson Valley Magazine*, July 23, 2014, https://hvmag.com/life-style/history/borscht-belt-hotels-catskills/.

265 Borscht Belt's heyday: *The Rise and Fall of the Borscht Belt*, directed by Peter Davis (1986: Villon Films).

265 *Postcard*: Philip Brown, "Pioneer Country Club, Greenfield Park, NY," Catskills Institute Collection, Northeastern University Library, https://repository.library.northeastern.edu/files/neu:m039zj50h.

266 they made plans: Lazowski, *Faith and Destiny*, 150.

266 the lady wouldn't hear of it: Philip Lazowski, author interview, March 3, 2019, West Hartford, CT.

267 Kiamesha Lake: Philip Lazowski; author phone interview, June 12, 2018; photo of Ruth and Gloria in boat, Rabinowitz family collection.

269 *He put a ring in her hand*: Ruth Lazowski, author interview, April 9, 2018, West Hartford, CT.

269 *Ruth and Philip's wedding*: "Ruth Rabinowitz Philip Lazowski Married Sunday," *Hartford Courant*, December 12, 1955.

270 *Morris and Miriam at the wedding*: Ruth Lazowski, author phone interview, February 10, 2021.

Epilogue

272 *Toby's candlelit wedding*: "Langerman-Rabinowitz," *Hartford Courant*, April 21, 1958.

272 always Mr. Morris: Alan Lazowski, author phone interview, summer 2020.

273 *Morris takes grandchildren fishing*: Alan Lazowski, author phone interview, June 2020.

273 *Miriam peeled apples*: Toni Langerman, author phone interview, January 4, 2020.

273 Morris teased Miriam: Toni Langerman, author phone interview, January 4, 2020.

273 "*Epes iz felndik*. There's something missing": Toby Langerman, author phone interview, March 19, 2020.

273 "Grandma, tell me about the woods": Ruth Lazowski, author interview, 2017, West

Hartford, CT; Ruth Lazowski, interview 25646, Tape 5, 1:30–1:50, Bloomfield, CT, VHA, February 9, 1997.

275 *Morris takes Miriam to Miami Beach*: Toby Langerman, author interview, August 7, 2019, Brookline, MA.

275 "I saved her in the woods": Ruth Lazowski, author interview, 2017, West Hartford, CT.

275 *Miriam Rabinowitz death*: Obituary, *Hartford Courant*, January 21, 1981.

275 *Morris Rabinowitz death*: Obituary, *Hartford Courant*, December 14, 1982.

Author's Note

280 *Cheery painting from Poland*: Ruth Lazowski, interview, July 31, 2016.

280 "I have longed to see my grandfather's house": Ruth Lazowski, interview 25646, Tape 5, 10:00–11:12, Bloomfield, CT, VHA, 1997.

281 "we should never forget": Ruth Lazowski, interview 25646, Tape 5, 2:50–3:45.

Acknowledgments

291 "gave him two such ringing slaps": "Eyewitness testimony 44. Tunnel Escape/Novogrudek," recorded by the Jewish Historical Commission in the Hindenburg DP camp, Germany, in 1945, in *Jewish Responses to Nazi Persecution*, edited by Isaiah Trunk (New York: Stein and Day, 1979), 252–255.

Index

Pete Kiehart

Rebecca Frankel is the author of the *New York Times* bestselling book *War Dogs: Tales of Canine Heroism, History, and Love*. She is former executive editor at *Foreign Policy* magazine. Her work has appeared in *The New York Times*, *The Wall Street Journal*, and *National Geographic*, among others. A Connecticut native, she lives in Washington, DC.